About the Author

Shirley Phillips met and travelled widely with her husband who was then an army officer. She worked as a voluntary nurse in a number of overseas countries and was involved in some of the violent results of insurgency. She carried out voluntary nursing in Ghana, Aden, Kenya and she occasionally lectured in the RIPAS Hospital in Brunei. With her husband, for five months in 1984, she helped him when he was with UNESCO on a project in Paris and Nigeria to aid disabled children.

Dedication

To my dear late husband, Derek, without whom this book would be at the bottom of my drawer, not read by others.

Shirley Phillips

THAT GOOD NIGHT:
MORE MEMOIRS OF A NURSE TEACHER

AUSTIN MACAULEY
PUBLISHERS LTD.

A CIP catalogue record for this title is available from the British Library.

ISBN 978 1 78455 524 5

www.austinmacauley.com

First Published (2015)
Austin Macauley Publishers Ltd.
25 Canada Square
Canary Wharf
London
E14 5LB

Printed and bound in Great Britain

Do not go gentle into that good night

Do not go gentle into that good night,
Old age should burn and rave at close of day,
Rage, rage against the dying of the light.

Though wise men at their end know dark is night,
Because their words had forked no lightening they
Do not go gentle into that good night.

Good men, the last wave by, cry how bright
Their frail deeds might have danced in a green bay,
Rage, rage against the dying of the light.

Wild men who caught and sang the sun in flight,
And learn, too late, they grieve it on its way,
Do not go gentle into the good night.

Grave men, near death, who see with blinding sight
Blind eyes could blaze like meteors and be gay,
Rage, rage against the dying of the light.

And you, my father, there on that sad height,
Curse, bless me now with your fierce tears, I pray.
Do not go gentle into that good night.
Rage, rage against the dying of the light.

Dylan Thomas

Contents

PART 1

Chapter 1

NANCY BAINE

It was by chance I began working for The Nightingale Nursing Homes: a complex of three purpose-built nursing homes for the elderly and the elderly mentally infirm. I went there to visit eighty-five year old Nancy Baine, the mother of my friend, Maureen Tate, who was on holiday with her family for two weeks.

Nancy was forgetful and might not remember that Maureen wouldn't be visiting her, although she had repeatedly told her. Maureen didn't want her mother to think she had been "put away" and forgotten.

Nancy was far from forgotten by Maureen but she was not the young, sprightly nurse she used to be. She had nursed her mother at home for as long as she was able. Nancy had had a cerebro-vascular accident (a stroke) resulting in the left side of her body being paralysed. The damaged part of her brain also brought about a change of her personality. Nancy sometimes became over-demanding and aggressive.

Maureen was a small person and Nancy was taller and heavier. Having been a nurse for many years, Maureen was experienced in the handling and moving of ill people but there was a limit to what she could manage at home.

She did so for over a year. Community nurses called, but an occasional twenty minutes was next to nothing when Nancy needed twenty-four hour care. She was not only partially immobile, but unable to dress, wash and feed herself and was incontinent.

She had a commode in her bedroom and would call out to Maureen to come to help her to cross the room to use it. Maureen responded to her calls, but more often than not found that when she got to her mother, her bed was already wet and fouled.

Nancy, during times of normality, was a gentle lady, but she frequently became confused as to time, place and people. She sometimes didn't recognise those who were dear to her. Tony, her son-in-law, the headmaster of a local school, became a stranger to her. When he greeted her on arriving home she became frightened. She would shout, 'Maureen! Quick! Come and show this man out of the house. Who let him in?'

Sometimes she didn't recognise Maureen or their two teenage children. It was hurtful.

In Nancy's periods of confusion she was frightened and at such times she would scream long and loud.

At that time, Wayne, Maureen's son, was fourteen and Sharon, her daughter, was seventeen. It was concerning to Tony and Maureen that their children rarely invited friends to the house any more. They were ashamed of their grandmother, who all too often smelled unpleasant. They feared their mother wouldn't have noticed the need to change Nancy out of soiled clothes and the sheet covering the seat of her chair in the lounge.

As much as Maureen sprayed air-freshener, the rooms never had a freshness about them, as they had before Nancy became the unpleasant burden that she had.

There were moments of lucidity when she realised what getting old had done to her and she would weep. She would continually apologise and promise not to be a burden.

'Don't have me put away in one of those terrible nursing homes, will you, Maureen? I will get well, I promise.' Then to Tony, 'I'm so grateful to you for coming to live here, Tony. I don't know how to thank you, except to say that all I have when I'm dead and gone will be yours.'

Tony, Maureen and the children had moved from their own small house into Nancy's smart, five bed-roomed, double-fronted house on the edge of the village. Tony regretted the move but if he had refused, Maureen would have found it difficult to help her mother with a half mile distance between their two homes.

He could see that caring for her mother was too much for Maureen, in spite of his help and the children's acceptance of the situation. At least, they had accepted the situation until they found that living with their old and ill grandmother was interfering with their lives.

One early Saturday afternoon, Sharon's heart-throb boyfriend, Cory, called at the house to ask her to his cricket's team get-together that evening. Nancy's comfortable chair in the family sitting room happened to be empty. She was taking an after-lunch nap in her room at the front of the house. It had been a reception room which had been converted into a bedroom for convenience.

Cory was asked to take a seat in the sitting room. Before Sharon had the chance to beckon him to sit on the big settee, he sat in Nancy's chair. It looked comfortable with its ample, plump cushions. He sank back on them, looking very much at ease. As if on a stretch of elastic, his broad grin of a laissez faire attitude dropped when he put his hands under the seat of his pristine cricket-whites, surreptitiously withdrawing them before looking at and smelling them. He had sat on a faecal and urine-soaked cushion.

Maureen hadn't got around to clean the chair when Nancy was out of it, as she usually did, to avoid the malodour lingering.

Cory then slowly rose from the chair by holding its arms and gripping their ends. His hands, too, became smeared with slimy faeces, which smelled, and it became clear where the smell was coming from. It was always in the air, anyway.

Cory's eyes widened and his raised brows arched as he stared at the faeces on his white shirt-sleeves. Revulsion turned his stomach; he retched as he leapt from the chair and made for the front door. He vomited on the doorstep.

Sharon was distraught. 'It's Granny. I'm very sorry. She's old.'

'That's OK,' he said, feeling at a loss for suitable words. 'I'll just get home and change.'

Sharon had accompanied Cory through the hall which passed Nancy's room. 'Maureen!' she shouted. 'Who's that?'

Sharon didn't attend the cricket club get-together that evening. She was ashamed. The humiliation filled her with thoughts of leaving home. For Tony, her father, that was the last straw but he couldn't think of the best way to put things right without upsetting Maureen.

Nature stepped in and helped him.

Maureen had battled on until she collapsed. She was ill and was admitted urgently to our local hospital. She'd had uterine problems for some time and underwent an overdue hysterectomy. (Surgical removal of the womb).

Nancy was taken to the Bedford Home of The Nightingale Nursing Homes for respite care; initially for four weeks, with the intention of giving Maureen time to recuperate after her operation.

Rehabilitation following a hysterectomy usually takes longer than that and Maureen hadn't been in the best of health before surgery. She had been ground down by trying to keep the household going normally, keeping Tony and the children happy and caring for her elderly, demanding mother.

When Nancy's physical and mental state was assessed at The Bedford Nursing Home before returning to her home, it was considered that she needed care that couldn't be provided by Maureen. No matter what help the social services were able to give, it wouldn't be enough. Arrangements were made for Nancy to remain a resident, indefinitely, at the nursing home.

The Bedford Home became Nancy's home where she was visited by Maureen several times a week. She felt guilty by having to admit that her mother had to be "put away" but she had almost forgotten how good life could be.

I was pleased Maureen had asked me to visit Nancy when she was on holiday. I had recently retired from the National Health Service and had time on my hands. I had visited her previously, at the same time as I visited Bronwen, an old friend who was also a resident there, but usually I was with Maureen.

Nancy seemed well settled. Her memory had deteriorated and she didn't always understand where she was and why we were visiting her.

At the time Nancy became a resident in the nursing home, horror stories of thousands of people dying in hospitals and nursing homes throughout the country from bad care or a lack of it, hadn't yet hit the headlines of the media. They did so with vehemence soon afterwards.

The Nightingale Nursing Homes had a good reputation. However, when I visited, I observed areas of nursing procedures and communication which had room for improvement. I was of the opinion they would continue, unless the powers that be discovered that the current nurse training would not result in heightening the prestige of our profession, as it was expected to, but denigrate it.

Myself and my erstwhile colleagues predicted this might happen. We repeatedly emphasised the disgraceful error of the bureaucrats and academics. I often wonder what possessed them. Was it an increase in power they expected?

When it was agreed that the NHS long-term care nursing homes were being sold to profiteers, our leaders could not foresee what the outcome of that would be. Fat cats who aimed to get fatter bought them. They did not concern themselves enough about the future care of the elderly and infirm. It appears they considered financial gain rather than care and protection of the elderly and infirm.

Most of our nursing homes are now privately owned and in the world of nurse training there have been erroneous changes the politicians and bureaucrats have been loath to admit to.

I was nursing long enough to be able to see this. It is basically a practical occupation, not an academic career. The words of my first tutor remain etched on my mind, "We want first class nurses not third class doctors".

No matter how much of the financial cake is poured into our valued NHS, patients will continue to die needlessly because of badly trained nurses. I have seen that they work hard but they appear to me, to lack the knowledge of the cause and effect of disease and the physical and emotional needs of the sick.

However; compassionate, dedicated and knowledgeable nurses still comprise the majority, and most of those are of "the old nursing school". Our salvation lies in the passing on of their skills and attitudes to those that follow them, before they, too, become a minority. In the past ten to fifteen years I have seen and experienced a decrease in their number.

The law stipulates that every nursing home must have a professional registered nurse in charge, day and night. More often than not, two registered nurses are required, dependent on the number of residents within the nursing home. The remaining staff is predominantly untrained nursing aides who learn their skills from experienced nursing aides. The latter have learned to recognise the needs of the elderly and mentally infirm as a result of long service. They are, usually, skillful and compassionate. It is said that they **must** be compassionate because the financial remuneration is ungenerous. They know the fate of the elderly and infirm if the wrong people are employed to care for them – and all too often they are.

Some months before I retired from the National Health Service after twenty-three years, Carole Jones, the Personnel Manager of The Nightingale Nursing Homes approached me on the way out, after seeing Nancy. Carole and I had been acquaintances for some time and she'd heard from Maureen Tate that I would soon have time on my hands. Carole asked me if I would consider working for them for a short time to organise a training programme for carers already in their employ who'd had no experience of carrying out personal care. I was surprised and thanked her, but I was beginning to enjoy having the days to myself, and Derek liked it. I explained this to Carole; she understood and the matter was forgotten – so I thought.

One evening I visited Nancy when Maureen, Tony and the family were on holiday. I was a little later than usual. I thought I would be a nuisance because it was just after six o'clock; the residents' supper time. Some called it "high tea" as we did at home in my young days. Whatever it was called the food smelled and looked mouth-watering and there was a pleasant atmosphere.

Nancy had a disposable bib on to protect her pretty blouse and a small table had been placed securely in front of her chair. A young carer brought the meal on a tray and placed it on the table as she spoke to Nancy. 'It's cooked ham, Nancy, and a couple of vegetables. Treacle pudding and custard for afters. Can you manage yourself or shall I help you?'

The carer was wearing a pale green, uniform dress and her hair was held neatly back from her face with a pony-tale ring.

'If you don't mind me being here at this time, I'll help Nancy with her supper, Nurse. I know the difficulty she has using her bad side.' I referred to her left side which was paralysed by the stroke she'd had some four years before. The carer blushed.

'I'm not a nurse, Mrs Phillips. I'm a part-time carer until I start my training.' She pointed to the name badge on the pocket of her dress. 'I'm Mandy. I know your name because my mother was here once when you came to see Nancy and she remembers you from when you were a tutor. She was a staff nurse in Nevill Hall then. Gloria Rees.'

I must have looked surprised. 'Well, that's making me feel my age. I remember your mother. Give her my regards and I hope you'll become as good a nurse as she is.'

'I intend to try but she says the training is not good now. It's all writing and research and I'm not so good at that.' She laughed. 'My mum said the trained nurses now are said to be "too posh to wash." They have degrees.'

Nancy tapped my arm. 'Shirley, what about my supper, then?'

As I spoke, I was using hand-sanitizer which I always carried in my bag before I took up the knife and fork from the tray.

'Sorry Nancy. Yes, Mandy, nursing is having very bad press; it's shameful. There is a minority who have no compassion and lack the ability and knowledge that are expected of them. But we mustn't believe all we hear and read. The majority of our nurses must be like you and your mother.'

'I hope so,' she replied. 'I'll leave Nancy to you, then. '

Nancy and I chatted as she ate. I was surprised she remembered my name, though she did ask after Maureen.

'You've forgotten she and the family are in Spain. They'll be back next week.'

Nancy looked offended. 'Maureen didn't tell me she was going away. Spain! That's across the water, isn't it? Who's looking after the little ones?'

'Yes, Spain is across the sea but they went in an aeroplane so they'll be back soon. And those little ones are teenagers now and they've gone with them.'

She continued to look confused. 'Well, never mind, I'm tired now and I want to go to the toilet. You'll have to take me.' I realised that was a hint for me to leave.

She held out her good arm and grabbed my hand. It was too late for the lavatory; she had already wet herself, but I called over a carer and explained. She smiled. 'All right, Shirl, I'll get someone to give me a hand.'

I was not enamoured by her unprofessional address of me but I supposed it was because the nurse in charge, Elaine Kenwood and myself were on first name turns. She had been a staff nurse on a surgical ward when I was at The Nevill Hall Hospital School of Nursing.

Two carers did what we use to call "the underarm lift". I cringed on seeing Nancy being scraped from her dining chair onto a wheelchair. The movement was called "the drag lift" for obvious reasons and known to be dangerous for lifter and lifted. Lifting aids were available in the NHS hospitals and had just become available to the private nursing homes. They were considered simple devices but were expensive for what they were, as was the training to use them, since extra staff had to be taken on to free the selected key lifters to attend the courses.

Before I left I poked my nose through the open door of the unit office to bid a good evening to Elaine Kenwood and to ask her to give my compliments to the kitchen staff because the meals were excellent. I made a point of mentioning the lifting technique used on Nancy.

'She's thin and incontinent; I'd hate her to have a pressure sore.'

I had the impression that Elaine was offended by my intrusion. 'Yes,' she said, 'we're actually having some lifting aids delivered next week and the rep will show us how to use them. And we are sending two of our carers from each of our three homes on a course as soon as we can. They will be "key lifters" and will train others.

'We already have lifting and moving hoists for the bathrooms and they're a Godsend but the residents don't like them very much.' Elaine chuckled. 'They feel as if they're flying through the air, which they are, and they're afraid of being dropped.'

I nonchalantly donned my gloves to leave. 'I expect you'll all get used to them. I hope so anyway. I wouldn't want to see any nurse end up with a back like mine. That problem never goes away. Anyway, since I'm here, would I be in the way if I popped up to say hello to Bronwen Morgan?'

'No, of course not. But I'll warn you not to stay long because you know it's National Lottery night, don't you?'

I nodded a grin. 'No, I hadn't forgotten. I hope she wins.'

Elaine walked from behind her desk and accompanied me up the corridor. I sensed she had something more important than the lottery to discuss.

'Shirley, now you've retired from the Service would you consider again coming back to work for a few months. I know Carole has already mentioned it when you hadn't long retired

19

from Nevill Hall School. An ad will be going into the local newspaper, hoping to attract someone with nurse training experience. People with your experience have become dinosaurs. Will you give it another thought? Carole said to mention to you that the boss will be coming next week.' She referred to Mr Miraj Rajiv, one of the directors. 'He lives in London so is not here every week.'

I had pushed Carole's previous request for me to consider taking the training manager's position to the back of my mind.

'Oh, I don't know. Am I really what you're looking for – because you know I have a back problem?'

'There'll be no hands-on. No lifting for you.' Carole didn't expect an immediate reply. 'Just think about it.'

Elaine held open the wide doors of Willow Lounge to let me through. I had been taken by surprise. 'I'll think about it but at the moment I expect the answer will be no. The spirit is willing but the flesh is weak. I'm not as fit as I used to be. Anyway, I'll just say hello to Bron. I won't interfere with the lottery.'

As I approached Bronwen Morgan, where she was sitting in a comfortable armchair facing the wide screen of the television, there must have been an unusual expression on my face.

Her wheelchair was beside her, within reach should she need it to go to the toilet or wander between the two lounges. She was able to move from chair to chair under her own steam of kinesis and wheelchair herself around. Her arms were strong.

Bronwen spent her daytime hours in Willow Lounge, where the more able residents did. Nancy was in Oak Lounge, with those who were totally dependent on others for care and constant observation.

'Hello, my lovely.' Bronwen was always cheerful in spite of her condition. She had been struck by poliomyelitis when she was a child of six. She miraculously lived through it but was left with no power in her legs. She described them as looking like broom handles. The muscles had been destroyed by the disease.

She beckoned me to a chair beside her. 'You look as if you've lost a pound and found a penny. But never mind, I'll have won the lottery tonight. You won't go short.' She never failed to make me laugh.

I'd known Bronwen since I was a ward sister; over fifteen years before. She had been admitted to the acute medical ward with pneumonia.

I replied. 'Oh, it's nothing. I've just been seeing Nancy. Her memory is getting worse. She'd forgotten that the family were on holiday.'

'Never mind, as long as she's comfortable. My chariot takes me up to make sure they're keeping an eye on her. The carers are lovely here – at least most of them are.'

I nodded. 'That's good.' I couldn't think of much to say; my mind was on Elaine's invitation to apply for the training position. Bronwen seemed to read my thoughts. We talked gossip for a while but I couldn't wait to get away to ask Derek what he thought about me coming back to work, though I knew he wouldn't be pleased.

'You feel a bit low again, I can see that.' Bronwen was one of very few who knew I was a depressive. 'You miss your work. I'd bet you'd get a training job in a minute, if you wanted. From what I'm reading and seeing on the telly the care in the hospitals is going to the dogs. Something will have to change.'

'I'm a bit over the hill for teaching nurse carers now, Bron. But as for the telly, I'll love you and leave you because you'll want to watch the run-up to the National Lottery.'

'Yes, my lovely. Come and see me for a bit if you come in the week, won't you?'

I did, indeed, visit during the week and I witnessed an event which made me realise the dire need for young carers to undergo basic training. I had been a nurse for so long that, I think, basic care came to me spontaneously and I expected everyone to be the same.

The following week I visited Nancy again. Maureen and the family hadn't returned from their holiday. I was chatting with her after the late meal had been cleared away and the unit was back to normal. All the residents of Oak Lounge were seated in their usual chairs, dozing or looking at the television, except for elderly Albert Thomas. He was still at the table in the dining area. He was sitting with his meal in front of him and a young carer standing beside him was trying to spoon food into his mouth.

'Albert,' she said for the umpteenth time, 'you've got to eat this. Come on, now, open your cake hole and let me get it down you. The suppers have been cleared away and I have a bus to catch.' His down in the mouth expression was pitiful.

I was appalled. I was reminded of my early training days at the mentally infirm hospital where residents were treated without an ounce of compassion and understanding.

I left Nancy and sauntered across to Albert's table. The carer was aware of my cold stare as she held the spoon in mid-air. She looked sheepish. 'He'll lose weight if he doesn't eat and Elaine has told us he must be encouraged to take his meals.'

'All right, dear. You'd best go and catch your bus.' She sensed my cynicism. 'I'll sit and chat to Albert.'

She had the nerve to cock a snoot as she slammed down the spoon, splashing food-bits onto the tablecloth. I considered she didn't mean to be unkind; she just didn't know how to approach Albert.

'If you don't want to eat, Albert,' I smiled, 'then why should a slip of a girl make you. She'll have a piece of cold tongue when I see her afterwards.'

To my surprise Albert was amused and chuckled. 'Aye, you're right,' he said. 'Can't feed myself with these,' he said as he held up his gnarled hands. 'An' I can't gulp it down the way I'm expected to. Cheeky little bugger.'

'Why not eat in your own time, then? The food is quite good here, isn't it?' 'Aye, and I'm partial to a nice bit o' cottage pie. Tha's wha' 'tis, aint it?'

'Yes. I'll get it warmed up in the microwave and you can give it a try.'

I took his meal to the open, wide kitchen hatch and asked the pristine, all-over white, uniformed assistant cook to get the meal micro-waved. She was at the end of the clearing up and looked suspicious until she recognised me from my several visits. She took the tray from me, did as I suggested and I returned to Albert with the meal. I scooped a small piece of the slightly spoiled meal onto a fork and put it to his mouth. He took it and slapped his lips.

'Nice,' he said.

I spoke quietly and slowly as he ate and he nodded and chewed. He ate the whole meal and the apple-crumble sweet.

Janet Daniel, Elaine's deputy, was in charge that evening. As I left she handed me a bulky A4 envelope. 'Carole asked me to give you this. Rajiv was here yesterday,' she said. 'He'd heard about your retirement from the Service and Carole told him about you.' The official-looking envelope contained an application for the position of a nurse training manager.

I had seen the advertisement for the post in the local newspaper and thought the position would have been taken.

'Have you not had any applicants, yet?' I asked.

Janet shook her head. 'No one that fits the bill. If we don't get someone to do the job soon, Carole said we'll be in trouble with the inspectors.'

The next morning I completed the application form and handed it to Elaine the following evening with the intention of speaking to the director to discuss a job description.

Less than a week later I received a formal letter of invitation for interview. I telephoned Carole. She had usually gone off duty when I visited The Homes. She told me Miraj Rajiv was most impressed by my curriculum vitae and was determined to encourage me to join them.

Carole spoke with a giggle. 'He came into the office swishing the air with your application form and CV and said he was disappointed with just a couple of GCSEs. He was joking and read out your qualifications. My, you've been around. You could do this training job blind folded. They are lovely girls, but young, and have to learn to recognise the needs of the elderly.'

'I'd need to keep my eyes wide open but thank you for the compliment. If I decide to accept the job I hope I can live up to your expectations.'

Chapter 2

THE HOMES

Having met Mr Rajiv I found him to be a pleasant, persuasive gentleman. I agreed to accept the position as training manager at The Nightingale Nursing Homes for the elderly and elderly mentally infirm on condition it would be for a limited period; no more than six to nine months, a year at the most. He and Carole were delighted and so was I.

The three homes are attractively purpose-built, situated on a steep hill.

The home at the top of the hill is the elderly care Bedford Home, named after the famous Mrs Bedford-Fenwick, the first Registered Nurse. The middle home, further down the hill is Bevan Home, after the great Aneurin Bevan, and cares for the elderly mentally infirm, (EMI) and the home at the bottom of the hill is the name of the homes, Nightingale Home, after the great pioneer of professional nursing, Florence. This, too, is an EMI unit.

Each of the three homes is of two storeys; ground floor, which is the living and working area and above are the residents' private rooms. Each building is in two sections, the centre being the wide hallway of the main entrance leading to the lift and staircase. On the left of the entrance is a large lounge and dining area, kitchen, the staff rest-room and a few ancillary rooms. On the right is another big lounge and a few single resident rooms.

The main kitchen is in Bedford Home, the interview and classroom in Bevan Home and the laundry in the Nightingale Home.

The rooms on the ground floor are favoured but are reserved, as necessary, for allocation to the terminally ill.

On my first day, Mr Rajiv happened to be there. He had travelled from London that morning. I assumed it was his gesture of courtesy. Carole, of course, was there and his secretary, Pat Todd.

It was agreed that my main remit was to formulate a short basic training programme for employees and to observe their practice.

At one point during the meeting, Rajiv became a little hesitant when he discussed a possible addition to the responsibilities of the post. He admitted he would like me to involve myself in marketing, of which I knew nothing, and a duty of which I **could** undertake – the assessment of the abilities of incoming residents.

I agreed. The multiformity of the position appealed to me, though I had to admit my apprehension of marketing. We discussed plans for the future of The Homes. He did most of the talking!

I felt elated at being back at work; satisfied that I had accepted the post. However, knowing Derek's feelings about me being back on the job, I repeated that it must be understood, it was to be a short term contract.

I was there for five memorable years.

I had been retired from the National Health Service less than six months. I was approaching sixty and should have been pleased to leave, but I wasn't. I felt I still had something to give to nursing. I didn't want retirement.

Project 2000 training had already been underway in a number of countries and we had followed. Changes already begun to filter down before I left the NHS.

My colleagues and I despaired of the radical changes. Many of us had predicted that the direction of nursing being organised from the lecture room, rather than at the bedside of the patients, was doomed to failure. We were correct and there has been much destruction of the prestige of our respected profession.

I had given a lot of myself to nurse training, often to the detriment of my family. I was sad leaving the NHS, especially The Nevill Hall Hospital. The sadness of tear-filled eyes around me as I left the school for the last time, told me that others were sad that I was going.

However, my departure was timely. Back pain had taken over my life and I had worked each day under the influence of potent analgesics. This had to stop as I was feeling one of its side effects – gastric irritation. Discomfort led to depression.

Clinical depression became acute and I was concerned about burdening Derek with my low spirit; his business was keeping him fully occupied. I reverted to something I had been determined not to – antidepressants. However, they helped and being at work at The Nightingale Nursing Homes was my salvation. Many of the residents made me feel a wimp and a hypochondriac. The depression I suffered was insignificant compared with the dire, deep abyss of many of the residents.

During the time I worked at The Homes I saw physical and emotional suffering that had been beyond my imagination. It made me wonder if, when I was in general nursing, I had displayed the compassion and understanding that patients with mentally disturbed conditions deserved.

When on medical and surgical wards I remember administering medication to relieve depression. I taught others to do so and explained the effect of the medication but didn't chastise when hearing the insensitive cliché, 'Why doesn't she just snap out of it?' I didn't then have the understanding I have now and I have to admit, it remains limited.

Being at The Nightingale Nursing Homes' three units, part of my mind was touched that would otherwise have remained dormant. I became involved in incidents which were bad and good, but more of the latter. I considered part of my remit was to correct that which was not good. I wonder if I accomplished what was expected of me, because hardly a week goes by without hearing of a hospital or nursing home atrocity. The media can be vicious but, necessarily informative. We have to know.

After a few weeks at The Homes, Nancy Baine died. She forgot her left side was paralysed and attempted to walk to the toilet unaided. She fell against the hot-drinks trolley that was being taken around by Mary, one of the carers.

Mary was pouring milk into a feeding-cup which was in her left hand, the right hand held the milk jug. The large hot teapot toppled over the rim of the trolley and piping hot tea poured over Nancy's face and neck, scalding her ageing, fragile skin, as she lay helpless on the floor.

Mary yelled and within seconds was being helped to raise Nancy slowly and carefully back into her chair. As well as being scalded, she had fractured her femur. She screamed with pain.

An emergency ambulance transported her to The Nevill Hall Hospital where two days later she underwent essential surgery to correct the fracture. She didn't recover.

It was a traumatic event which should have been avoided. Mary, Maureen and others became ridden with guilt as well as sadness. A guilt complex struck me; I thought it might have been my punishment for not giving Nancy more time, or not being at home helping Derek. He assured me I was wrong and sensed, as I did, an oncoming phase of acute depression. However, my work at The Nightingale Homes helped me to shrug it off.

Those residents in community private nursing homes remain under the auspices of the National Health Service. The Nightingale Nursing Homes have their own general practitioners within the NHS who can be called upon when necessary and The Homes' nearest hospital is The Nevill Hall Hospital. In spite of its increasing faults we are fortunate to have the NHS. Millions of people are alive and happy, thanks to its services and in spite of the damning media broadcasts.

The rule of the elderly and other vulnerable groups being given the influenza immunisation is one of the essentials provided throughout the nation by the NHS. Many of us tend to forget its immense protection and take it for granted.

The majority of residents of The Nightingale Nursing Homes received their "jabs" by visiting nurses and GPs. By appointment, a selected number are taken in small groups to the nearby health centre. It provides an opportunity for the chosen residents to get out for a short time.

I became involved in an unusual event during the first winter I was at The Homes. I smile to this day when something brings it to mind – jab day.

One bright, sparkling October morning, Janine Jarvis, one of the senior EMI .I. carers and I, volunteered to take four residents to the nearby surgery to get their flu jabs. We decided it would be good for them to be out on such a beautiful day; their outings were rare. The four residents selected were delighted; it was a treat for them. Iris and Bill from Bevan Home and Horace and Pricilla Jane from Nightingale Home.

Pricilla Jane was a victim of Down's Syndrome. She was in her late thirties but looked younger; a characteristic of the condition. Liam Drew, one of the registered psychiatric nurses in charge of Nightingale Home, knew that the psychosis of the four we were taking was controlled. I hadn't given that a thought. They all seemed as "normal" as myself.

I saw Pricilla Jane as a delightful lady. As a ray of sunlight; she was always happy, smiling and affectionate. Everyone loved Pricilla Jane.

However, Liam Drew once told me that when Pricilla Jane moved into one of her "rages" it took three of them to restrain her; to prevent her harming herself or others. She could be dangerous and I found that difficult to comprehend, so I shut my mind to it.

Off we went in the sunshine to keep the eleven o'clock appointment. We had decided to miss our elevenses. After the immunisations, Janine and I decided to take the four residents into a nearby café to have drinks and cream cakes.

We all made an extra effort to look smart. Janine wore a well-pressed uniform, I had shed my white coat and wore a good skirt, sweater and jacket.

The immunisations were administered uneventfully and it was pleasant afterwards, tripping the short distance to a nearby café where we had decided to have refreshments.

We were a group of six but squeezed around a table for four. Janine and I ordered coffee and sponge cake, our four companions chose soft drinks and jam doughnuts to be followed by ice-cream.

There were others in the café. The fine weather had enticed the local people out to enjoy the autumn sunshine

I was taken aback when a woman with a face of daggers stared at me. She was sharing a table with three other people and a little boy.

'Disgusting,' she huffed. 'People like that shouldn't be allowed to come into the town.'

Janine and I ignored her. Our companions didn't seem to sense, or care about, the resentment. They went on enjoying the refreshments.

The woman, loudly, repeated her remarks and I decided she should be responded to. I turned to face her to let her know I was about to speak.

'People like that,' I said through clenched teeth, 'are as good as you and better, since your nasty tongue doesn't stay in your mouth.'

The woman cocked a snoot and I thought the argument was settled. Calamity arose when the little boy, who was sitting beside the woman, approached Pricilla Jane, stuck out his tongue and punched the arm which held her ice-cream cone. She was about to lick from the top of the blob when her arm was jerked and it fell to the floor.

Pricilla Jane yelled and began to cry loudly. She attacked the little boy and began to strike him heavily about his face and head.

She screamed and punched, screamed and punched. I feared Pricilla Jane was entering one of her psychotic rages.

While this was going on, our other three companions were shouting obscenities at the woman and threateningly raised their fists to those at her table and others in the café. Big Horace, the fourth of our residents, picked up the boy as he would have a kitten and threw him at the nearest woman. The boy began to yell and the situation had become nasty.

'Call the police!' someone shouted. The man behind the counter was struck motionless but he shook himself and made for a phone that was on the wall behind him.

Janine intercepted. She held up her hand and shouted. 'That won't be necessary, we're leaving.' She lifted the lid of a large, chest freezer which was against the wall just inside the doorway. She scooped out a handful of iced lollies and forced them onto Pricilla Jane. She calmed immediately, smiled and, unfortunately, wet herself. Urine pooled on the floor and trickled in several directions. I thought afterwards that Pricilla Jane must have a large urinary bladder.

We left the shop, omitting to pay the bill. Before we were half way back to The Homes everyone's demeanour had returned to normal, as if nothing out of the ordinary had happened.

Our adventurous outing became well known at The Homes and resulted in a lot of laughter.

Chapter 3

THE FLU JAB

Derek and I were given appointments on the same day for our immunisations against influenza. We both agreed that we were lucky to have this magnificent service available to us. Others waiting in the queue seemed to disagree. They seemed to have forgotten the importance and reason for being immunised. I enjoyed myself; it was a pleasant social gathering.

It was on a Monday, when Gilwern, our home for over thirty years, is usually like a ghost town. Only the Post Office and the chemist is open all day and the doctor's surgery until noon.

When Derek and I passed the surgery to get our influenza vaccinations we wondered what tragedy had struck the village. A crowd of people stood outside the door.

I parked opposite the old antique shop, about twenty yards from the surgery. It was a bit far for Derek to walk but he said he could manage the distance. He would use his crutches.

Not only was the surgery packed with senior citizens but there were also those who waited outside. It was a good thing the November day was fine.

Derek and I eventually got into the surgery but all the seats were taken in the waiting room and the floor space was crammed with those standing.

When Derek tottered in with me close behind him, a man sitting near the door stood up and offered him his seat. We thanked him. It was Dudley Crow, an old acquaintance.

'Hello, Dudley. Haven't seen you for ages.'

He and Derek chatted, though Dudley did most of the chatting because he was as deaf as a post and would not have heard what Derek had to say.

Dudley complained about having to come to have needles stuck into him at his time of life and about the swine 'flu which he believed was being made too much fuss of. Derek simply smiled and nodded.

I looked directly at Dudley so that he could read my lips and mimed that we were not there for the swine 'flu vaccine. He looked surprised.

'No? What're we here for then?'

I smiled. 'Don't worry. They'll explain when your turn comes.'

Looking around I saw a number of people I knew. I spotted Betty and Bob Townsend. They'd popped in our house for tea the day before. She came across to me and said she was surprised that Derek and I were there because I hadn't mentioned it. She hadn't told me they would be there, either. Apparently, she hadn't thought about it until she looked at her kitchen calendar that morning.

She, also, complained about having to be there. She thought it was for the protection against the swine 'flu virus, otherwise she would not have come. She was having her son and family arriving that afternoon and had a lot to do.

She and Bob had already had their 'flu jabs; they had got there early and I wondered why they were still in the waiting room. Bob had joined us so heard me asking.

'You tell us,' he said, 'you're the nurse.' I explained it was a precaution, in case of a reaction to the serum.

I realised, then, why the waiting room was so full and whispered to Betty that it would have made more sense if those who had been treated waited outside. She looked around doubtfully and agreed. She made for the door beckoning Bob to follow her.

Martin Pike, who had kept the village pub before handing over to his son, complained about the fact that we had all been given the same appointment time. He said he thought it a shambles; Martin was a champion moaner. So was his wife, Hazel. She muttered something about being treated like a lot of sheep.

Ted Powell, retired solicitor, grumbled his agreement and suggested the appointment times should have been staggered.

I told him that I thought nine o'clock till twelve was pretty flexible and it was for our own good we were asked to stay a while. He sneered and stormed off.

I heard a few other muttered complaints and there was an exodus from the waiting-room of the people who'd had their injection.

Anyway, I had a seat. The others sitting down were reading magazines and journals. I just sat and looked around.

The room was bright and warm. An old saying of my grandfather passed through my mind: "*look more at the roses and less at the greenfly*". It was not until I was older did I realise he was not thinking simply of the roses within the boundary of his small allotment but about life in general. Some of us forget what our surgeries had to offer in "the good old days". They weren't so good.

I was born and went to school in a mining valley where life was hard. Poverty was rife. When I was cold and hungry there were plenty of others around me. I accepted hardship and illnesses as the norm. We had no National Health Service.

As I sat in the surgery waiting-room I reminisced about a time when I went to the surgery with my mother. I was five and it was November 1939.

My mother and father had quarrelled the evening before. He had caught sight of her ash-tray overflowing with cigarette ends and ash. He was a miner and the thought of his hard-earned wage going up in smoke angered him.

He picked up the ash-tray and flung it across the room at my mother. She didn't move out of the path of the flying ash-tray fast enough and it caught her a glancing blow on her neck. She gasped and for a few seconds she couldn't breath.

My father grabbed his coat from a hook behind the scullery door and darted off. He decided to escape the following scenario.

The next morning my mother's neck was so swollen and painful she could hardly move her head. Aunty Hilda, who lived next door, advised my mother to go to the doctor's. My mother took her advice and kept me home from school to go with her.

Getting there was a few pennies' bus-ride. The bus-stop was directly outside Doctor Richards' surgery. Whoever needed to see him wasn't expected to make an appointment. We simply went and waited.

The surgery and waiting room was a converted end-of-street house, similar to the one we lived in but bigger and in better condition; no leaking roof when it rained.

The house belonging to Doctor Richards was made clear by the gleaming plate on the front door. The polished brass plate bore the doctor's name and medical degrees and was all that cheered the front of the surgery. The flaking brown paint and chipped brick-work didn't deter the constant flow of disease-carrying humans who attended there for morning and evening surgeries.

The front room had become the waiting room with a small reception desk behind a half door that looked like the entrance to a stable. Behind it was a small pharmacy where a woman dispensed medicines. The scullery at the back of the house had been converted into the doctor's consulting room.

When my mother and I got to the surgery we found it packed. Wooden benches, warped at their centres under the strain of the hip to hip squatters, lined the walls of the waiting room. Snorting, coughing people were elbow to elbow.

The queue to see the doctor extended through to the passageway and out onto the flag-stones of the front path. It was half-past eight. Surgery didn't open until nine o'clock. My mother wondered whether we should go home. She was worried about the fire going out and getting everything done before my father came home from work. The dinner had to be cooked and his boiler of bath-water warmed. And she had to call into the shop for bread.

Over an hour later, my mother acquired a seat in the fusty, smoke-filled waiting room. Most of the waiting men rolled their own from strong, shag tobacco into a Rizzla paper, then lit the straggling end and inhaled deeply. They puffed out the throat-catching smoke, coughed and spluttered. I was glad spitting wasn't allowed in the surgery.

Babies, some with colic, running noses, coughs and rashes, cried fretfully in the arms of their mothers.

Mrs Thomas, the receptionist, with hands, mouth and nose peeping through a hatch of the make-shift records' office beckoned my mother to come forward. My mother plonked me onto the bench so that no-one could take her place.

Mrs Thomas asked some personal details. While Mam responded in a hoarse whisper, my attention was taken by a girl of about fourteen. She was kneeling on the floor, in front of her share of the bench, resting her elbows on the seat. Her face was clean, pink and acned from forehead to neck. There I noticed a tide-mark, the demarcation between a washed face and an unwashed body.

She smiled broadly, displaying a row of even, but decaying teeth. She asked me why we were there.

The girl looked to the reception desk where my mother was standing, answering questions in a lowered voice through the cubby-hole.

I wanted to satisfy the girl's curiosity but I was ashamed of what had happened. I distracted her and asked her why she was there. The girl was willing to tell all.

She had boils. Two under one arm, one under the other and three on her bum, but she said she wouldn't mention the ones on her bum to the doctor because she didn't like to. She said she could rub the same stuff on her bum as under her arms. I guessed it was because she wasn't wearing knickers.

She went on. 'But it hurts awful, even to touch, let alone rub stuff on it. That's why I can't sit on my place on the bench.'

I nodded, showing my understanding.

My mother came back from the receptionist and moved me off the bench to take her place again. The girl asked her what was wrong with her neck.

My mother looked frostily at the girl and didn't answer.

The girl's cheerful smile dropped. She rose from her haunches and straightened her back. Supporting her buttocks, she slowly turned her back on us and gave her attention to the man sitting on that side.

Eventually, my mother's name was called. She grabbed my hand and marched me through into the doctor's room.

Doctor Richards sat behind a large desk, an ash-tray at arms' length, filled with dead cigarette ends. He looked up as we entered, taking a last puff on the cigarette he was smoking and stubbed the remainder into the ash-tray.

He beckoned my mother to the chair in front of his desk and turned to his writing, dipping a pen into the inkwell on the stand in front of him.

My mother sat down and pulled me close, waiting for the doctor to speak. He placed the card he was writing on into a wooden box at the side of him.

He smiled at me before addressing my mother. 'What can I do for you, Mrs Meredith?' He glanced at her and saw the angry wound along her neck. He moved from behind the desk and came towards her.

He held her neck and prodded around the swelling. She winced. He asked her what had happened.

I thought she was going to say it was an accident. I was wrong. She told the doctor her husband had thrown an ash-tray at her.

The doctor tutted. 'Well, I think you've been lucky.' He bent towards her, looking closely at the swelling.

'No major damage but another half inch it would have severed the carotid, an important artery here.' He prodded again and again she winced.

He went back behind his desk, sat and scribbled on a slip of headed paper. 'You must bathe the swelling in cold water then rub on the ointment Miss Rattrey will dispense for you.'

My mother nodded.

'Then I suggest you and your husband behave like adults. Here's the prescription. Good morning to you.'

We left the doctor's room and went to the cubby-hole where Miss Rattrey, the pharmacist, hid behind the shelves which supported demijohns of coloured liquid. She appeared and my mother handed her the piece of paper. She disappeared behind the shelves again and after a few minutes returned with a small jar of ointment. At the time I thought it to be a magic remedy but I've realised since it was simply Vaseline. Miss Rattrey asked my mother for her full name and wrote it in a ledger before telling her it was sixpence and that it would be stopped from my father's pay.

When we passed back through the waiting-room it was still crammed with people.

It was nice getting out into the air. It was damp and cold but better than in the sick-filled surgery. My feet felt like blocks of ice. No socks; they were being kept clean for school.

When we got home the fire had gone out so I had to go next door to Aunty Hilda for a kettle of water to wash our dishes. My sister, Rosy, came from school soon afterwards and helped.

When my father came in from work I told him my mother had been to the doctor's and explained that he had said her carrot arty was nearly broken. My father was unperturbed and asked my mother if the doctor gave anything to put on it.

I answered for my mother and held up the small pot she had put on the dresser-shelf. He grunted. 'I suppose that'll be taken out of my pay.'

Rosy interrupted, informing him that soon we won't have to pay anything to the doctor or for any medicines; everything would be free. She had been told at school of the approach of a national health service. She told us there'd be new hospitals and new doctors' surgeries.

I remember Rosy saying that as if it were yesterday. The National Health Service came into being almost ten years later.

My thoughts were broken into by the receptionist calling Derek and me into the clinical area to have our vaccinations.

There were still mutterings and grumblings as we passed through on our way out. I thought, perhaps, more respect should be given to the progress of the last fifty years and of the millions of us walking about today who would otherwise be dead.

I remember the suffering and premature deaths of my past and I think of my grandfather's philosophy; look more at the roses and less at the greenfly. We have a lot to be grateful for.

My grandfather worked down a coal mine until he was sixty-five – the age miners were allowed to retire, if they lived until then. Pneumoconiosis (coal-dust on the lungs) took many before they had the privilege of getting old. Miner's lung was a common disease among men of the mining valleys. "Occupational hazard", it would be referred to now.

It was accepted as the norm; to be expected. So there was little or no treatment available for those who suffered with it, except home brewed remedies. A towel-covered head over a bowl of steaming water straight from a boiled kettle to which would be added tincture of balsam or oil of eucalyptus; two common methods which I remember my grandmother concocting. There was no long acting effective treatment available or offered by the mine-owners.

'My little bit of Heaven,' was my grandfather's description of his allotment. He spent all his leisure time there, breathing in "God's fresh air."

He died at the age of seventy-two. I have always been of the opinion that it was his allotment which allowed him to live to that "good age".

He was a dear man who turned his eyes from greenfly – except when they were on his rambling roses. We knew his suffering only when he gasped from a tight chest and coughed up black sputum into a spittoon. He had no qualms about expectorating into it when with us, his family, in the living room. My grandmother insisted he didn't feel that he had to go into the back yard but he most often did.

Chapter 4

THE BLACK DOG

I am a victim of clinical depression. Sir Winston Churchill was too. It was he who referred to it as "The Black Dog". I admit to my affliction. It is said that self-recognition is part of the cure. There is "no cure", but these days there is help for those who will accept it. I know, in retrospect, that my mother was a depressive and she had no understanding from myself, my sister, my brothers, or indeed, my father. She had no help, either, as I do; though I have had it suggested to me that I should, "snap out of it," as my mother had said to her many times. We considered her to be a hypochondriac when she was in a long, black mood. We were wrong. I am, now, twisted with guilt and remorse when I think of her suffering made worse by the attitudes of others.

'I feel so awful,' she often said. 'I wish I knew what is making me feel so bad.'

She struggled to meet her domestic responsibilities and often failed. She went to bed to escape from the world and everyone in it until her mother, my grandmother, or some other member of the family succeeded in getting her to "pull herself together" and get up and out.

Her depressive state came and went as mine does. Derek diagnosed my depression to be clinical a long time before I would admit to it. It was he who suggested I look back and think of how my mother had, at times, suffered. He became an educational psychologist and only in retrospect did he think of her illness and put a tag on it.

The psychosis in me became apparent after I had injured my back. Having a congenital spinal curvature, I had been warned to be careful but I worked and lived as if it were normal. Constant pain is an evil companion and lets the "black dog" in.

After a successful spinal fusion surgical operation to remove two dead discs in my spine I felt ill when I should not have. The operation was successful. It was the post-operative depression which made me realise I had inherited something from my mother that I had considered a weakness.

When the depression is with me, I wish it were a simple matter of being miserable, down in the dumps, feeling sorry for myself, worried, anxious or sad. It is not. I am content with my life: a happy marriage, a healthy family, a fine home, friends, work I enjoy. But, there is something inside me which I cannot explain. Certainly, sitting here at my computer writing about it helps – and the pills. I rely on medication, but it is not a panacea.

'Catch me taking antidepressant?' I had said to myself in the past, and indeed, to others. 'Never! I know the trouble they cause can sometimes become worse than the original complaint.' I have eaten my words, digested them and am in no position to repeat them.

On two occasions I have stopped taking the pills; tried without them, thinking I could "snap out of it" and there would be no change to my psyche. Each time I was wrong. The first time I was glad I still had the pills in my bedside draw, not having thrown them down the lavatory, as I almost did. I began taking them again and after three days I felt better.

The second time I stopped taking them I **did** destroy what I had left of my monthly supply so that they wouldn't be available should I weaken again.

After about two weeks I felt physically ill. I couldn't say exactly why, or put my finger on a cause, so I knew it was clinical depression. I guessed I was feeling particularly bad because Derek had been diagnosed with heart failure.

However, we lived a happy, exciting life. I continued to fear that anxiety and pain might exacerbate my depression and I went back to my GP to start prescribing anti-depression medication again.

'Just give me the 25 milligram dose,' I suggested, 'and only to carry me through this bad time with Derek, then I'm determined to stop them for good.'

'Why?' Dr Field asked, 'If they help, why not stay on them. And if you're going to take them I suggest the seventy-five milligram dose.'

'I just thought it would be easier to give up the weaker strength.'

'I'll give you the higher dose and I suggest you do not try to stop them until the spring.' The month was February and I agreed.

Before I left his surgery he passed comment that aroused shame in me. 'You know, Shirley, we all feel down sometimes. You, of all people, I would expect to know that. When you get back to your work at the nursing homes, take a look around you and try to consider how many of them must feel. The depression you feel is nothing compared to their despair.'

'I do know that.' I replied. I felt patronised and must have sounded offended. 'I have clinical depression and it is not a simple feeling of being miserable, is it? I wish it were.'

'No, I know, it's a chemical imbalance. Take the pills. You need them.'

As I walked hurriedly to my car, away from the clinic, tears welled up my eyes. I felt a wimp and remembered that Donald Field also had health and family problems. He might have been feeling worse than I did.

That was fifteen years ago and I'm still taking the pills. He need not have suggested that I look around at the residents at the nursing homes. I did so every day. I knew all their names and they knew mine. The atmosphere in the three homes was pleasant and companionable. The carers enjoyed their work and were tolerant of the mood swings of some of the residents who could be "normal" one hour and aggressive the next. They followed the examples of approach they were taught by the experienced, trained nurses.

The three homes were comfortable, clean and well appointed. The residents had their own rooms; small but adequate and some personal items of furniture and nick-knacks from what had been selected from their own homes. There were dressing-tables and wardrobes and more often than not, the residents had their own clothes.

There was a number who had been in institutions for years before, who didn't have their own personal pieces of furniture, but usually had their own clothes. They were some who had no relatives, either. Or if they did, they never visited. We, the carers, were their friends and they were treated as such.

I found the skill, dedication and compassion that went into the care most gratifying. A far cry from those days at Pen Y Heol Hospital where I was placed during my training.

When I was at The Nightingale Nursing Homes the carers' remuneration was, predominantly, at the lowest end of the pay scale and increased when the legal current scale did. The satisfaction from the work made up for the poor salary.

The carers had their favourite residents but cared well for all. That is something I have witnessed which has become sadly lacking in recent years in nursing homes and hospitals.

At The Homes I had my favourites. My friends were not only the people who managed: Carole, Erika the household manager, the administration, kitchen and laundry staff, but especially the residents.

One of the residents, Bronwen Morgan, and I had been friends for years. I knew her before she had herself admitted to the Bedford Home. She was young at sixty five for an elderly care unit but she was paralysed. The muscles of both her legs were severely deformed.

The "black dog" was sometimes her companion but only I knew. The difference between her and myself was that she had reason to be depressed.

Bronwen had herself admitted to The Bedford Home because her daughter, Beryl, didn't have the ability to care for her mother and the household.

Bronwen was thirty-eight when she had Beryl. The birth was long and hard; Beryl's intellectual development was affected.

I enjoyed sitting beside Bronwen when I had some spare time. She had a personality which brightened Willow lounge. No-one would be bored in Bronwen's company. She kept the black dog's company for when she was alone in her room.

Another such friend was Myrtle. She was in one of the two EMI units. She was a severe manic depressive; a condition I knew existed, but I had no idea of the full extent of its effect. Her mood swings, from high to low, were extreme and difficult to manage.

When she was "on a high", as the mood was described, Myrtle, strode at speed, up and down the long corridors, around and around the dining rooms and lounges and, unless observed continually, she would stride through areas which were out of bounds to her. She went into an aggressive rage when finding the front door was locked to prevent her going onto the forecourt. Should she have been able to get out she would have been down the hill to the busy main road like a bat out of Hell.

As she wandered wildly about the unit, she shouted and sang hymns at the top of her voice, getting on people's nerves. She would hit out at others if they got too near to her.

There were times when she became too manic and had to be sedated. Sedation was avoided; undertaken as a last resort when there were signs of Myrtle harming herself or others.

She walked with long, fast strides for hour upon hour until she dropped with fatigue, then slept for many hours. She was carried to her room, undressed, washed and put comfortably down to sleep.

She lashed out at the carers when they had to disturb her to ply her with fluids or to change the bed-sheets when they became wet and soiled.

Although appearing like a living skeleton she was surprisingly strong. She was thin to a point of emaciation. We worried about her refusal to eat and drink. The only way to get food inside her was for two carers to walk, one each side of her, and spoon food into her as they trotted beside her.

When her manic state passed she was too depressed to take anything, no matter what method was attempted.

Her face was as grey as her sparse, lank hair. But inside her were the remnants of a keen mind and a sharp personality. She had been a seamstress in her time and, apparently, a good one, with a successful business which she ran from the front room of her house.

When she was well enough at The Aneurin Home, she did embroidery. I still have a tray cloth she made for me.

'It's not my best,' she had said, when she proudly handed it to me. 'Don't use it when you have Prince Charles for tea.'

When she awoke from a long sleep she became ridden with guilt for hitting her carers. It was unsure what she remembered but the carers tried to comfort her. When on a "down period" nothing could comfort her. At such times she asked for me.

We had become friends and had long talks – when her mood allowed.

The first time she asked for me, I was in the Bedford Home where the main office is. I went to Bevan Home and found her with her face pressed against the panes of the front door, waiting for me. The door could be opened from the outside, though it was always locked on the inside.

She cried and cried. Her old face, thin and gaunt, was soaked with tears and mucous.

I put my arms gently about her and wiped her face with a paper tissue which I took from my pocket.

'Feel bad today, Myrtle?' I remember asking.

She sobbed. 'Oh, gel. I feel bad.' The depth of her despair was in those few words.

I am a depressive but compared with Myrtle … I cannot describe… There but for the grace of God … I have never felt as bad as she did.

There were several residents who suffered with Myrtle's devil-inflicted psychiatric condition and other diseases of the mind which tore at the fibres of their being. They were helped by the understanding of the trained nurses and medication. Myrtle refused to take her medication and that was her choice, but when she became acutely manic she was forced to take it. The staff were reluctant to do that. She believed the medication was poison.

In well organised nursing homes the residents are not sedated to calm difficult behaviour unless it is for the safety of the resident. It is not for the convenience of the staff. The resident with a raving episode of mania is sedated as a last resort, to prevent injury to him or herself and others. Sometimes to relieve their tortured minds.

I have seen that all homes do not abide by this principle. I have witnessed it being done when I have been in no position to intervene. I should have, and cannot justify my weakness.

There was something about Myrtle which pulled at my heart strings. She had no teeth, having thrown her dentures down the lavatory pan. Her grey, withered, sunken-cheeked face was always gaunt and cheerless, except for the very occasional smile which beamed from bead-like blue eyes when she was lifted, for a minute or two, out of an abyss of Hell.

Myrtle died with that smile on her face. I'm glad I was there to see it.

Myrtle had been a resident of the Elderly Mentally Infirm Nursing Home. The staff who managed it were Registered Psychiatric nurses. That trained, experienced nurses are given charge of that type of unit is a legal stipulation. The number of nursing-aides depended on the number of residents. Each of the three homes had thirty-two residents when they were full, but that was not always the case. People died and their rooms remained empty for varying periods.

The owners didn't like unoccupied rooms; it was not cost effective. There were times when nursing-aides were made redundant on the premise to be recalled when needed again. Inevitably, they sought employment elsewhere, invariably in positions which paid more and didn't come back to The Nightingale Homes.

New staff, who had not done the work before, were taken on and trained to carry out basic care.

The Government introduced the NVQs to bridge the gap in a current lack of apprenticeships. They are work-based awards achieved through training and assessment.

The Nightingale Nursing Homes organisation had a generous training budget. My remit was to supervise and teach candidates as they studied to acquire NVQ Levels 1 and 2 in Direct Care. I also taught basic first-aid and cardio-pulmonary resuscitation. (CPR).

The atmosphere in The Homes was more casual that in the general hospital. It had to be; it was home to those who were cared for there. It was good for me at that time, as the rigidness of the wards and classroom would not have been. In The Nightingale Nursing Homes I was one of the team with no obvious concern about formality.

A professional distance had to be subtle to maintain discipline between the carers and the nurses in charge. The principle aim was to be respected as well as being liked. I enjoyed close relationships at The Homes with staff and residents.

I still have contact with the friends I made within the staff and we visit each other from time to time. The friendships I had with the residents ended when I left. This was because I never went back. I could have, but I feared that I would not be remembered or they had died. They were elderly or elderly and infirm. "In God's waiting room" is often the cliché used. If there is such a place, are we not all there?

At The Bevan Home I became a friend of one of the youngest residents; Pamela Granger. She was a manic-depressive; the "black dog" was always with her.

She was in her early sixties but looked hardly younger than the other residents who were all, at least, ten years older. A hard life had knocked youth out of Pamela. The difference between the residents and her, was that she was physically self-dependent. She was a very private person and valued the amount of independence she had. The staff respected that.

Pam had to be coaxed to take a bath and she did so at night when everyone was asleep, including the less diligent staff.

Night duty at the Homes was a second job for some carers and qualified nurses. It was not unknown for them to arrive for night duty having been working elsewhere during the day. They would snatch any opportunity to sleep for a few hours. Anyone caught sleeping on the job could be dismissed, but as far as I knew, no-one had been. There was the excuse of "resting during their break-time".

I did a night shift from time to time to ensure all was well. There were a few NVQ candidates on permanent night duty.

One night I approached the entry to find a naked resident banging on the inside of the door wanting to get out of The Bevan EMI unit. It was a good thing the doors couldn't be opened from the inside unless a code was pressed out on a device on the wall just inside the door.

I let myself in, greeted the naked lady as she flagged her knickers in the air, and led her into the lounge. The Registered Mental Nurse who was in charge was asleep in one of the comfortable lounge chairs. I shook her roughly; she should have been watching out for the confused and vulnerable residents. She didn't awaken when I shook her; she was fast asleep. I shook her again, more roughly. Her eyes snapped open. She was disorientated and couldn't find words to explain her neglect.

'Oh, um, um Shirley. What are you doing here. I must have dropped off for a few minutes. Where are Judy and Edgar?'

'Your carers are upstairs circulating the rooms to make sure everyone is safe. That's what you should be doing down here. Now, take Sadie to her room and dress her.' The uncaring nurse blinked sleep out of her eyes and sprang to her feet before scanning Sadie's nakedness.

'Yes. Sorry. Won't happen again,' she said as she took Sadie's hand. She said nothing to Sadie to ease her obvious, fear and misery as she was led zombie-like out of the room.

I had heard that this particular nurse slept for long periods and wondered if the complaint had been exaggerated. It had not and the nurse was dismissed.

Chapter 5

DANGEROUS FRIENDSHIPS

Pamela Granger's mental condition warranted residency at one of the EMI units; she was psychopathic. She had the ability to self-care, had a normally, quiet and gentle nature, so was admitted to be among elderly residents rather than those who were mentally infirm. When admitted she was in her late fifties and refused to be admitted to the EMI unit. Flexibility of the law was the best solution.

Pam was sixty-five when we met. After reading her case history I thought it was little wonder she looked older than she was. However, on discretely observing her, I sensed remaining touches of elegance and pride. The record of her past was heart-rending. During much of her early life she had experienced bad, cruel treatment and I found little evidence of a normal existence in her records.

To me, the abhorrence of her life partly explained her behaviour, but being at The Nightingale Nursing Homes, I learned that her life story was not unique.

She had long, thinning, fine hair which wilted like an old dust-web down her back, almost to her waist. She hadn't had it trimmed for years. It was dull-grey with reddish streaks. A sign of its former glory. It was held back at her neck with a pony-tale ring or a piece of ribbon in an untidy bow.

She was emaciated and her clothes, which at one time, must have been neat and smart, sagged raggedly about her tottering frame. The only time she walked was between her room and her chosen, comfortable chair in the far corner of the lounge and to and from the lavatory.

She stooped as she walked. Had she stood upright she would have been a head taller than my five feet two. She rarely looked anyone in the face except when she had to speak. That wasn't often. Her red-rimmed eyes were the same colour as her hair; a dull grey. Her sad face must have been attractive but she did nothing to enhance her appearance, except to manicure her long, hard, talon-like nails. They were the longest any of us had seen. When she walked she bunched them together and twiddled and clattered them in front of her as if she were defending herself. Sometimes she had cause to defend herself; the other residents hated her and would try to trip her on her way to the toilet. She ignored the bitterness and stepped aside to avoid tripping over outstretched legs. She ignored everyone and spoke only when she had to. No-one spoke to her except the carers, but only when they had to. I pitied her and spoke to her whenever I happened to be near her.

Initially, she ignored me.

Perhaps the other residents didn't like her because they were afraid of her. When riled, and she was riled with anyone who, inadvertently, entered her personal space, her fingernails became dangerous weapons.

Pamela had a tormented mind and should have been in one of the EMI units, where there were people who understood her abnormality, but she would never have settled. She knew the difference between the home for the elderly and the home for the mentally infirm. She objected to the stigma of being known as "mad" or "insane".

She was on a regime of potent medicines. She was allowed to reside at the Bedford Oak Lounge with the elderly as long as she agreed to take her medication, which helped to control her mania. She was wise enough to comply.

One morning, when she'd had a bath the night before, I asked her if she would like me to cut her toenails. Elaine, the nurse in charge, told me that one of the night-staff, who was keeping a discrete eye on Pamela in the bathroom, noticed that her toenails were so long they began to curl under her toes. So

I asked her, quietly and humbly if she would like me to do this small thing for her.

'No!' she snapped. 'My toenails aren't bothering me. Mind your own business!'

'All right, Pamela. Of course, it's none of my business. But if you change your mind, just let me know. I do my husband's toenails because he likes me to and I do some of the residents when they have problems. When any of the staff has corns or in-growing toenails I am asked to help them, too. They often like me to help if they have blisters from wearing new shoes.'

I noticed *The Daily Telegraph* on her table had most of the crossword completed. 'Gosh,' I said, 'you've nearly finished *The Telegraph* crossword. I enjoy doing that one myself when I have the chance.'

She snatched up the newspaper and hid her face behind it.

'I'm sorry,' I said. 'I won't bother you again.'

The following afternoon, when I passed by close to where she was sitting, she held out her arm to attract my attention.

'I'm sorry I was rude,' she said. 'You were nice and if you could spare the time I would like my toenails cut, but in my room.' Normally, foot-care was carried out in the treatment room.

'Of course. I'll do them after tea, if you like.'

I had taken an interest in chiropody when I was at the school of nursing. I had attended a short course on the subject, so I was considered an authority on foot-care. That was far from correct but I was, perhaps, a little wiser than the carers and indeed the registered nurses. Care of the feet has never been a popular task.

That afternoon, in Pamela's room, I had the impression she didn't want a lot of talk so I said little and let her lead the conversation.

'Is your husband not well?' she asked.

'No, he's not in the best of health now but we cope all right.'

'Is he a doctor?'

'Yes, but not a physician. He's a psychologist.'

'He must be very clever.'

I smiled. 'He'd like to hear you say that.'

'I had a husband, you know. He was clever, too, but he was wicked.'

My concentration left Pam's feet and I looked up at her. I was surprised and it must have shown on my face.

'Wicked? In which way? You are so gentle, I can't imagine anyone being wicked to you.'

'Well, he was. Have you nearly finished now?'

I sensed the conversation had ended. 'Yes, I hope they feel all right.'

'Yes, they do. Thank you. I must pay you.'

'Oh, no. I don't want payment.' She was already standing. She walked to the door and held it open whilst I packed up my equipment. I realised she intended to remain in her room.

After that day I sat beside Pam in the corner of the lounge whenever I had an opportunity to. I could check NVQ files and keep an eye on the residents. It freed the carers to carry on with other jobs that had to be done.

I said nothing except in response to what Pamela said. It was always when the other residents were asleep in their armchairs or had gone to their rooms for an afternoon nap. We did the crossword together. She was sharper than me with words.

Pamela had had an unhappy childhood. Her education had been important to her father and she wasn't allowed to miss a day of school. She defied him on hockey days when she would have had to undress in front of others in the gymnasium changing room. She hid herself away until it was time to go home. The fact that she was unnaturally averse to taking off her clothes unless in private, was mentioned in her notes. It was connected to a reporting of her father making her undress to nakedness before sexually abusing her.

There were many psychiatrists' and psychologists' reports between the covers of the thick folders which revealed the dark secrets of her life.

In her young days she was an isolate; no friends were allowed into her home. She was used as a slave by her mother, who knew that her church deacon father abused her, physically and sexually.

Pamela ran away from home when she was sixteen. She was attracted to the bright lights and excitement of the big City of London. Her intention was to seek a glamorous life in one of the big departmental stores she'd read about in glossy magazines. She imagined herself behind the counter of a perfumery or in one of the famous fashion houses.

She hadn't been in a big city before, except Cardiff, when she'd been taken as a girl to a pantomime. She found London frightening; not at all as she had imagined. She was lost; had no idea where she was and wandered the streets aimlessly. She became destitute.

One day, when she had sunk to the lowest level of existence, she was approached by, what she thought was "a nice woman" who took her into her own home.

Pamela hadn't heard of "trafficking" or "prostitution" but soon became acquainted with that seedy side of London life. She became a slave in a big house with girls like herself who had been taken in by evil people. One of the victims tried to escape by climbing through a window. She was caught and severely beaten.

However, Pamela decided to take the risk; she was determined to escape. She managed to squeeze through a small window and, she thought, had got away. She hadn't and was caught the following day by "her owners". She, also, was badly beaten but not taken back to the evil house. She was found in the gutter of a back street by a member of a benevolent society. She was taken care of until she was well. She hated London and decided to return to her home; she had nowhere else to go. She returned to her parental home to find that her father had died. Pamela continued caring for her mother until she met a charming, financially well-off man who asked her to marry him.

It didn't take her long to discover he was neither charming nor wealthy. He was no better, even worse, than all the other men she had known. He beat her and became a pimp more evil than the ones she had run away from.

One night she got home to him with no money. She had lost the money she earned scrubbing floors and washing dishes in a restaurant. At night, her husband expected her to traipse up and down the main street, trying to sell her worn out body. She couldn't do that.

When she came home with no money he beat her and that night she fought back. She stabbed him with a sharp kitchen knife. He died and Pamela was sentenced to fifteen years imprisonment. She was in prison until diagnosed as being psychiatrically ill.

Pamela had lived all her life in loneliness and fear. She hadn't known love or happiness. Now, in the nursing home, she shut herself off and lived in a world of her own, where she must have felt safe. She never laughed, nor even smiled. Her mind had been twisted into blankness.

Eventually, when an invisible barrier between Pamela and I began to crumble, little by little, she spoke to me in response to a couple of words now and then.

'Is the TV too loud, Pamela?'

'What are the headlines in *The Telegraph*, Pamela?'

'Do you want another cup of coffee, Pamela?'

No-one had taken that much notice of her before. She had given a strong impression of not wanting communication. When I had time to sit in a vacant chair which happened to be next to hers, I said nothing.

I was surprised when she eventually began saying a few words of what was in the newspaper. When she asked me how Derek was, I was even more surprised.

'He's all right, thank you, Pamela. He has good and bad days, as we all do.'

'I heard you say he wasn't well.'

'I didn't think you took any notice of what anyone said, Pamela.'

'Well, no. I don't. Why should I?'

I eventually got her to join in simple quiz games the carers held in the lounge some evenings. She knew most of the answers and couldn't resist calling them out, especially when no one else knew them. She had a wealth of general knowledge which must have been gleaned from the many books she read. A mobile library called once a month. The newspapers were delivered daily. *The Daily Telegraph* was especially for her.

One afternoon I asked Pamela if she would like to come home with me to see where I lived.

She was aghast. 'Oh, no. I couldn't do that!'

I was surprised by her reaction. It was the first time I'd seen a change in her demeanour. Her manner of speaking had been persistently monotone with no apparent change of emotion. I thought I had offended her.

'I'm sorry, Pam. I meant no offence, but why not?'

'You haven't offended me but I'm not good enough. You don't know me. You don't know what I've done. Anyway, I'm not allowed out.' I felt relieved that she hadn't considered that I knew about her past; I had read her case notes. I feared she would have considered that intrusive.

A week later, when Derek was away on a conference, I invited Pamela again. I didn't expect her to accept but I wanted to give her the confidence of knowing her worth. I wanted her to know that I thought her good enough. I was surprised when she agreed. She smiled for the first time. It was a little tilt of her lips, but definitely a smile.

'I didn't think you'd ask me again. Yes, I'd like to see your house.'

'Good. I'll leave early today, at four o'clock. Don't have tea here. I have a fruit loaf at home.'

The staff told me the following day that she had gone to her room to find something suitable to wear. Lyndon Payne, the male nurse in charge that day, helped her; she had no idea of what to wear. I thought it strange, that apart from myself, Lyndon was the only one she would relate to. He was a registered psychiatric nurse so I assumed his type of training gave him the knowledge of how to approach her. They chose a skirt, blouse and jacket from the worn-out selection in her wardrobe. He helped her to do her hair. He twisted the flimsy strands onto the top of her head and it looked surprisingly smart. I think, for the first time in many years, Pamela felt anywhere near human.

When I was waiting for her in the duty room, I glimpsed Lyndon through the glass partition, coming out of the lift. He had left Pamela to complete preparing herself for, what to her, was a grand outing. She hadn't been outside the home for several years. He joined me in the office and took his chair behind the desk.

'Mrs Phillips,' he said, 'would you mind a little advice?' Since he addressed me formerly I guessed he had something important to say.

'Of course not,' I replied. I think my expression must have been quizzical.

'I think it very kind of you to take Pamela out. It will be good for her. But I must warn you – be careful. I would advise you not to turn your back on her. I speak from experience.'

I was surprised; he was telling me that Pamela could be aggressive. I knew that; I had read her case-notes.

'Thank you, Lyndon. Perhaps if she were taken out more often her state of mind would improve. We'll be all right.'

Lyndon Payne was, what was described as, "double trained". He was a registered general nurse as well as a registered psychiatric nurse. I found him to be a sensitive, clever man. Unfortunately, we all knew Lyndon was fast becoming an alcoholic. He didn't allow his weakness to interfere with his work except for calling in sick on some of his early morning shifts.

When Pamela and I walked to my car, I noticed she'd applied a touch of rouge and lipstick to her sallow complexion.

When we arrived home she sidled out of the car looking anxiously around. 'Don't worry,' I said, 'there's never anyone about at this time.'

When we got in, her enjoyment was obvious. She looked about her with an expression of brightness that I hadn't seen before and she made no effort to disguise her curiosity. It was as if she'd forgotten about an existence outside prison and institutions.

She asked if she could look at the photographs I had on the walls of one of my sitting rooms where I kept all my favourite family photographs and snaps. Placing them in one room avoided them being scattered all over the walls of the house or being tucked away in drawers, although I do have a few scattered here and there.

We sat in the lounge. 'How very lovely,' she said.

'Thank you, Pam. We like it.' I didn't add that I know my lounge is nothing special because she seemed to think it was. She wasn't aware of the changes in décor that had taken place since the last time she was in a normal home. What she had missed in life flashed through my mind and I pitied her.

She ate two pieces of warmed currant buttered loaf, drank two cups of tea and helped to wash the cups and plates afterwards. I have a dish washer but I sensed she wanted to do the dishes.

I took her outside the kitchen door to see the back garden, although the summer flowers had gone. The early autumn made the little garden look pretty and she remarked upon the beautiful colours. She actually smiled broadly. For the first time her teeth were revealed. She had dentures and one was chipped but was not unsightly. I knew that wasn't the reason for her not ever smiling. She was a sad, lonely and bitter woman.

'Would you take me back now, Shirley. It will soon be supper time.'

I sensed she was being careful not to wear out her welcome. I dropped her outside Bedford Home. She let herself in and went straight to her room. No-one saw her for the rest of the day except Lyndon. He took a tray of sandwiches and a cup of hot milk to her room; it was her usual nightly drink.

I should have felt pleased that the afternoon had been worthwhile and successful, but I didn't. Pamela had had a snatch of what life should have been. For a few days afterwards she was in a deep depression. Her bird-like appetite went to nothing. She drank only when I sat beside her and said nothing. However my time was limited: my commitment to training had to take priority.

The staff didn't interfere with Pamela's daily routine unless they had to. They told me they preferred to see her in a depressed mood than in one of the raging tempers she was prone to. She continued to live in seclusion in the corner of the lounge with her book and newspaper.

One morning, on entering Bedford Home at ten o'clock, I sensed a strained atmosphere. I was allowed a late start because I, cynically, explained that my arthritis didn't awaken at the same time as I did. I was no longer a youngster and a late start to my working day was one of the agreements when I accepted the job.

'Shirley! Shirley!' Pamela was calling me from her far corner. Her chair was beside a tall window which overlooked the forecourt. She had been watching out for my arrival.

Elaine, the senior nurse, came out of the duty office to where I stood in the hall. Her expression told me she was under stress. There was no, 'Good morning, Mrs Phillips,' as was usual.

'Shirley,' she said, 'we have to move Pamela Granger. It's not safe for her to be here in Bedford Home. I can't take the risk any longer. She needs to be with those trained to deal with her.'

I was surprised. 'Why?'

'She's unstable and dangerous,' she said. 'We don't have enough staff for someone to be with her all the time. You spend more time than you should with her.'

Elaine's remark offended me. 'That has nothing to do with you,' I said sharply. 'I decide what time I spend with anyone. I well know my responsibilities.'

Elaine recognised my displeasure. 'Yes, I know. I'm sorry for saying that but I'm rather wound up and not pleased with what I've let happen. Our residents are feeble and unable to cope with the onslaughts Pamela gives them. She attacked little Bessie Gate and stabbed her with those talons of hers. I should have had them cut whether it was her choice to keep them or not. You just go and see the scratch marks on Bessie. I hope they don't become infected.'

I hadn't yet taken off my coat but I went to Bessie Gate, a small lady well in her eighties. Her face, from her eye to her chin, had three deep scratch marks, as did her right forearm. She looked curiously up at me as I stood beside her chair. She wondered why I was looking at her; she had forgotten about the unpleasant tussle she'd had with Pamela. It was her habit to wander aimlessly around the big lounge and meddle with items on other resident's tables.

'Shirley! Come here, will you?' Pamela shouted across the room. 'Don't talk to the stupid woman! She's mad!'

That morning, when Pamela had arrived back at her table after going to the toilet, Moira was tottering around Pamela's armchair and table. She had spilled Pamela's glass of squash over her newspaper, taken her box of tissues, scattered them on the floor and was about to go off with Pamela's book.

Pamela was distraught, especially about her newspaper. She went into a rage and attacked little Moira with her weapons –long fingernails – before pushing her to the floor.

'She'll have to be transferred to Bevan or Nightingale unit.' Elaine gave me the impression she wouldn't enjoy doing what she had to.

The units she referred to were, of course, the EMI units of The Nightingale Nursing Homes. The nurses in charge there were Registered Psychiatric Nurses and were trained to deal with residents with psychopathological illnesses. I was involved in the basic training in the three homes; nothing to do with the causes and effects of the illnesses.

However, when I was not working with the NVQ candidates or taking small seminars, I helped in other ways: feeding the helpless residents, wound management, foot care and any other general tasks which didn't involve anything physically strenuous.

I responded to Elaine's suggestion of Pamela having to move to an EMI unit. 'She's going to hate it. I'm sorry for Bessie. She wouldn't understand Pamela's moods. I'm sure you know how to deal with this matter. I'm not in a position to interfere but thank you for discussing the matter with me.'

Carole appeared at the top of the stair. The door of the office had been open and she had heard the fracas. She knew what was causing it and thought she would rescue me from Elaine's wrath. She called out to me as she leant over the banister of the stairs leading from the hall to the second floor. Before I took heed of Carole's call I went to the open door of the lounge, waved to Pamela and mimed that I'd go to her in a minute. She was in a state of hysterical weeping.

'They're putting me in the mad house!' she screamed. 'I'd rather die than go there!'

When I went into the office with Carole I found that she, too, was not pleased with me or what had happened to Bessie Gate.

'Elaine is right, you know,' she said. 'And Pamela's movement to Bevan Home is not your concern.'

It had been years since I had been put in my place for stepping out of line. It didn't feel good.

'I know, Carole. I'll keep my nose out and won't argue with you. I wouldn't do anything to spoil the relationship between you and me or anyone else here. I know my place.'

In spite of the unpleasant event, Pamela was not transferred to an EMI unit, but I knew nothing of why she wasn't moved except that she had threatened to run away at the first opportunity; and she would have. She knew the combination of the device which opened the main doors. However, I know she had promised to conform to all that was expected of her. One promise was that she would allow me to cut her fingernails.

When I was in the office with Carole behind the closed door, Carole said something which hurt me again.

'Elaine is right, Shirley. You are spending too much of your time with Pamela. I know nothing about psychiatry but Pamela is her own worst enemy. She'll never change.'

Silence was my response to Carole and my damaged pride soon healed. I was determined not to damage my relationship with Pamela but learned that I should have.

One afternoon, soon after the nail-cutting session, Pamela spoke after we had been sitting in silence for about ten minutes. Though no words had passed between us there was a closeness. What she said caused me unrest.

'Let me come and live with you, Shirley. I could be your maid. Do your cleaning and cooking. I'm a good cook, you know, as long as it plain cooking. I wouldn't get in yours or Derek's way.'

I was taken aback and at a loss for words. 'Pamela, what a lovely person you are. You're too good to be waiting on us and I know Derek wouldn't agree. It's too small a house for a servant even if we could think of you as one. You and I are friends; not mistress and servant.'

'Yes, you're right. I'm sorry. Just a little dream I had.'

That was one of the longest pieces of conversation I'd had from Pamela for a while, but I guessed it must have been thought of long and hard before being put to me. Her despair saddened my day.

'Would you consider coming to my house for tea again, Pamela. I've talked to Derek about you and he would like to meet you.'

She turned to face me. She didn't smile but her downcast expression lifted.

'Oh, are you sure he would? I'd like to come to your home again. Your garden must look lovely with all the autumn shades still on the trees. Winter will soon take them.'

She was right. Our copper beech, which was a sapling when Derek planted it, is now above the rooftop and glows golden into the front rooms of the house.

'Why not come home with me on Friday? He works at home on Fridays.'

'That will be lovely. I'll put on a good frock. Would it be all right if I painted my nails?'

'Of course it will. We just don't want you to have long sharp nails.'

On the Friday of that week I drove Pamela home as before. One of the carers acquired nail-varnish for her; her own had spoiled. She helped Pamela to dress and groom her hair. She looked happy.

Lyndon made a point of speaking to me in confidence before we left.

'Please, Shirl. Bear in mind what I told you. She is one very sick lady.'

I nodded a response to, what I considered, an over-reaction.

Derek welcomed Pamela and his kind manner made her feel at ease. He made a point of talking about himself and me, rather than asking questions of her, though she did offer information about herself. She talked about the type of music she liked and issues of interest she'd read in *The Daily Telegraph.* She asked him if he'd be going abroad on business again.

'No, thank goodness. I'm getting too long in the tooth for long journeys. I like being at home with Shirley.'

We had tea and Pamela joined me in the kitchen to help to wash up the few dishes. She stood beside me in silence as she wiped up. Derek came into the kitchen to pass through to our toilet which is beyond the utility room.

Something snapped.

'Pamela snatched up my sharp vegetable-slicing knife, propelled it above her head and was about to lunge it into Derek's chest. She bared her teeth like an angry dog and there was evil on her face as she thrust the knife towards him. I became stiff with fear and dropped a wet plate I had taken from the sink and it shattered on the hard kitchen tiles.

Pamela seethed, 'Why do you have to stay here? Why don't you go away? Leave Shirley alone!'

I screamed. 'Watch out, Derek! Watch out!'

Derek had been a soldier for over twenty years; the first two as an ordinary rank. His reaction was dynamic. He knocked her arm aside and grabbed the wrist which wielded the knife. It must have hurt because she instantly dropped the knife which would have penetrated his chest.

A deathly silence followed the shattering of the china plate. Pamela collapsed onto her haunches and threw punches at the floor about Derek's feet.

'What have I done? I don't know what I've done! I'm sorry, sorry, sorry! I want to die!'

I recovered from what seemed to have happened in a flash of time. Derek seemed unmoved by the fact that Pamela had tried to kill him. He leant down to her, put his hands on her elbows and pulled her to a standing position, but she crouched like an animal and couldn't look at him.

'It's all right, Pamela, it's all right,' he said.

'I'm so, so sorry,' she sobbed. 'Please don't let them put me in a mad house. Please don't tell anyone that I'm mad.'

'It's all right, Pamela,' he repeated. 'I know you didn't mean it.' Derek was so gentle. I was speechless. He could have been stabbed to death and it would have been my fault.

He looked at me. 'Come on, Shirl. No big deal. Just get Pamela's coat and we'll take her home.' He put his arm about Pamela's shoulders. 'I know it's not you, Pamela; it's the way you are made. We're all different.'

A grey, wrinkled, tear-stained face looked up at his with an expression of disbelief. 'But I could have killed you. There's a devil in me. Why can't I die?'

'Because life is good. And you must come here again. Come on, now, it's time you went back. They'll think we're keeping you too long.'

I couldn't stop trembling when I helped Pamela on with her coat.

Derek sat in the back of the car with Pamela beside him as I drove to the nursing homes.

Lyndon and Mary, the carer, met Pamela and I in the hallway. He sensed, immediately, that something had gone wrong. Pamela looked wretched. The pins had fallen from her long, straggling hair, her make-up was smudge by tears and she was hunch-backed as she, Lyndon and Mary entered the lift to the floor above.

'Thank you, Shirley. Pamela can stay in her room, I'll take some supper for her. Mary will help her to bed. We'll see you on Monday unless you want to speak to me before that. I'm on all week-end.'

I didn't know what to do or say. How should I handle the horrible event? Thank God for Derek. He knew what to do and Pamela remained in Bedford Home. Derek advised me to treat Pamela as if nothing had happened.

I did as he advised but I felt a wave of despair ripple through me, warning me of an acute depression approaching. I had got used to it and recognised when the black dog lurked.

On a cold, bleak morning in February, 1997, I went to work to find Pamela's chair in the corner of the big lounge vacant. She had the 'flu and was confined to bed. The day became bleaker when I was told.

'She refused to have the 'flu jab,' Elaine said. 'I should have done more coaxing but you know how determined she is.'

'Yes, I do, but it was her choice. You could do no more.'

'She can still have the jab. Will you talk to her? She'll listen to you.'

'I will, Elaine, but you know I'm not her keeper.'

I was shocked when I saw Pamela. Her face had shrunk and drained of what little colour it had. Her dentures were in a pot on her dressing table. I hadn't seen her without them before, nor do I think anyone else had. She looked very, very old. She was sixty-seven; not much older than myself.

'I thought you'd never come, Shirley. I've been waiting for you.' Her voice was hoarse and weak. 'I would like to die. I feel so awful.'

'Please don't talk like that, Pamela.' I felt full of pity and I could not stop my eyes becoming tearful. I continued to have the occasion fit of depression and it didn't take much to put me into the doldrums.

'Here, take a sip of this orange juice and I'll sit quietly beside you for a while. When you're feeling better you must think about having the 'flu jab.'

'I won't need it. I'm going to die.' She sounded too ill to speak. 'Come closer; I want to tell you something.'

I sat on the edge of her bed. 'Don't tire yourself. It can wait until you're well, whatever it is.'

She murmured on. 'I've made a will and you will have all my money.'

I was taken aback. 'Pamela, you shouldn't have! Money is one thing that I don't need. Anyway, you're not going to die. It's only the 'flu you've got.'

'Please take it as a gift for being nice to me.'

I helped Pamela to take her six o'clock medication before I left. Derek didn't ask me why I was late getting home. He could see I was particularly low in spirit.

'Don't feel so good, Love?' he asked.

'I'm fine. Pamela's quite poorly, though.'

'You know, Shirl, I wish you didn't let yourself get so involved with the people you care for.'

'Sorry. I can't help it. Compassion is the key; remember?'

'Yes, Love, but I've seen it choke you. Please, you've done your bit. Let it go now.'

Pamela's influenza became pneumonia. Her lungs had not been all that strong; she had smoked heavily in the past. She died in her comfortable bed at The Bedford Nursing Home. I managed to get to her before she closed her eyes for the last time. I held her warm, still alive, beautiful hand. She didn't know I was there.

What could I say. 'Sorry, Pamela. You were unlucky. Life is good.'

I inherited her life's savings: twenty pounds. It went into the residents' fund which financed small trips, birthday and Christmas presents.

Chapter 6

ALL THE NUMBERS

One Saturday afternoon, Carole telephoned me with apologies for calling at home. There was a staffing problem at Bedford Home and would I do her a favour? Elaine had been called away urgently; her son was in The Accident and Emergency Department having been involved in a road traffic accident.

I guessed what was coming. Carole went on, 'Would you come in and take charge until the night staff come on? You are the only RGN I can get hold of but I've managed to get an extra carer so you won't be involved in any lifting or anything heavy.'

Derek had gone to a rugby match with my brother. It was in Cardiff so I knew he wouldn't be home until late evening. I wouldn't be long after him getting home if I solved Carole's problem.

'Carole, of course I will. I'll be there before the afternoon shift goes off. How awful about Elaine's boy. I hope she'll keep us informed.'

'I'll be calling her from home if I don't hear soon and I'll let you know. I'd be grateful if you circulate between Oak and Willow lounges. Janet will finish the nursing report; she's already started it.'

Janet Daniel was the SEN back-up for Elaine. She was undertaking the NHS Conversion Course at that time. She would be doing the weekly check of medication in the treatment room, then in the office doing the documentation for much of the shift.

I was Jan's mentor and adviser for her academic work for the Conversion Course; enrolled nurse to registered nurse. Being there, I thought I could work with her for a time, unless something unexpected happened. I hoped not; it was a long time since I was in charge of a ward or hospital unit.

It was cold and dark when I left the house so I put the porch light on. I thought Derek might wonder where I was when my car wasn't on the drive so I left a note on the kitchen work-top, just inside the kitchen door, where he would be sure to see it.

Oak and Willow lounges of The Nightingale Nursing Homes were snug and warm. From outside, the yellow-curtained windows glowed golden in the cold, damp, air of late autumn; attractive to visitors and would be residents.

Each day at The Homes was barely different from the one before. When someone died the atmosphere was gloomy, but a little interest was aroused when a day or two later the residency welcomed a new client.

Saturday was different. It was the night of the National Lottery Draw and the eyes of most of the residents on Willow Lounge were on the television screen waiting for the programme to start.

Bronwen Morgan, my friend, had once won ten pounds. It gave hope to every lottery player in Willow Lounge to win ten pounds; possibly more. That would have caused a stir. I used to wonder what any of them would do with a lot of money.

From time to time shopping outings were arranged for the more able residents but The Homes' bone-shaker bus couldn't take them much further than the local market or superstore.

I once asked Bronwen what she'd do if she won a lot of money. She said she'd buy a bigger and smarter headstone for Lewis's grave because she would be "under" it when her candle went out. She laughed when she said it so I didn't know if she meant it or not. In retrospect, I know she did.

'You have a wicked sense of humour, Mrs Morgan,' I teased her.

'And I'd give the rest to my Beryl,' she replied. 'She'd spend most of it in the hairdresser's and mail order catalogues.

Until Beryl, her daughter, came to visit, Bronwen usually dozed in a lounge chair with her wheelchair, as always, within reach in case she needed to go to the lavatory or down the corridor to Oak Lounge. There, she knew, the residents needed constant supervision and spent all their day-time hours without a change of four walls, except when they went to the lavatory. Bronwen knew the ones who liked to chat. She once told me that seeing those more debilitated than herself, and talking to them, prevented her "going into the doldrums", as she referred to her depression.

She was getting older, though, and the manoeuvre of her wheelchair up and down the long corridor began to weary her.

On National Lottery Draw nights, she remained alert. She hoped to win. She could do with a few hundred pounds to meet the debts her daughter incurred. Beryl couldn't resist a mail order catalogue.

As well as the possibility of winning, I know Bronwen, enjoyed, as I did, listening to the banter of what her companions would do if they won. Carole had asked me to make myself available on Saturday evenings before that time and I always stayed to listen to the National Lottery programme. I participated myself and I, too, had once won ten pounds.

I didn't sit near Bronwen and her close companions; I needed a spot where I could observe everyone.

In spite of the disabilities, most of the residents of Willow Lounge played the lottery. Some of them had secret desires, too late to achieve, but it made them forget they were old.

'Bronwen, what would you do if you won a million?' a voice called across the room.

Bronwen faced her questioner. It was the diabetic, Tom Daly; two lower limbs amputated in his fifties.

'Give half to you, Tom. What would you do?'

'If I win,' Tom replied, 'you and me would travel the world in luxury before either of us leaves in Roberts Undertaker's limousine.'

Bronwen jokingly challenged him. 'How would we travel, Tom, when we haven't a good leg between us?'

'Well, I wouldn't mean us to walk. I'd be rich and rich people don't have to walk.' A burst of laughter interrupted the casual chat.

Another pitying voice softened the atmosphere. 'How much must be won to buy a miracle?' Blind, paraplegic, Henry Bliss thought he spoke to himself but he was heard by those around him. No-one replied.

'What would you do if you won a pile of money, Tillie?' Bronwen asked Tillie Market, as she was called. Tillie earned her nick name of "Market" from being the owner of a home-produce market stall for many years in the town's open market. She had worked hard to give her five children a good life. She worked for longer than nature intended and collapsed on a market day – her last one. She had a stroke which rendered her partially paralysed and ended not only her market days, but her ability to care for herself.

'Hug,' Tillie scoffed. 'What would I do with a pile of money with this?' She referred to the paralysed side of her body. 'But my lot of kids would soon make short change of it.'

'Shut up, the lot of you,' someone shouted. 'If we don't have a bit of hush we won't hear them call the numbers, let alone win.'

Bronwen responded quietly to Tillie, sitting opposite. 'You know, Tillie, if I won a million I'd go to America. Me and Lewis often talked about it, especially after we'd been to the pictures.' She paused, 'Eh, my Beryl is late tonight, isn't she?'

Tillie nodded. 'She'll come waddling in in a minute.'

Bronwen turned her head and said nothing. I knew Bronwen didn't like the way Tillie described Beryl's way of walking. It hurt because it wasn't far from the truth.

Bronwen closed her eyes and, no doubt, wondered how Beryl would cope when she had no-one to love and guide her. She had confided in me that the worry of it kept her awake at night. Bronwen's health was deteriorating. I had noticed she tired easily.

'Shirley,' she called out to me, 'if I drop off, give me a shake, will you, Love?'

She told me later that she closed her eyes and must have dozed off before the lottery numbers were called and dreamed of winning millions of pounds and setting up Beryl for life.

I hadn't noticed her going into a deep sleep. I went to a window, plucked the curtain aside and looked out onto the forecourt to see if Beryl was on her way up the hill. She was.

Bronwen's thirty-four year old daughter, Beryl Morgan, was scurrying up the steep hill to the entrance of the home. She was later than usual so her mother had been wondering what had happened to her. Not that anything but the mundane every happened to Beryl. A lackluster, lugubrious personality and being overweight by more than two stones didn't attract interest to her ordinary, everyday life. Going too often to the hairdressing salons didn't help, either. She let the trainees practice on her, resulting in dull-coloured, over-permed, straggly hair.

Bronwen had become crippled in childhood. She was six when poliomyelitis struck her. The scourge destroyed the muscles of her legs. She had resigned herself to a life of spinsterhood until one night after the pub, her father took home Lewis Morgan to share their supper. Bronwen fell in love with him but never did she think he would have the same feelings for her. She was a cripple; lifeless from the top of her thighs to her ankles. To her joy Lewis wanted her in spite of her ugly deformity.

He proposed. 'Please, Bronwen, will you marry me?'

After the wedding, Lewis moved in with Bronwen and her parents. They were blessed with Beryl late in the marriage. It was a long difficult labour which resulted in Beryl's impaired intellectual development. She was labelled "simple" by those who didn't understand the reason for her learning difficulties.

However, their lives were filled with joy for twenty-five years; until a heart attack took Lewis. Bronwen's parents outlived him, but not for long. First her father, then just months later her mother passed away.

Bronwen was unable to cope. Beryl was out of her depth when caring for her mother or for helping to manage the home.

Bronwen made the reluctant decision to be admitted to the nearby nursing homes. Beryl didn't object. The house became hers to live in as she pleased. She could stay abed for as long as she wanted, eat what and when she wanted and do housework when she felt like it. That wasn't often.

She visited her mother at the nursing home every day and that became the main event of her social life.

After her energetic dash up the hill to Bedford Home, Beryl pressed the brass bell at the side of the locked door. She'd hardly caught her breath when a uniformed nurse-carer opened it.

'Oh, that was quick,' Beryl gasped.

'Come on, Beryl,' the carer snapped. 'I'm on my way to Willow to take the lottery numbers. She ran off entrusting Beryl to ensure the self-locking door was closed after her.

'O' course,' Beryl said to herself. 'I forgot it's lottery night.'

She fumbled in her handbag for her own lottery ticket as she walked down the corridor to Willow Lounge. She stealthily pushed one of the heavy double doors ajar, crept into the room and tip-toed to where her mother was sitting in her usual armchair.

The lottery programme hadn't started when Bronwen had nodded off so Beryl didn't awaken her. She'd wake up herself when the programme started

Indeed, the sound of the lottery numbers being called stirred Bronwen out of her reverie. When they'd been put in numerical order she gasped with excitement. She was certainly well awake.

'Beryl! Look!' Bronwen shouted, looking down at her ticket. 'I've got all the numbers!'

Beryl was distracted by her mother's behaviour. It wasn' like her to be anything but calm. Bronwen held her breath as she listened to the silken voice of the announcer. '*There is one lucky jackpot winner, to receive ten million pounds.*'

'Oh, my God.' Bronwen held her hand to her chest. 'Here, Beryl, call out these numbers.' She pushed her pad into Beryl's hand.

Beryl concentrated hard and read out the numbers.

'Yeeeeeh!' Bronwen screamed.

Everyone in the room stared at her, surprised at the unusual outburst.

Bronwen decided to call on her close companion, Geraint Lloyd-Davies, to confirm she had all the right numbers. He'd been a successful accountant in his day. He would know.

'Geraint! Where are you? Come and check these numbers. Quick!'

Eighty-five year old, Geraint Lloyd-Davies, had missed the calling of the lottery draw. His prostate let him down at the least bit of excitement; he had to go to the lavatory.

'All right! All right! I'm coming as fast as I can!'

Geraint, carrying his Zimmer frame rather than let it support him, tottered towards Bronwen. He flopped into his chair beside her and took the lottery ticket from her. He put on his horn-rimmed spectacles, which he kept dangling on a chain around his neck.

'Geraint!' Bronwen shouted, 'For God's sake, check my numbers!'

Geraint looked at her with surprise. He's never seen her so excited in all the years he'd known her.

'All right, Bronwen, calm down.' He turned to a bewildered Beryl, who, with blank expression, stared wide-eyed at the slip of paper in her hand. He snatched it from her and handed it to Bronwen.

'Now call out all the numbers that were called. You took them down when the numbers were announced on that piece of paper in your hand, did you?'

'Yes, and I'm positive these are exactly the numbers that were called.' She looked across at Tillie. 'Tillie, give me the numbers that you took down when they were called.'

Tillie handed her paper to Beryl to pass to Bronwen. Bronwen checked them. 'Yes, they're exactly the same as what I took down.'

Bronwen did as Geraint bid. She called out the numbers, slowly and clearly. Geraint's eyes widened in his wizened face. 'No, it can't be right. Call them out again.' She called out the line of numbers again.

'My goodness. You have all the numbers. I wonder how much you've won.'

A shout from across the room answered the question. 'Ten million pounds!'

The voice confirming the figures came from Tom Daly. He stretched his neck over the heads of those in front of him to cast his gaze on Bronwen. Like the lid of a boiling pot he bounced on his wheelchair with excitement.

'I knew you'd win one day, Bron. Shall I make the call for you? That's what you have to do.' He was the only resident who possessed a mobile telephone.

'Yes, Tom, make the call.' Bronwen assumed Tom would find the number.

Beryl began to stir out of a trance. 'How much is ten million pounds, Mr Lloyd-Davies? Is it more'n hundred pounds, 'cause tha's awful lot of money.'

Geraint looked at Beryl with astonishment. 'My dear, it's many, many times more. Your mother has won a fortune.'

Tillie scoffed and shook her head in disbelief at Beryl's ignorance. 'Hell's bells, Bronwen. How can a scholar such as you have such a dunce of a daughter?'

For a moment the thrill of winning was spoiled. Bronwen was hurt. 'There's not one of yours would make Brain of Britain, Tillie, so I wouldn't call anyone a dunce if I was you. Anyway, let's wait until Tom's got through to them lottery people.'

After a few minutes Tom got through to Camelot. He told them who the lottery winner was. 'It's Bronwen Morgan,' he said. 'She's living here in The Nightingale Nursing Homes. She said I was to phone you.'

There was another pause as Tom listened. He covered the mouthpiece and called out, 'Mr Lloyd-Davies, quick! Bring me Bronwen's ticket. They want to check.'

Geraint forgot his Zimmer. He snatched Bronwen's ticket, dashed across the room and plunged it into Tom's outstretched hand. Tom read out the numbers.

'Yes!' he yelled. 'Thank you! Mr Lloyd-Davies, take my phone to Bronwen. They want to speak to her.'

Geraint grabbed Tom's phone, shuffled back to Bronwen and thrust it into her hand. She held it in the air and looked at it as if it were extraterrestrial. She hadn't used a telephone for years and then it was attached to a long cord.

'What do I say?' she asked everyone in the room.

'Put it to your ear and answer their questions,' someone said.

'Hello!' Bronwen called out in a high pitched-tone. 'Here are my numbers.' Geraint thrust the ticket into her free hand. She read out the numbers of her winning ticket before asking, 'Have I won anything?'

Bronwen paused and listened. 'Yes, thank you.' As if in a trance, she dropped the phone.

'Yes,' she said, looking around at the sea of expectant faces. 'It looks as though I've won the lottery. I'll have to spend like there's no tomorrow. All of you will have whatever you want. I'll buy a miracle if I can, Mr Bliss. And Beryl, now I won't have to worry about you when I'm dead.'

A loud cheer filled the room. It awakened Bronwen from a deep, short nap. I watched her blink the sleep from her eyes.

The cheer was for Tom who had won ten pounds. Bronwen told me later that she had dreamed of herself winning the National Lottery. Reality penetrated her brain like a devouring smog as she struggled with disappointment. She hoped it didn't reveal itself in her expression. Others would mistake it for jealousy over Tom winning.

She heard Geraint's voice from a distance, although he sat in the chair next to her. 'I've checked your numbers, Bronwen. No luck, though.'

Down the corridor Jan, the assistant manager, was completing her writing of the daily report when the loud cheer reached her from Willow Lounge.

She was amused when she went there to hear it was for Tom, who had won ten pounds. Bronwen looked disappointed.

'Never mind, Bron,' Jan said. 'Shops shut tomorrow and, anyway, it's too cold at this time of the year for long shopping sprees.' She winked at me before returning to the office to finish off her writing.

I noticed Bronwen still looked dazed. Something was troubling her. Beryl's future I guessed.

'I'll push you to your room, Bron. You look tired,' I said.

'Yes, please, Shirl. This wheelchair needs oiling. It's getting stiffer by the day.' Wheeling herself had become strenuous for her ageing body.

I raised my arm to get the attention of the nearest carer to let her know I was going up with Bronwen.

When in Bronwen's room I glanced out at the scenery as I closed the curtains. It was dark so there was nothing to see beyond the glow of the lights of the nursing home but I know what was below.

'The view is lovely from here, Bronwen, even though your room overlooks the cemetery.'

'That doesn't bother me, Shirl. Lewis is down there waiting for me.' The remark saddened me. 'I won't drop off to sleep as easily as when I was in the lounge. That dream of being a millionaire must have flashed through my mind in seconds, as dreams do.

'I don't particularly want to be rich. It could cause problems, but it would have put my mind at rest as far as my Beryl's future is concerned.'

'She'll be all right, Bron. She'll cope better than you think.' I tried to console her. 'Anyway, we don't want to lose you for a long time. You worry too much.'

'Yes, I expect so, but I wish Lewis was with me. I fall asleep every night thinking of him. And if he was here I know what he'd say and I can hear him as clear as if he was beside me.'

'What would he say, Bron?' I asked as I helped her into bed.

'He'd say, Bron, my lovely, we lived as happy as millionaires when your purse was empty and I didn't have two pennies to toss in my pocket.'

'Yes,' I would say, 'I know what that means. We know what to do when we have nothing in our purse or pockets – manage until pay day. We wouldn't know how to manage millions of pounds. I tell you what, though, I wouldn't refuse the opportunity of trying.'

I was glad Bronwen laughed before I left her room.

Chapter 7

IRIS AND BILL

When I met twins, Iris and Bill Brewster, they were in their sixties. They were residents of Bevan EMI unit. To me they didn't seem elderly or mentally infirm, in spite of the fact they had been institutionalised since early childhood. They were both diagnosed as being of unsound mind.

When Trevor Ellis, nurse in charge, told me of their background, I realised why they had behaviour disorders.

They were toddlers when their mother hanged herself from the attic rafters with the clothes line from their back garden. They were left to be reared by their father, a drunkard, and their older brother, an imbecile.

For a time the neighbours left the Brewster household to its own devices. At that time it was socially unacceptable to interfere with how parents treated their children.

However, a "nosey" neighbour couldn't stand by and watch the two four year old children die of hunger or disease. One morning she saw Bill crawl from the open front door of his home and drink the rain water which had pooled in the gutter. Iris, his sister behind him, dabbed her small, unclean hands in the water and lifted them to her mouth.

The neighbour, Mrs Miller, was kind as well as inquisitive. She knew the children were there but had never seen them. She often wondered why, until the day she saw them toddle out of their front door and could hardly believe the terrible sight of them.

She took a mug of cold, sweet tea and a slice each of bread and jam from her own table. Both children grabbed the food and gorged it. The mug of tea spilled as Iris grabbed it before it reached her mouth. The children were starving, filthy dirty, covered with sores and bruises. Rags covered part of their bodies. Mrs Miller thought they could have died in that house had their brother not carelessly left their front door open so were seen by her.

She left the little ones, half-naked and perishing, to wallow in the filthy wet gutter. She watched them from her front window, wondering when they would be taken in by their brother or father. She saw neither.

Bill and Iris crouched on the doorstep and clawed at the door which had slammed shut. The day was damp and cold.

Mrs Miller couldn't tolerate what she saw. It was wicked. She strode to the children, took a hand in each of hers and led them into her house. She and her married daughter, who lived there, washed the children and clothed them in old vests and jumpers before feeding them.

The little ones made not a sound. They shook or nodded their heads when spoken to. Their behaviour was far from that of four years of age.

Mrs Miller expected that one of the Brewsters would come to get them. She kept a close eye-out; she hoped to see one of the men come out of their house to get the children. She feared that Mr Brewster would be alarmed at not seeing them and would look for them. Mrs Miller didn't want to be accused of kidnapping.

By six o'clock, keeping a watch on the Brewster's home had become tedious. The twins had cuddled closely together and fallen asleep on a comfortable fireside chair in the warmth and comfort of Mrs. Miller's home. It wasn't a big chair but both children fitted into it with space to spare.

'Poor little things,' Mrs Miller said to Stella, her daughter. 'Shame to awaken them but you'd better go to the Brewsters' and tell them where Billy and Iris are.'

Stella frowned. 'I'm not doing that, Mam. Can't we wait until Brian comes home' Brian was Stella's husband.

'No, Love, they might pick a fight with Brian and blame us for keeping the kids. You go.'

Stella reluctantly walked up the street to the Brewsters', three houses away and knocked on the door. She knocked several times before banging the door with her fist. There was no-one in. She was glad. Teddy, the son, frightened her. She ran back to her own house.

'Do you mean to say, they're out and haven't even missed the kids?' Mrs Miller asked with surprise.

'Looks like it. What're we going to do, Mam?'

'I don't know, Love. I suppose we'll have to keep them here. I can't take them to an empty house, can I? Let's wait until Brian and your Dad are here.'

When the men came home they were both angry with their wives.

'You must be daft to bring the kids in,' Brian complained. 'We can't keep them here.'

Brian went to the Brewsters' and banged hard on the door. Teddy, the son, appeared and Brian told him what had happened.

'Kids are upstairs in bed,' Teddy said. 'Wait a minute, I'll go up and see.'

Brian didn't have to wait long before Teddy returned.

'Not there,' he shrugged his shoulder. 'I don't know where they are. They're not with our dad. Keep 'em till the morning, will 'ou?'

Brian was aghast but kept his temper; afraid to speak his mind. He said nothing and walked away.

Neither the children's father or brother came to get them the next day. Mrs Miller took the children to their home. Mr Brewster answered the door, grabbed the children and pushed them into the passageway.

'What are you doing, you nosey old cow. Leave my kids alone.' He slammed the door on her.

Mrs Miller was worried. The twins were Brewsters but the treatment of them was beyond the acceptance of social decency. She couldn't rest until she had reported the cruelty and abuse of the twins to the local policeman. He, apparently, passed on the information to the authorities and Iris and Bill were taken away to be cared for by the NSPCC.

Iris and Bill's records, filed in the unit's cabinet, were the thickest and heaviest I'd ever held in my hands. I couldn't find the time to go through the mound of documents and forms but I had read large sections.

The children had gone from one institution to another, sometimes being split up. They both had committed a number of atrocities. When they were apart their behaviour had been at its worse. They had been examined by doctors, psychologists and psychiatrists and the diagnosis of their state of minds was conclusive.

One of the kindest decisions made for their care that I read, was of someone being compassionate and wise enough not to split them; to let them stay together.

When the building of The Nightingale Nursing Homes was complete, Iris and Bill returned to their home town, Bryncelyn, and were the first residents of Bevan EMI unit. It was a happy ending to a tragic, cruel existence..

They were always together. They held hands as they walked down the corridors or out on short outings with staff members. They shared a room and lived as man and wife. They had been sexually intimate before being admitted to The Nightingale Nursing Homes and no-one, as far as I know, objected.

I wasn't aware of their sexual intimacy until a day when Helen Young, also an RMN, who alternated with Trevor Ellis in taking charge of Bevan Unit, enlightened me. I knew, of course, that incest was illegal but existed, and was sometimes socially accepted. Jennifer Worth wrote of it in her classical novel, *Call the Midwife.* Her characters, Fred and Peggy, lived as man and wife and brother and sister. They lived a life full of love and happiness after their hard beginnings in the workhouse.

One afternoon, when I was cutting Iris's toenails in the treatment room, she confessed a fear of being without Bill. Her feet were small and plump, just as she was. Her round, dimple-cheeked face always had the hint of a smile, but not on that day.

From her appearance no-one would think that she and Bill were twins. The only feature they had in common was their height.

Bill was on the skinny side and narrow; his clothes sagged and he didn't care about his appearance as Iris did. He had enough hair to run a comb through but his lean face had a fixed frown. He hardly ever spoke; Iris did the talking for them both.

'What would I do without him, Shirl?' She spoke quietly. Bill was sitting on a dining room chair outside the open door. Helen Young, the nurse in charge at the time, wasn't happy about that. Bill had a chest infection and he didn't care about coughing his germs into the air and the possibility of spreading his infection to others. But he wouldn't allow Iris to stray from his side or close behind him. He was jealous and would throw a tantrum if she spoke too long to others or others to her.

Bill was prone to chest infections and Iris was worried that it would cause his death. I heard him coughing and understood why she was thinking that he would die.

'Well, now,' I replied with a fast ticking mind; anxious to find the right words. 'You have lots of companions here, Iris. You'd never be on your own, everybody loves you.'

Iris shook her head and looked sad. It was an expression I hadn't before seen on her. 'I know, but it wouldn't be like having Tom. What would I do without him?'

'I don't know, Iris, but I know you'd be looked after. You must know we all have the same thoughts that you're having. Anyway, Bill could outlive you, couldn't he?'

'Oh, no. He couldn't live without me.'

I didn't respond to that but steered away from the subject of death.

'There, toenails are cut. You can put your shoes and socks on now and take Bill to tea.'

'Thank you, Shirl. Don't tell Billy what I said, will you?'

'No, of course not,' I replied.

I watched her rise stiffly from her chair and grunt slightly as she made for the door. I guessed her stiffness was one of the contingencies of ageing – arthritis.

However, I did speak about it to Sister Helen Young later. Iris had saddened me. It was quite possible that she would lose Bill; his health wasn't good and Helen told me that each chest infection Bill had was worse than the previous one.

'This time,' she said, 'his chest is very bad and when Dr Davies comes I'm going to suggest he gets Bill admitted to hospital for some aggressive treatment.'

'I think you're right, Helen, but Iris will want to go with him and that's not possible.'

'No, but it will be good for her, too. Iris will have a rest.'

'What do you mean by Iris having a rest?'

'Shirley, you should see her when she's undressed. Her thighs are covered with bruises. If you'll excuse the crudeness, he's bonking her until she can't walk straight. If she hadn't been put on "the pill" years ago she would have produced like a rabbit. She used to have a spring in her step but now she walks as if she needs hip replacements and she doesn't.'

I was flabbergasted. 'I thought I'd seen everything. Rape, abuse, assaults of all sorts, but nothing like this.' I was at a loss for words but Helen went on.

'And that's not all. We've noticed that Bill is even more unwilling for Iris to be out of his sight since Melvyn Baker joined us.'

At the age of seventy-five Melvyn Baker had been transferred from a sheltered institution for offenders. He had been imprisoned for rape. He had served his long sentence but it was considered he was too mentally unstable to be set free into the community.

Helen went on. 'To put it bluntly, Melvyn is a sex maniac and Bill found out that he had raped Iris in their room. Bill won't let her go to their room unless he's with her. Mind you, that's always been the case. When we know their room is in a filthy state we have to tempt them out and keep them out until it has been cleaned. Shirl, go up and see it for yourself.'

'No, I won't do that. Bill and Iris haven't the understanding of neatness and of being orderly and clean. I wouldn't wonder that being here is the nearest they've ever been to a home.

'I'm beginning to see how ignorant I am about the lives of people who are here at The Nightingales. I've worked in the community, hospital wards and departments and hadn't given much thought to EMI nursing homes until now. Psychiatric nursing has never appealed to me. I haven't been aware of the complexities in your part of the nursing world.'

At that point, the sound of a rumpus broke the quietude of the lounge when all the residents were peacefully awaiting afternoon tea. Both Helen's and my sights turned sharply to peer through the glass partition which divided the lounge from the office.

After her foot-care Iris left the treatment room and made straight for her usual comfortable chair in the lounge to await Bill who always sat next to her. He had gone to the lavatory; the only place he went without her.

On going towards his chair beside his sister he went into a snarling rage. Hardly a sound was ever heard from Bill but on seeing that Melvyn Baker had moved from his usual chair in front of the television and sat next to Iris, Bill became murderous. Melvyn had his hand on her plump thigh.

Bill shouted as loud as his small voice allowed, spitting forth a tirade of foul words directed at Melvyn. Melvyn smirked until Bill reached out, picked up a half-full water-jug from the small table nearby and smashed it heavily on Melvyn's head. It broke into two pieces, a sharp edge piercing Melvyn's scalp.

In seconds, blood trickled down between his eyes onto his nose. As he leapt up from the chair, he pulled back his arm, raising a large fist into the air about to thrust it down onto Bill's nose.

Iris screamed. The water from the jug had splashed over her and it dripped from her hair as she forced herself between the two men. Melvyn's fist, which was meant for Bill, landed full-force onto her nose.

The sound of booing, laughing and clapping of the "spectators" filled the room as two carers interrupted the fight. The two men were separated by force. Melvyn, whose tall frame towered over everyone, was pulled back by the two carers, and thrown kinetically into his chair in front of the television. He was held there whilst another carer calmed Bill and pushed him heavily onto his usual chair.

I was impressed by the swift and skillful method used by the carers to ease the viciousness and hatred. They were, obviously, familiar with having to deal with such events. In minutes the lounge was back to its normal, controlled atmosphere. Peace reigned.

'I must go and sort those three out,' Helen said. 'You look quite surprised, Shirley. That event is not rare, you know. We're used to it. We have worse than that to deal with.'

'I'm glad my responsibility here is to teach basic care. How on earth are you going to deal with Iris and Bill's situation? Or keep Melvyn out of trouble. I shouldn't say it, but he gives me the creeps. I passed him on the way in.'

'I know what you mean. He makes me cringe, though he doesn't know it. But he's sick and that's what we're here for.'

'Helen, I admire you and thank God there are people like you. Thank you for enlightening me about Iris and Bill, too.'

'And thank you for doing the chiropody; I don't like dealing with feet. And thanks, too, for doing the wound dressings. I could never do your job either.'

'I only do those procedures when I have a learner with me. That's my job. As a trainer, there's no point in carrying out care or treatments on my own, is there? But I understand it's sometimes difficult for you to spare a learner to be with me.'

'I know, but we have to make it possible,' Helen replied.

On my way into the unit that morning, I had to pass Melvyn Baker who was smoking in the hallway; the only area where cigarette smoking was allowed. We exchanged a few words but I was glad to be out of his space. He came as closely as he could into mine and I shuddered.

There were times when I had passed close by him when he was sitting next to Iris and Bill in the lounge. They had become a threesome. I wondered if they would patch things up after the fracas I had witnessed.

Melvyn was bulky and taller than six feet in height. He dressed in sweat shirt and jogger bottoms. He must have been handsome in his time but having been told of his past by Helen, I saw him as evil.

I didn't like the way he looked at me every time we were in each other's sights. It was a hungry expression but not hungry for food. I knew then what he was hungry for.

I hoped he'd leave Iris alone because he was twice the size of Bill, who was gentle and quiet. Bill would attack Melvyn again if he became riled.

As I walked slowly up the hill to the haven of the office I shared with Carole at The Bedford Home my mind was on Iris and Bill. Mother Nature can be cruel and I realised she was being exceptionally good to me. How long would it last?

Chapter 8

SOME LIVE, ALL DIE

When I got back to the office from Bevan Home, Carole was busy at her desk speaking to someone on the phone who was creating aggravation. She signalled an hello and raised her eyes to the ceiling.

'I've been on this phone for over an hour and have got nowhere. I'm on to the Home Office but I think it would be easier if it was Buckingham bloody Palace.'

'I'll go down to the kitchen and make us a pot of tea,' I said. 'Do you want anything to eat?' She shook her head as she shouted down the phone. 'The Nightingale Nursing Homes! I was speaking to someone who deals with employing immigrant nurses! Who am I speaking to now?'

That was it for me. I escaped the tense atmosphere. We were having difficulty getting qualified staff and Rajiv and his associates had decided to take on staff from overseas. He'd left for his London office after giving Carole instructions on what to do.

'Yes,' she snarled, after he had left the room, 'he's given me instructions of what to do but not how to do it. He most probably doesn't know himself.'

When I got back from the kitchen with a tray of tea Carole had ended her call and was studying intricate-looking forms. I admired her ability. Official form filling is one of my pet hates and I was glad Derek did all our domestic administration.

'You shouldn't have carried that tray up them stairs, Shirley. You know it's no good for your back.'

'It's all right. I came up in the lift. Don't worry; I'll do nothing to annoy my back. It's a blooming pest, though. And it's easy to forget.'

'I can understand that. Where've you been up to now? There's a list of phone calls for you. I didn't know where you were to put them through.'

'Sorry, I should have told you. I've been down Bevan Home doing the chiropody and talking to Helen. She's been telling me about Iris and Bill Brewster. I was shocked. Do you know they, sort of, co-habit?'

'Yes. I thought you knew, too. Trouble is, there's not enough time to read the case-notes. There must be a lot we don't know about and perhaps that's a good thing. How does Marlene Phelps look?'

Marlene was a senior carer in The Bevan Home. 'All right, to me. Why, has she been ill?'

'Well she's pregnant. Didn't you know?'

'No. I thought she was putting on a bit of weight. And I thought she and her other half had separated.'

'They have. She became preggers after a one night stand with Stan Jones.'

I almost shouted. 'That horrible Stan Jones, the male carer?'

'Yes, that's him. They all got together – about a dozen of them – at The Bridge pub to celebrate his birthday and things went a bit over the top. Both must have been drunk out of their minds, at least, I think Marlene must have been. They had it off against a wall down the gully. It beggars belief, doesn't it?'

My jaw dropped. 'And she's keeping the baby? Well, I admire her. I don't believe in terminations, myself ... but there are times ...'

'I admire her, too. But I can't understand how she could bear him touching her. And she already has two children. She and the kids live with her parents.'

Stan Jones was short and thick-set. He was sly-eyed, kept his sparse, brown greasy hair at shoulder length and had no front teeth. He had dentures, didn't wear them or clean those teeth he had. He had halitosis and was uncouth. I couldn't comprehend why he was employed as a carer except that he was a close friend of the other male carers at The Bevan Home.

Marlene Phelps had started studying for the NVQ I had had several sessions of helping her with the written work which had to be accomplished.

She was, and no doubt still is, pretty and gentle. She was popular among the residents and staff. She displayed interest in completing the course and seemed to have the ability to succeed. She had never mentioned the fact that she was pregnant. She was slim and shapely so was able to disguise the pregnancy with a loose, uniform tunic.

Two weeks after my knowing that she was pregnant, Marlene came up to the office at Bedford Home to speak to me in confidence. Carole and I guessed what she wished to talk about so Carole, tactfully, excused herself.

I greeted Marlene, told her to take the chair beside my desk and tried to create an easy atmosphere. Her cheeks pinked; I sensed her embarrassment and I thought she wasn't sure how to begin what she had to say.

'Is it about the NVQ Marlene? I asked.

'Yes, Shirley. I expect you know I'm pregnant and who the father of my baby is. I'm the main topic of gossip throughout the place and, I expect, half of Bryncelyn. And I know many here think I should have a termination.'

'Yes, I know, and for what it's worth, Marlene, I think you are very principled to want to keep the baby.'

'Thank you. But what I want to know is, if I'll be able to complete the NVQ after I've had the baby and come back to work, because I'm determined to do something to better myself. I'm thirty-two so I need to get on before I'm too old. My mother will look after the baby.'

'I'll see that you can carry on with the NVQ as soon as you're back,' I replied. 'You might be interested to know that I didn't start nurse training until I was thirty six. Having the

NVQ will be an advantage if you wish to go into professional training.'

'You were thirty six?' She sounded surprised. 'Thank you for telling me that. It gives me more hope of getting into training.' Marlene got up from her chair. 'I mustn't keep you. You've told me what I want to know and more.'

'I'll let Deborah, the co-ordinator of Age Concern know. I expect you know they are one of the chief bodies of the NVQs in this area and it's her I deal with. I'll see that she'll keep you on the course. There is no limit to the time it takes to qualify, so contact me as soon as you get back after your maternity leave.'

'When I start back I promise it won't take me long to complete it.'

'I know. Good luck with the baby. It will be loved and have a good mother.' I felt sad for her. I wouldn't have coped with that difficult predicament as she seemed to.

Our office window overlooked the forecourt of The Bedford Home and the top of the hill. I watched Marlene Phelps's back as she walked down the hill to return to her work at The Bevan Home. Her dark hair was short and neat, her uniform tunic pristine and smart, in spite of her being near seven months pregnant. I wished all nurses, already in posts in the hospitals I'd visited recently with Derek, had Marlene's principles and courage. She walked steadily as a thin layer of snow sparkled on the tarmac.

Bryncelyn was prone to the first finger-tips of winter. Its sea-level was high as was the spirit of its community, in spite of the high unemployment after the mines and steel-works closures. It was December with Christmas around the corner. They would pull together and make it merry and gift-giving, no matter what.

Bryncelyn is a close-knit community of large families. Brothers, sisters and cousins live with their families in the same street or near-by streets, as do their mothers, fathers, and grandparents. There is security within extended families. I know because I was born into one. When trouble strikes, help is within walking distance.

I was born into an extended family in the early days of coal-mining. I knew no other until I met and married Derek. I travelled widely with him and returned to the U.K. to an area of nuclear families. We have many friends and colleagues but no near relatives.

My nearest relatives abide in the valley which I left on marrying. Ruby, my closest relative lived twenty miles away and her daughters and grandchildren surrounded her. She would not have accepted residence in a nursing home so she had the support not to have had to think about it. Ruby had plenty of loving relatives within walking distance to care for her in her ground floor council flat. She was adored by everyone, including myself. All my life I had enjoyed a relationship with Ruby.

She died at the age of eighty-three when I was working at The Nightingale Nursing Homes. I hadn't thought of Ruby being dead. I was brought up with her and still miss her but it helps to be in touch with her large family of off-springs.

The road is good between Gilwern and Cwmdare, where she lived until she died. I visited her often and she made me promise that she would not "be put away" in any nursing home if an unlikely situation arose which prevented her children caring for her. Not even to The Nightingale Nursing Homes, where I worked.

I knew she would always be looked after by her girls and die in her council flat but she took a lot of convincing that there was nothing frightening about our nursing homes.

I hadn't noticed that Ruby had become elderly and debilitated and the thought of her dying hadn't entered my mind. I had difficulty accepting the fact that she had.

I was devastated. I had to "pull myself together" to attend her funeral. I was overcome with depression but, as Derek said, I had to attend the final farewell. It would offend her family and I would always regret it if I didn't.

At ten o'clock, on the day of Ruby's funeral I drove down through the valleys. I took the back roads as far as I could.

They were roads which were familiar to me, before I would turn onto the main highway which took me to where Ruby lay in her coffin. Having turned onto the highway I steered into a spot to park out of the way of other traffic and let my thoughts go back to Ruby's and my early days.

Ruby was my mother's young cousin but it was she who mothered me. There were no secrets between us. She made me, what is termed, "street-wise", not that I had, by any stretch of the imagination, been sheltered.

Ruby and I were of a poor, humble background. We had lived in a rough, tough environment of a mining valley. Those early days were poverty-stricken but since we knew no other there were more happy days than sad.

There were no nursing homes that I knew of, but the threat of the dreaded workhouse; the social stigma of the elderly and poor. It cannot be said that living was for the survival of the fittest because we all pulled together. The strong helped the weak.

Bartering was done over garden walls. 'Kate, lend me a cup of flour to make our gravy.'

'Aye, I can do that, Hilda, but you'll have to spare me half a loaf and a bit of butter until I come from the shop, tomorrow.'

When my mother and Aunty Hilda couldn't help each other out there were three other neighbours in our street who would lend or borrow until the following day.

Our street, Vale View Terrace, was a row of five houses. Not living in a house, which would be exactly the same as ours but in a street of fifty or more houses, made us a cut above them. That was a life-time ago.

When I turned my head and stretched my neck from where I was parked I could just get a glimpse of the chimney pots. Chimney pots but no smoke; gas or electric fires now.

On the day of Ruby's funeral I left home with the intention of seeing her go and bidding a last farewell; but I couldn't. My emotions ran riot and I was held back by something inside me. I should have taken the new road. I would have missed seeing the valley streets of my old terrain. Memories of the past saddened me.

From the main highway the cemetery is seen across the valley. It is the first sign of my old home where I lived until I married. The year had entered April and a Spring breeze nodded through the scattered wild daffodil patches which surrounded the high grey walls of the cemetery. More than half a century of sweet and bitter memories stirred my mind.

Only by someone who knew the valley and where to cast the eyes could the graveyard be glimpsed from the side of the highway where I had stopped and switched off the engine. I needed a pause to steady myself before taking the road at the next left turn which would swing round and descend to the narrow streets.

I loved Ruby. In dire sadness it was, and still is, hard holding back tears. To a depressive, which I am, it is harder. The cliché "pull yourself together" has worn out long ago. But for the sake of others one has to try.

When I was growing up, Ruby and I were close friends as well as second cousins. My mother bore me, fed and clothed me as best she could and loved me in her own way, but it was Ruby who nurtured me. Ruby was part of my growing up and I, part of her growing old.

Four years before she died, Ruby had her left leg amputated above the knee; it had become gangrenous. She was then seventy-nine and living with Dave Miller, her "partner" of thirty years.

Following that, she managed for a time to get about with a false limb and crutches but her poor health had become complicated by a paralyzing stroke. During her early eighties she was bound to her small, comfortable ground-floor flat and a wheelchair. She often had to remind me that she would soon be joining "all the others" up the cemetery. I pushed the thought out of my mind.

'Where's your fight to live? You've got years left in you. I'll never forgive you if you go before me,' I joked. 'I have to run up the corridors after residents years older than you.'

'Well, they must be well looked after, but you make sure I won't be put in with them,' she had said with determination. 'I have plenty of my own kids to look after me here. Don't you dare let them put me away.'

Many elderly people have a dread of "being put away". Fear of nursing homes and "being put away" has been driven into the hearts and minds of the elderly and incapacitated citizens who have died alone in their homes, rather than accept the warmth and comfort of a nursing home.

Ruby considered herself fortunate to have many willing hands about her. Her official carer was Sarah, her twenty year old grand-daughter, unmarried with two girls. Ruby had financial help from the State. An attendance allowance is available to those dependents who are sixty-five or over. It is meant to pay a personal carer. Ruby had attendance allowance and paid her granddaughter to care for her. Sarah couldn't be with Ruby for twenty-four hours but with the help of several other member of the family Ruby was well cared for.

I had visited Ruby frequently, but now my visits to the valley are rare, although I still have my uncle and his family there, a few cousins and one surviving old school-friend.

Ruby lived her last years in a flat which was allocated to her by the social services when she left the home of thirty years with her "partner" Dave Miller.

Ruby had never loved Dave but he had given her and her three daughters a home when she left her Irish husband because of his infidelity and cruelty. She was fond of Dave and he had once adored her. He was eleven years younger than she but didn't appear so. He'd had a face spoilt by years of contesting in a boxing ring. Ruby's daughters amused me by describing his face as looking like an old potato and that, I thought, was an apt description. He would have been devastated had he known because he had a good self-body image. Ruby was modest about her beautiful appearance. Most of her life she bloomed with health and even on her death bed there were remnants of her beauty.

Dave had managed a pub which was on the decline before Ruby moved in with him. She had taken pride in it and made it profitable. Her sparkling personality made it a favourite for miles around.

Dave's mother then lived in a rented tiny terraced cottage. Dave had always paid the rent and the rent-book was in his name. When he and Ruby retired from the pub they moved into the cottage and eventually bought it in joint names. Ruby loved it, especially its patch of garden at the back. It was something which we didn't have when living at Vale View Terrace. She turned it into a little haven of herbs and flowers.

However, the heavy work of the pub had ruined her health. Dave had left all the heavy humping and dumping of barrels to Ruby while he drank most of the profits.

As Ruby aged and became ill, Dave could not, would not, care for her. He was a bully and became alcoholic. When drunk he was violent and vent his spleen upon Ruby.

When she became dependent on others for her care he didn't provide it. Dave used her incapacity to humiliate her and made her life intolerable. He went off on a holiday to Thailand and came back with a thirty-two year old Thai wife. He was sixty-eight. Ruby was delighted and had good reason to request a social service apartment for herself. She was glad she had refused his many offers of marriage to her.

Ruby was granted a ground-floor flat within visiting distance of relatives and friends. Not me, though. It was a twenty mile drive from Gilwern but I didn't mind; I was her frequent visitor.

Sometimes, one of her daughters and granddaughters lifted Ruby from her wheelchair onto the front seat of my car, put her wheelchair in the boot and we went shopping at the supermarkets. The transferring process to get her home was reversed, as necessary. Ruby overspent her state allowance every time, buying things for everyone but herself. Her purse seemed to be bottomless.

I'd kept in touch with relatives and friends in the valley mainly through Ruby. We gathered from time to time at her flat. Funeral gatherings predominated, but I didn't think one of them would be Ruby's. Not yet.

As I sat in my car overlooking the valley I wondered if I could escape saying a last fair-well to Ruby. I know she would understand my reluctance, but her large family of off-springs expected me to be there. I glanced up at the cemetery and caught sight of the tombstones clawing their way up the side of the mountain which rose abruptly from the backyards of the street-houses below and I felt choked with memories.

As children, me and my sister, Rosie, often visited that cemetery. There were many graves of people we knew to refresh with wild flowers we had gathered on the way there.

When I was a little girl of seven I went on my own. I fell asleep over the mound of my grandfather's freshly dug grave and nearly froze to death. It was on an icy November evening when I was unhappy and lonely. Aunty Hilda, my friend Tom Bolt and Rosie risked their own safety to find me. But for them I wouldn't be here today. Yet, Rosie is dead. It came to my mind that she was among those tombstones and the thought opened the floodgates of my eyes and I wept. I was alone so was allowed to.

On my first ward in nurse training, that was a principle of my ward sister. She had seen my tears more than once and had sensed my avoidance of being involved in carrying out "last offices" of the dead. This is the procedure of washing and straightening the body and the putting on of a shroud.

'You may shed tears, Nurse Phillips,' she had said, 'but ensure there are no witnesses. You will do your duty as a nurse and be grateful that your patient died in peace and comfort. Your compassion will be in giving strength to the loved ones.' So I wept alone, without a feeling of guilt, to ease my own sadness for losing Ruby.

I just couldn't tolerate the thought of Ruby going to the cemetery. Something inside me objected. I turned my car at the passing point and drove home. I decided to take flowers at another time.

I wasn't at home the hour she died. I was out shopping, getting a few things I needed at home for Derek and myself. As I was taking my bags from the car, Derek had appeared on the drive to help me unload, as he usually did.

'Leave this to me, Love,' he said. 'Your cousins have been trying to get you. You'd better call Ruby's straight away.'

He knew what I would hear and thinking back, it was strange that I didn't consider Ruby had died. I had been with her two days before and realised she was worsening but assumed she would pull through as she had with all previous serious illnesses.

She had pneumonia and seemed to be responding to the antibiotic therapy. We didn't talk much. I had sat beside her on the pretty duvet cover and let her speak when she felt like it; when she had something to say. She was weakening and her words were few.

She pointed to the top of a small chest of drawers against the wall at the bottom of her bed. 'Press the button at the back of that narrow strip, there above the proper top draw, Shirl,' she said. I did so; there was just enough of a slit to get my fingers to the button. A secret drawer sprang open.

'Only you and Sarah know about that but watch out for her. Watch in case she takes advantage. She'd spend it in a week if she had her way and I mightn't be here to stop her. It's to be shared between them.'

I heard her quiet words but didn't look at her as she spoke. My eyes must have looked ready to pop onto my cheek-bones. The narrow space between the secret drawer and the top of the dresser was narrow but every inch was packed tightly with wads of notes.

'Must be nearly ten thousand pounds,' Ruby said. 'Dave's house was in both our names. He knew I did most of the work to keep it going so I got him on the phone to give me a share of its value or I'd take him to court for it. He knew I'd get more if I did, so he brought it here in a carrier bag. It's the only time he's been here and no-one saw him, as far as I know. There was more money there but I've been dibbing into it. Sarah and me were going to Australia to Jacci and Richard's.' Jacci was

Ruby's second daughter. She and her husband and two children had emigrated two years before.

'The way I feel now, though, I don't think I could stand a jaunt to Tesco's, let alone to Australia and it would be too hot for me there, anyway.'

The lengthy dialogue seemed to have taken the last of her strength. She sighed and sank back into the pillows.

I gasped. 'Ruby, you can't keep all this money here! If thieves broke in they'd find that drawer in no time. I'll take you to the bank to put it in and just keep some of it back.'

'No, I want it here so I can see and feel it and give bits away when I want to. Shirley, I won't be here much longer. I should have gone to God or Old Nick years ago.' She recited a line of Dylan Thomas's poem, '*Do not go gentle into that good night.* I'm tired, Shirl. No more fight in me.'

Her words saddened me and I had to turn away to hide my tears.

'Neither God nor Old Nick want you yet. I've warned you before; I'll never speak to you again if you die before me.' She managed a faint chuckle.

As I drove home the thought of Ruby dying didn't enter my thoughts; I was worried about the money she had in her secret drawer. I supposed she'd go on spending it bit by bit until it was gone and I expected her to live until then. Looking back, I must have realised she would die but my mind wouldn't let me look at the obvious.

When I had the message that Ruby had died my hands trembled as I dialled her home number and I had an unpleasant gut feeling. Bridget, Ruby's eldest daughter had answered immediately. She was crying.

'She went peacefully about two hours ago, Shirley. She's still warm. I wish you were here.'

Something inside me snapped. I screamed. 'Oh, no. Not yet. Ruby, not yet!' I slammed down the phone and rushed back to the car.

'I'm going to Ruby's,' I called out to Derek. He was in the kitchen unpacking the shopping bags. He dropped what was in his hand and came out to me.

'Please don't go yet, Love. You're too emotional to drive over twenty miles and back. There's nothing you can do.' He knew why Bridget had called.

'I must. I won't be long.'

When I got to Ruby's flat the door was wide open; the room was full of relatives and those she had been close to. They all lived within a stone's throw of where she lived and the bad news had got to some of them when it was known her life was ending. Everyone moved out of my path to let me through to where she lay – where I last saw her. I kissed her and embraced her warm, dead body and sobbed.

Anita, a dear second cousin was manicuring Ruby's nails. She had beautiful hands even though she had done rough work all her life except when she was, a "call-girl in London". She had been loath to use the term "prostitute." She went to the bright lights for a while, looking for a better life than the valleys had to offer, when I was fourteen; the year Rosie died. It was only I who knew how she had been caught up in a dirty business. She spent a few weeks working for a pimp.

'And that was long enough to let me know that it was safer to get away from the big, rotten City,' she had told me.

To all others she had worked as a maid for a rich family. Ruby had sworn me to secrecy when she told me about her adventures in London. I remember the day she returned home. I was dazzled by her glamour. She'd brought her clothes. She had the loveliest frocks I'd ever seen and her fingernails were long and varnished a bright red.

As I embraced Ruby's still warm body, Anita, manicured her nails. 'She'd want her nails to look their best,' Anita sniffed.

I stayed with Ruby for just minutes. She looked peaceful, gentle and lovely, even in death. Derek had been right; there was nothing I could do.

'Let me know if there's anything I can do, won't you, Bridget?' I embraced her and gently pulled her ear close to my mouth; she's a head taller than I.

'I hate to mention this at such a time but you must know there's a lot of money in a narrow draw below the top of her chest of drawers. You'd better take it if you're going to leave tonight.'

'Don't worry, Sarah's told me. I'll deal with it as she would want me to and I'll ring you every day until she goes.' She was referring to the funeral.

I didn't attend Ruby's funeral and I don't regret it. She was ready to die. There was no more fight in her.

Chapter 9

THE PIANIST

I did not attend Ruby's funeral but when working at The Nightingale Nursing Homes I attended many. I had become well acquainted with the residents and there was always sadness when someone died. Perhaps, I became too acquainted with some. I was repeatedly warned by Derek and I knew he was right, but I couldn't stop myself from wanting to know all about them. I needed them to know they were valued.

There was just not enough time.

In every coffin lay an untold, unique life story; past memories of a fruitful, adventurous life. What might have been considered exciting and eventful to some, was peacefully satisfying and uneventful to others.

I wish I had the time and talent to write all the stories which are crammed into my small mind of the five years I worked in The Nightingale Nursing Homes. In retrospect, five years was a flash in time. Perhaps, that is because the older one gets the more quickly the years seem to pass.

The passing of residents did not help my scourge of depression. I tried to justify this and blamed back pain, which became worse when I was stressed. The curvature of my spine was deteriorating though my work involved nothing physical. The director who invited me to take the post of Training Manager assured me he would expect no "hands-on" work. He referred to the moving and handling of dependent residents. During twenty five years in general nursing I mistreated my spine – pretended it would heal, but it was the reverse. *"There is none so blind as she who does not want to see"!* That old proverb perfectly fitted my attitude. I didn't care about the torture of back pain as long as I could take a pill which would ease it and let me carry on working. I decided to concern myself with it when it got in my way. Payback time was with me in The Nightingale Nursing Homes but it was bearable. It hadn't yet beaten me.

The number and type of analgesics I was taking increased to no avail, except to cause gut problems and I discontinued the anti-depressants. I was determined to beat the depression.

Derek advised me to resign but I was enjoying the work and it was good for me to see so many with mind disturbances which made mine seem like nothing; a painful twitch that would or would not go away. I was self-diagnosed as being introverted and emotionally weak and I was depressed, not unhappy. Being among very debilitated, elderly and elderly mentally infirm people made me realise how puerile my depression was.

However, I was correct in labelling myself a depressive and I knew that I would, most probably, be a depressive for the rest of my life – as my mother was.

In all ways my marriage and home life were perfect. I certainly had no financial problems, Paul was well and happy and my husband was among the finest men that ever walked. What more could I expect? Yet I sometimes felt physically wretched, had convinced myself that it was a temporary surge of clinical depression after the death of Ruby and the effect of unrelenting back pain. Analgesics are not a panacea, but we can thank God we have them. Various drugs took the edge off my pain.

I got used to not travelling to see Ruby and, gradually, the heartache of her loss eased. As they say "life must go on" and for me it went on very well. I had my work and my writing and the love and support of a family that couldn't be bettered.

I had been the nurse training manager at The Nightingale Nursing Homes for three years when Ruby died, so I was no stranger to death.

The average age of the residents was said to be eighty years. Inevitably, some died. No matter how aged, there is always sadness and grief. It is easy for relationships to become close between resident and carer but good care must be given to all.

That wasn't and isn't always the case; the media has made it clear. I have been caring for people long enough to say that there is more of the good, but there is no Utopia. From what I read in the newspapers and what I hear on the radio news broadcastings, the care of the elderly, the elderly mentally infirm and patients on hospital wards is in danger of further deterioration.

When is someone going to call a halt?

I, and any of the staff available at The Nightingale Nursing Homes, attended the funerals. Sometimes we were the only ones, when there were no relatives, acquaintances or old friends. They, too, would have passed on or be too old and decrepit to attend a funeral, even if they wanted to. There are those who see no benefit in making the effort to say the last farewell.

There have been times, when there has been an inheritance to be dealt with. Unknown or unheard of relatives have, surprisingly, turned up at The Nightingale Nursing Homes.

There was an occasion when I witnessed two people squabbling across the bed of a dying lady. They argued about who had done most for her and the entitlement of the proceeds of the sale of her house, her jewellery and money left in her bank account.

The passing of that lady is etched on my memory; Mrs Martha Haines-Jones. She had been a famous pianist.

She was breathing her last in the room she had called her own for over eight years. It was overlooking the field at the back of the building which she appreciated when she was admitted into The Bedford Home for the elderly, but for her last two years she had been blind. Her age was one hundred and two when she died.

One of my hated clichés is, *"Well, she was old and decrepit. She's out of suffering now."* Surely, every hour, every day in this world is precious. This was, certainly, the attitude of Mrs Haines-Jones.

One morning I knocked the door of her room and entered. She wouldn't have heard me knock without her hearing aids in. I told her that I had knocked. I knew she appreciated courteousness. I bid her good morning and she recognised my voice.

It was after ten o'clock; she was left in bed until she rang the bell for assistance. At her age she was allowed the privilege of breakfasting in bed and not in the dining room, if she so wished.

I recognised that one of the carers had been in to check on her because the curtains were open and her commode had been emptied and sanitised. It was expected that one morning someone would go into her room to find that she would never awaken again. She was very much alive on the morning of which I write. She responded brightly to my greeting.

'Good morning, Mrs Phillips. What a lovely day,' she said. She was one of few who, sometimes, addressed me by my surname.

'It is, isn't it?' I agreed. 'Even though it's cold and raining.'

'You know, Shirley, each day I awake, I thank God that he's given me another day to listen to my beautiful music. Perhaps I'm being greedy but I still have a strong will to live.'

'I'm of the same sentiment Mrs Haines-Jones. Life is a precious gift that we must treat with respect.'

What she uttered next stopped my movements. *"Do not go gentle into that good night,"* It was a line of Dylan Thomas's famous poems which Ruby had recited shortly before she died.

'That is one of mine and Derek's favourite poems,' I said, 'and that's the second time I've heard it being recited in a short time – when a dear relative passed away. She fought on for as long as she could.'

'Dylan Thomas, our cleverest of poets,' she said.

'Yes,' was all I could say for some moments. 'Anyway, Mrs Haines-Jones, Elaine has asked me to give you a pedicure. Would you like me to come in just before lunch to cut your toenails?'

'Oh, yes, please, Shirley. My pedal toenail is giving me trouble.'

Later, when I had made her and myself comfortable, I took out my instruments and prepared to cut her toenails. I hadn't cut them before that day and had quite a surprise to find her piano pedal toenail was a huge claw. She sensed my surprise and chuckled.

'I know, my dear, it's like a big eagle talon, isn't it?'

'Yes, and it looks as if you haven't had it trimmed for a long time. I think it must have given people a lot of pleasure when you used it.' I spoke as I put a little pressure under it with my instrument.

'Oh, my goodness!' My voice rose with anxiety. 'It's dropped off.'

She chuckled again. 'I'm not surprised. I tried to bend down to it but couldn't reach it. When I touched it with my grabber I found it was very loose.'

I completed Mrs Haines-Jones pedicure and, with her permission, kept the toe-nail to show my colleagues.

The dropping off of her piano pedal toenail was an omen. When I next went on duty Mrs Haines-Jones was dying. She had bent over to adjust her radio, fell and bumped her head. She had become unconscious and would never hear her beautiful music again.

The following morning she was in a deep coma. Her death was expected at any time. I happened to pass her room during the afternoon and heard raised, angry sounding voices and from the few words I heard I understood the subject of their argument. I didn't knock on the closed door before entering. The squabbling stopped abruptly; my hard, stony stare made the two women realise I had guessed what was going on. 'Mrs Haines-Jones is not yet dead but for all we know she can hear what is going on. Your behaviour is disgusting. I doubt she would recognise your voices because in the time I've been here neither of you has visited or telephoned.'

'How dare you!' the plump, over-dressed, over-painted faced women said. 'I have often visited Martha. She is my aunt through marriage and I have kept in touch.'

'Oh, no you haven't,' the other lady argued. 'And you are in no way related to her, through marriage or any other way. It is I who have been constantly visiting.' A woman who reminded me of a runner-bean; tall and haggard in a green beret, a heavy, well-worn green, tweed suit argued across the bed in which Mrs Haines-Jones was breathing the end of her life.

I kept my voice low. 'We keep a record of all visitors and messages. You wouldn't know that but I know she wouldn't mind me asking you to please leave the room. Mrs Haines-Jones needs her care now.' I leant down to be close to Martha's ear, ignoring the visitors. 'Annie and Frieda are coming in now, Mrs Haines-Jones, to make sure you're comfortable.'

I opened the door and beckoned the two avaricious women to leave. There is not always sadness when someone dies. Greed causes conflict in many a family.

When there are sons, daughters, grandchildren or other relatives, we weep with them, but I have, sometimes, recognised crocodile tears. Relatives of the dead are sometimes relieved to be rid of the responsibility of visiting and financing.

All too often I have heard, 'Well, it's a blessing. She'll be glad her suffering is over now.' That cliché certainly wasn't suitable to Mrs Martha Haines-Jones existence. She loved every day.

She had been a well-known professional concert pianist. She had entertained throughout the kingdom with her wonderful gift and had given a lot of pleasure. The people of the valley she was born into were proud of her. She was famous for her parts in the National Eisteddfods, too. She became wealthy and hadn't needed to sell her property to maintain her existence at our nursing home.

She was one of five children but had outlived them. She had married and had children herself; two sons and a daughter. Sadly, one son died in his teens, one in a road traffic accident and her daughter died of breast cancer when in her forties. Martha and her husband had celebrated their fiftieth wedding anniversary shortly after which he, too, died.

After a sad family life she continued to think of the happy days and enjoyed every day through her music.

She was able to walk a few steps on her own using a Zimmer walking frame, which was a blessing, because with a little help she could go to the toilet and could get to Willow Lounge when she felt like having company. Her sight was bad but she was able to feed herself, also with a little help. Her hearing was poor but with hearing-aids she listened to music all day, switching over only to hear the national news.

In her own elegant, smart house Mrs Haines-Jones had a living-in companion for over thirty ears, Blodwen Pugh. Blodwen was a little woman but was able to fully care for Martha until her mobility became limited. Martha stumbled and fell too often. Eventually, Blodwen became unable to raise Martha from the floor when she fell. Also, elimination, which is apt to become a problem in the elderly, began to affect Martha's independent existence.

Blodwen went on living in the house after Martha was admitted to the nursing home.

'I'll keep it spick and span for you, Martha, and see everything is safe,' Blodwen wept as she waved Martha away in a taxi, loaded up with her essential personal belongings to The Nightingale Nursing Homes.

'Don't cry, Blod. It's only for a few weeks until I'm more my old self.'

Initially, her admission to a nursing home was intended for a short respite period but she was surprisingly comfortable in The Bedford Home. The carers were kind and thorough in maintaining her physical needs and she had her music player and radio.

Blodwen had no other home and no relatives. Martha had no qualms about telling Blodwen that her home was hers, where it had been for the past thirty years. Blodwen had looked after Mr Jones and the children when Martha was on her concert tours.

Blodwen visited Martha several times a week, until she, too, suffered the contingencies of ageing.

After Martha's death a number of strangers appeared to pay their last respects at the The Nightingale Nursing Homes. Having been a famous pianist, her death was announced by the media. That was how the human leeches knew of her death.

Blodwen faintly remembered one face from many years before, but apart from her, she recognised no one. As many of the staff who could be spared, as well as those off duty were at Martha's funeral, so there was quite an unexpected large congregation. Those residents who could walk the distance did so and six of our staff came on their off-duty days to wheelchair residents who had known Martha for a long time. There were others who knew of her famous life and were proud to have met her.

I can imagine the scene at the reading of Martha's will. There was a legacy of valuable jewellery, cash investments, antique furniture and ornaments and the house itself, which was probably the most valuable item. There must have been much disappointment on finding that Martha had left the house and all its contents to Megan.

Many tears were shed over the passing of Mrs Haines-Jones.

'We shouldn't cry for her,' one young carer said, who hadn't known her until recently. 'After all, she was well past her sell-by-date. Gone a hundred and two!'

That carer was given a number of dirty looks.

Chapter 10

CLARICE'S STORY

The day I witnessed the unpleasantness of the fight between Bill and Melvyn with Iris in the middle, Carole was a long time out of the office after Marlene Phelps left. I was impatient to relate what I'd witnessed. Carole had been at a meeting with Elaine, Janet, and a few carers and residents, planning the Christmas festivities.

When she came back to the office it was near the end of the shift; time to go home. She explained, briefly, some of the ideas for making the atmosphere Christmassy and jolly in the three homes.

'What we did last year was magnificent, Carole,' I told her. 'We could do the same thing.'

'We have more money in the residents' kitty this year,' she replied, so we can make it extra magnificent. Firstly, we have to find three Father Christmases.'

'Well, neither your better half nor mine could play that part because they are both as skinny as bean-poles.' She agreed with a chuckle.

I went on. 'There's someone's birthday to think of first. We must think of our lovely resident, Clarice Davies. She will be eighty on the twenty-third of December. It will have to be subtle because she won't expect us to have remembered and she doesn't seem the type to want a fuss.'

'Oh, yes. Good thinking. You seem to have got to know her, so you can deal with that, will you? She seems to have taken to you.'

'Yes,' I replied. 'I've cut her toenails a couple of times. She's beautiful inside and out, yet she never married. I'd love to know more of her past. Her case-notes don't say much.'

'Ask her then. I'm sure she'll enjoy telling you. She might tell you what she'd like for her birthday.'

'Yes. I'll try discretely to find out.'

The following day, when Clarice was sitting in a comfortable lounge chair in Willow lounge I took the chair next to her. She was reading an Alexander Cordell book. I apologised for interrupting before asking if she were feeling more settled at Bedford Home.

'That's nice of you, Mrs Phillips,' she said. 'When you spoke to me shortly after I arrived you kindly said you hoped I would. I told you I wasn't sure. If I'd been truthful I would have said I was frightened. Had I made the right choice by leaving my home? The change has been quite difficult, but at my age, what can I expect? But, yes. It's warm here, the meals are good and the company, especially, I enjoy.'

'I'm glad about that, Miss Davies. So many bad things are said about nursing homes these days. I know it makes elderly people afraid of giving up their homes when they can't manage to care for themselves, so they remain lonely and in discomfort.'

'Well, now, I have it in mind to write to the local press and express my opinion about Bedford Nursing Home. I'm lucky I still have good enough eye-sight to do it. I would advise people to make the change before they become my age. I should have accepted the opportunity to come here over a year ago but it was hard to leave the home my brother, Gareth, and lovely sister-in-law gave me. Memories, you know? Sentimentality can be a foolish friend. My brother was the last of us to meet his maker. I thought I would soon follow him but here I am.'

'What happened to your mother and father, Miss Davies?' I paused. 'I don't mean to be too inquisitive. I enjoy listening to the interesting lives our residents have led.'

'No, you're not.' She shook her head. 'I like talking about the past. I grew up without my mother, Maud. She died when I was five. It was awful and if I live to be a hundred, I shall never forget the terrible loss.

We were living in a mining area called Pontycwm then. My father and brother were miners and we moved to this part of the world when Gareth became an under-manager of a colliery, not far from here.'

A look of surprise crossed my face and she noticed. 'Why are you surprised, Mrs Phillips?'

'I'm surprised because, I too, was born and lived in Pontycwm until I married.'

'Well, I never! Our ancestor must have known each other.' Her remark amused me.

'Anyway, time marches on and I'll soon be eighty. Who would have thought I would last this long? Certainly not me.'

'Miss Davies, it's your birthday I'd like to talk about. We want to do something special for you. A gift that would give you pleasure. Have you anything in mind – something that you've always wanted and couldn't afford; bearing in mind it can't be hundreds of pounds.'

My cynicism made her chuckle. 'Nothing. I have everything. I've got older by the year but I've never had a birthday. And please call me Clarice, Mrs Phillips.'

'And I'm, Shirley. My father was a fan of Shirley Temple and you will be one of few people I meet these days, outside The Nightingale Nursing Homes, who has heard of her.'

Clarice nodded. 'Pretty little film-star Shirley Temple.'

She went on, 'My birthday was never celebrated in the house of my birth, 6, Wyndham Terrace. I was born on 23rd December, 1917 during the first Great War.

'Thoughts were always on Christmas, though when I was little, my father always slipped a penny or two and a few extra walnuts into my Christmas stocking.

'It was Christmas time, 1922, when my lovely mother was very ill and died. I remember it as if it were yesterday.

'But I mustn't bore you or keep you from your work. You'll have heard sadder stories than mine.' She added 'I'll have to get used to calling you Shirley.'

'You are not boring me in the least. My hobby is writing short stories. I would like to hear a little about the time you lost your mother. If I can put it into readable words I'd like to write about it, if you wouldn't mind.'

'I'd like that, too. I'm flattered by your interest. Let me tell you a little now, until our supper time, and continue when you have time, is it?'

'Yes, go on until supper comes, then I have some writing up to do before I go home.'

Clarice took a long sip of her squash which she had poured into a glass from the jug her carer had put on her side-table. Clarice began her story.

'On Christmas Eve, 1922, I pegged my stocking onto a piece of string which served as a clothes-line above our fire place on which my mother aired our freshly-ironed underwear.

I stood tiptoe on the edge of the hearth and stretched my arms to peg the stocking. I remember thinking it too small. I would have cheated and hung up one of my brother's if he hadn't been there.

I gave my mother a fright. "Watch!" she screamed across the room. Grab her quick, Gareth, or she'll end up on the fire!"

A lot of children got burned by tripping onto unguarded open fires in those days. I was five then and small for my age. It could have happened to me if our fire wasn't guarded for most of the time. The four of us were at home so the fire-guard stood in the corner until Dad put it back when we went to bed.

Only my stocking hung there. Gareth was sixteen. He considered himself to be a man having worked down the coal-mine since he left school.

We were a family of only two children. The trend then seemed to have been for a fertile woman to have babies, one after the other, until she was worn out. It wasn't so with my family. There was only Gareth and me.'

Clarice paused and chuckled. Behind her spectacles I saw her unblinking, blue eyes stare at nothing as her mind filled with scenes of her old, happy home.

'I teased my brother. "Hang up your stocking, Gareth. Father Christmas might put something in it." Clarice paused at times, smiled and nodded. I guessed she had pictures in her mind of that night.

'Gareth glared at me. "Clarice, I've told you a hundred times, there is no Father Christmas and I've been a collier on the coal long enough for him to know I'm not a little boy, so shut up."

Gareth looked older than sixteen. He was already nearly as tall as our Dad and, since hewing coal, he'd filled out. He was handsome and would have been more handsome had his teeth not yellowed from chewing tobacco-twist during the long working hours and had there been better facilities for washing off coal dust. This was a long time before pit-head baths appeared. Beneath his fair, curly hair his scalp was encrusted with a black scab. Only on a Saturday afternoon did he use his nails and pumice-stone to scrape it off.

It hurt our mother, Maud, to see the spark of youth doused from her son.

"Why don't you wash your hair properly every day, Gareth?" she asked more than once. "And I don't know why you chew that old 'bacco twist. It's not as if you smoke. Others only chew it because they can't light up some baccy."

"If I scraped my scalp every day, Mam, I'd soon be as bald as our Dad. I want to keep my curls for my girl to fancy me. I chew twist to keep the dust from my throat. Anyway, I've given that up so my teeth will soon be beautiful again". Gareth was being facetious.

"Yes, Mam, he's saying the truth. Morffydd Top Shop's got a real fancy for him."

'I was looking at Gareth in case he'd catch me by the scruff and shake me for embarrassing him. I knew he wouldn't hurt me, though. He loved me. He would give his last penny to buy me a lollipop, and not only as an excuse to go to the shop to see Morffydd.

My father said nothing. He sat in his fireside chair, deep in thought, sucking an empty pipe.

"Penny for your thoughts, Tom, Love," Mam asked.

He took another suck on his pipe. "I was thinking," he replied without looking at her. "I hope our Gareth keeps well in with those at the top shop because there's talk of another strike at the pit." "Oh, no." My mother's cheer dropped. "We're still in debt after the last one, Tom. I don't think we can survive another strike."

My father's pipe-holding hand fell onto his knee. His eyes followed it. It looked as if it knew something he didn't. He felt guilty because he was one of the gang-leaders who spoke out against the low pay and dangerous conditions in the mines. It wasn't uncommon to hear of men, and indeed, young colliers not much older than schoolboys, losing a foot or a hand or worse.

"We've got to stand up for what is right, Maud. Big pits are still being sunk and when men are in rat-holes under the surface things could go wrong. They say there could be more pits sunk in our valley before long. There'll be lots more of big machines, dangerous ones and precious little fresh air to breath, if we accept things without a fight. God knows what will be next."

The world was hungry for coal and there were those who became rich by satisfying that hunger. Dazzled by wealth, the mine owners all too often closed their eyes to how the coal reached the surface.

"I thought you wasn't going to say anything about it until after Christmas, Dad." Gareth sounded displeased. He didn't want the festive season to be spoiled with bad news.

At the age of five I was sensitive enough to feel the atmosphere souring. A strike meant many families in Pontycwm would feel the pinch again, especially those of men working in the mines. Disease and death weren't new to the valleys. Large families were crammed into small houses where sanitation and clean, running water were not considered essentials of their tenancies.

We Davieses, as others in our streets, were lucky. We had running water from a tap in our yard and a shared lavatory. It should have been flushed down every day with buckets of water and lime but the trouble was, no regular arrangement was made for the flushing of the lavatories. I hated going. I only went when the call of nature was urgent.

"We'll get through," my father said, with more confidence than he felt. "You three go to bed now. I'll lock up here. I won't put the fire-guard up tonight in case it'll stop Father Christmas coming down the chimney."

I hugged him. "Thank you, Dad." I smiled but he knew I felt sorry for him. 'I'd better go out the back to the lavvy before I go to bed, though. There won't be a long queue there now.'

"I want the lav, our Clarice," Gareth said. "I'll come with you."

The lavatory was shared with three other families. Sitting on the cold, wet closet seat for a longer time than having a quick wee-wee caused uproar and a hammering on the door. When I, and others in our street had diarrhoea, we were glad there was a grass verge in front of our street and a hedge. Not much comfort, mind, but better than the hurry of the lav when I had to get off before I'd finished.

"You use the chamber under the bed, Clarice," my mother said. "Let Gareth go up the lav on his own 'cause they won't cheat the queue with him like they do with you. I'm going to use the bucket in the scullery and you can, Tom. I'll empty them early in the morning before people start going to chapel for Christmas Service."

"I'll empty them, Love. You look all in. No chapel for you in the morning."

They both knew my mother was too weak to empty the chamber pot into the zinc bucket, carry it and its content to the lavatory, empty them away, then rinse the bucket until it was clean enough to go back into the scullery.

My mother didn't use the lavatory to relieve herself in case she passed blood and others would notice. Her monthly period lasted two weeks and would start again in less than two weeks.'

Oh, here we are, Shirley, supper is here.' A smiling carer put Clarice's meal on the bright, green-checked table cloth before her. The food smelled delicious and digestive juices rose into my mouth. I remembered I hadn't eaten since breakfast.

'And it's time I left you in peace, Clarice,' I said as I stood up from my chair beside her. I have lots of NVQ files to check but I think most will be left until another day. One good thing about the NVQ is that there is no limit to its completion.'

'Thank you for your time, Shirley. I've enjoyed talking about myself but I hope I haven't bored you.'

'Quite the opposite. If you don't mind, I'll write what I remember of your story and I hope you will tell me more. You ended by telling me your mother was ill and why. I hope you'll tell me how you lost her. You've made her sound a lovely Mam.'

'She was. And I'd like to go on whenever you have the time to listen.'

'That will be soon. And in the meantime you must think of something nice we can get for your very special birthday.'

She smiled before she put food to her mouth. 'All right. I will then.'

The following afternoon I helped Janis to check and lock away the weekly delivery of medication. It was almost the end of my shift so I'd glanced into Willow lounge to see if Clarice was awake and not snoozing as many of the others were. I asked if I could join her to hear what remained of her Christmas story until supper arrived, as I had the day before. I considered her age and hoped her memory hadn't deteriorated by time. It didn't seem to have. Quite the contrary, she was articulate and seemed to have a better memory than I have. The pleasure of my interest in her story was expressed on her lovely face.

I reminded her again of where she left off the day before. 'It was where you said your mother's heavy monthly periods came every two weeks rather than normal.'

'Yes, I remember very well where I'd got to. It was Christmas Eve, 1922.'

'That morning, Mam had taken me to the shop in the main street to get groceries for the day and a few extra bits and pieces for the next day's Christmas feast: flour, lard and dried fruit to make mince pies. I helped my mother to carry the shopping bags. She found them heavy and could barely manage. She soon became breathless.

'She'd got all the vegetables a few days before and a joint of pork from the milkman that morning. The size of the joint was generous for what she paid; Mr Jenkins the Milk had a fancy for my mother. Her big blue eyes and bright smile pulled at his heart-strings. She was the exact opposite of Mrs Jenkins, who was fat and strong and had a voice like a fog-horn. I suppose it was needed since she had to steer in a herd of cows and milk them at dawn and every evening in preparation for Mr Jenkins to churn the milk for his round.

'Mam would have swapped all her prettiness for a small part of Mrs Jenkins' health and strength. Mr Jenkins didn't think Mam was too pale and thin, which she was. He saw her as being frail and delicate with a kind nature.

'My grandmother, Nanna and grandfather, Gramps, were coming for Christmas day and they would bring a chicken, well stuffed with sage and onion. I hoped Mam would be well enough to make the mince pies.

'At the age of five I knew about monthly periods though they weren't monthly for my mother. Gareth, myself and our Dad knew about my Mam's frequent menstruation, as did her sister, Alice. Mind you, I didn't know big words like that or why a woman had to have that every month. I put two and two together, as is said, when I was older.

'Aunty Alice, Uncle George and my five cousins lived next door. Our two houses were near the end of the street so we

didn't have far to walk to the hill which passed two other streets on the way up to the main road, where the shops were.

When Mam and I waited in the shop queue that morning, Aunty Alice stood a few paces behind us. She came to Mam and whispered into her ear,

"Get an extra loaf on tick, Maud. Two loaves plenty for you but I can't get enough to fill my lot. Get an extra two if you can. Don't forget shop's shut tomorrow."

Of course, Mam remembered that; she answered with few words. "Yes, all right, Alice"

Aunty Alice had three daughters and two sons and didn't want any more. My mother had only Gareth and me. She'd resigned herself to the fact that there was "too much wrong with her insides" to have more babies. In the early 1900s, there was little sympathy and understanding of such a condition.

There were women who were nervous every month when their period was due and despaired when it didn't come. Some women we knew thought my mother was lucky not to be constantly plagued by the thought of becoming pregnant again.

After the grocers Mam ushered me to the butcher's, where again Aunty Alice was standing a few people behind us. Alice left her place in the queue and stood beside my mother.

"You look dying on your feet. You like that again?" She referred to my Mam's monthly period.

"No," she replied. "I've only just stopped, thank God."

"Then you'd better take a look down at the bottom of your skirt. There's blood trickling onto your boots."

"Oh, my God. Not so soon again, for God's sake. I thought I'd stopped. Don't let anyone see, Alice. Don't let me be shamed."

"No-one's noticed; pull your skirt down a bit so the hem is covering your boots. You go home. I'll get some scrag-end off Benny Butcher for your dinners. You can pay him again."

My mother grabbed my hand and stalked out of the shop. I could barely keep up with her. The force of her emotions were stronger than her physical debility.

Alice spoke to her as we left the shop. "You get to your bed before you drop and send our Clarice into my girls with the mince and they'll make your pies."

When we got home from the shops, Mam went straight to bed, as Aunty Alice told her to, after she had padded between her legs with strips of rag. She saved suitable worn out clothes from any of us to cut down to use as sanitary towels. I hadn't heard the term "sanitary towels" then. They came as a luxury when I was older.

Aunty Alice put dinner for us that Christmas Eve. She cooked a saucepan of broth on her own fire and brought it into our house after Dad and Gareth came home from work and had bathed. She insisted my mother save her strength and to stay in bed until supper time. She would need to feel well to enjoy the following day and I think she did.

It was a fun-filled, happy day. My stocking had been replaced by a pillow-case and I had presents from my Mam and Dad, Aunty Alice, Uncle George and the girls. There were Christmas presents from all my grandparents; on Mam's and Dad's side.

Gareth received a pack of playing cards, a book and new socks. My father had new socks and from him to my mother the prettiest necklace I'd ever seen. It was a string of blue beads. Glass, of course, but at that time I took them to be real gems.

During the late afternoon and evening our house was full of family. They came from Dad's side of our family as well as Mam's.

Aunty Alice brought what was left over from their dinner into our house and with what we had left over as well, everyone was able to have pickled onions with something on a thick slice of bread.

The men gathered in our parlour, which was the front room, with their flagons of beer. The women gossiped in our kitchen drinking cup after cup of tea and eating mince pies and Christmas pudding that was full of candid peel, currants and sultanas. There was, also, a three-penny piece which they let me find.

By ten o'clock my mother looked tired and weak but she tried to keep smiling. She'd only moved when she had to, because the more she moved the more she bled.

When everyone had gone except Alice, Mam rose from her chair and walked slowly to the door to make her way to bed. Alice helped her up the stairs and I followed. Nothing was said until my mother was lying down with her eyes half closed.

"Alice, I feel awful bad." Her voice was weak. "I don't think it's my period. I think I've had a mis' again." She referred to a miscarriage; a word which was outside my vocabulary at the time.

"I think you have, too, my lovely," Aunty Alice replied. "And it looks as if you're going to have the flux for ever and a day unless we do something about it."

"I don't know what," Mam murmured. "I took that tonic the doctor gave me. It tasted awful but I took it 'cause I didn't want to waste the two-pence we paid for it. It made me sick."

"Well, day after tomorrow is Sunday and me and our Violet are going to take you to Quaker's Yard to see Gwenny Getbetter."

I interrupted Clarice at that point. I was surprised by what she said.

'Clarice, I know Quakers' Yard and I heard my Nanna talking about Gwenny Getbetter. We used to go to the fair at Quakers' Yard every Whitsun. I remember it was a long walk from where we lived but we went every year until my grandparents got too old.'

'That's right. The big fair came every year. It was a big, special day.' Clarice was pleased that I knew of the place she talked of. 'Then you'll have a picture in your mind of where we were.'

'Yes, please go on. Supper won't be long. I hope you'll finish your story.'

Clarice went on.

"Gwenny Getbetter will have something to make you well again," Alice spoke as she turned her eyes to me. "You must come as well, Clarice, 'cause we don't want anybody to know

where we've gone and I won't ask you to tell lies. Anyway, we'll need your help.

"There won't be many about if we go early, Maud, so no-one is likely to think you're going to Gwenny to be put right. We'll have to miss chapel and people will talk. But let them. Talking about us will give others a rest."

It was years later I learned that Gwenny Getbetter was an abortionist and she "put girls right" when they found themselves with unwanted pregnancies. I think there were quite a few of those women who did that in those days.

Gwenny lived in a wooden hut in the corner of a field outside the village of Quakers' Yard. At the front she grew herbs and vegetables. At the back, there was a chickens' cot and behind rusty chicken-wire she kept hens and a cockerel. Gwenny's house was a little more salubrious than the cot; but not much.'

I laughed at her description of Gwenny's house.

'Gwenny was a recluse but known to everyone in Quakers' Yard and surrounding villages for her healing and illicit abortion abilities. She was often seen out and about with a big basket in which she collected leaves, weeds and substances from the soil. It was said she boiled them up and made portions which cured all ailments.

"Alice," Mam sighed, "I don't think I can walk to Quaker's Yard. I feel too bad. Can we wait until the fine weather?"

"By the looks of you, you won't see the spring. You're worse than pale now; you're grey, and I know that's not good."

I'd noticed for some time that Mam's feet and ankles were so swollen she wasn't able to put her boots on without a squeeze. She couldn't do up the laces, either.

"You won't have to walk," Aunty Alice said. "I've asked Dan Rag an' Bones to take us on his horse and cart. My Violet is strong and she and Clarice will be in the cart with you to see you're kept warm."

Mam was too weak to argue. I spoke for her. "Yes, Aunty Alice, we'll come. I want my Mam to get well."

On Sunday morning, Dan, the rag and bone man, sat on the buckboard of his crumbling cart, waiting at the end of the street. He couldn't be seen inside his old greatcoat with a greasy, flat cap on top. We knew he was inside the coat because his spade-sized hands were outside the sleeves, holding onto the reins of the old nag.'

Here, again, Clarice chuckled at the picture she had in mind of Dan Rag and Bones. I, too, was amused at her subtle description which left little to the imagination. My mind turned back the clock of memories of the rag and bone man squeezing his horse and cart up the gullies between the streets where I lived as a child. Clarice had a way with words which put my own attempts at story-writing to shame.

'Aunty Alice sat beside Dan up at the front of the cart. The cart must have been as old as the poor horse. Violet and I sat in the cart with Mam. We started out before most people were up for chapel.

It was a hard journey to Quakers' Yard. It was about three miles as the crow flies but seven through the lanes and over the rough, stony road. We were lucky Dan knew the short cuts over the fields.

Violet and I sat each side of Mam with our arms entwined about her. We'd wrapped her in blankets and cuddled close to keep warm. We were all wrapped up well with shawls but were shivering with cold when we got to Gwenny Getbetter's.

I was glad she was at home and pleased to see us. She was on her vegetable patch and saw us approach. People looked down on Gwenny because of the way she lived and the facts she was reputed to be guilty of – until they needed her.

"Well, well, Alice Evans. Haven't seen you for years. You don't come every Whitsun now, when the fair comes, do you?"

"No, Gwenny. Nanna and Gramps too old now. Didn't like to come without them."

Gwenny's ample petticoats and rough, wool skirts were hitched up to a piece of rope around her waist to prevent them trailing in the dirt. Her hair, the same colour of her drab, grey clothes, was in plaits, one over each shoulder. She had no teeth but the brightest of smiles from sharp, shining eyes.

Before she gave Aunty Alice time to finish her reply Gwenny greeted Dan.

"How be, Dan, my lovely. You're still alive, then? Good job, too, 'cause this lot would never have walked here."

Aunty Alice gave her reply. "No Gwenny. Got a houseful of kids so I got too much to do. They come, though. I've brought my sister to you today. She's awful bad. Every month she pours out her life's blood. I want you to give her something to stop it."

"I can but try, Alice, my lovely. Come in out of the cold and get warm for a start. Dan!" she shouted. "Go and tie up the horse to the fence and come in for a warm. I hope he won't pull the fence down, though."

My mother was helped down from the cart by Violet. I picked up one of the blankets she was wrapped in to put over her as she walked into Gwenny's house. There was no passage. It was a step straight into her living-cum-kitchen-cum-bedroom.

A big pot was bubbling on the bricks of her fireplace. A strong smell of elderberry filled the Spartan shack. On the bare wooden floor in front of the fire there was a rug, commandeered by three fat dozing cats.

There were two tired-looking fireside chairs and four spindled kitchen chairs at a wooden table, each held together with string and wire. I thought it was cleverly done. There were wooden shelves bracketed to the walls here and there, covered with bottles and jars of various shapes, sizes and colours.

The chickens had been allowed into the room and clucked on the top of the table. Gwenny brushed them away with a long, skinny arm and chased them out of the room before closing the door.

"Come you." She beckoned my mother to a make-shift sofa covered with crocheted blankets. I think it must have been Gwenny's bed.

"Lie down there. You look all in, my lovely. But don't worry, I'll find something to buck you up." Gwenny sounded confident but the look she gave my Aunty Alice spoke words which indicated otherwise.

Without waiting to be asked, my cousin Violet plonked herself into a fireside chair. "I'm blooming knackered," she gasped.

"You sit down there, my lovely," Gwenny told me, pointing to the other fireside chair.

"Thank you, Mrs Gwenny," I said as I sat. I guessed Mrs Getbetter was a nick name and I didn't want to risk offending her. She was such a nice woman.

She and Aunty Alice sat at the table, after she had wiped it over with a damp rag and put a clean cloth on it. She reached under the table and brought out a bottle.

"A drop of the elderberry. Better than what's brewing ' 'cause the berries were fresh when I brewed this." She spoke as she went to a wooden box on the floor under the window and brought out two half-pint drinking glasses.

"Only got two glasses. Dan! Pass me some of them cups from off that shelf. One for you as well and make yourself comfortable while you sip it."

Dan did as he was told. "Ta, Gwenny." It was the first time he had spoken since we left home.

He held out a chipped cup as Gwenny poured the wine into it before going to the far wall of the hut to squat on the floor.

We all had some elderberry wine. I didn't like it but I didn't say. Violet drank it for me. Aunty Alice told Gwenny about Mam's never-ending periods.

"No wonder she's so bad," Gwenny said. "Her poor body don't have time to make more blood before the next flux. It's never ending. She's slow bleeding to death. She needs something to make new blood."

My Mam heard. She sat up on the hard wooden sofa and smiled. "That's right," she said with excitement in her tone. "Alice, Gwenny's right."

Our spirits lifted. My Mam was going to get better.

After a meal of hard boiled eggs and stale bread we prepared for our journey home. I guessed Gwenny's hens were good layers.

What was of most importance was wrapped up safely in the blankets wrapped about my mother to keep her as warm as the cold December day allowed; a precious bottle of dark red, almost black, liquid.

"She's to take a good swig of this morning and night," Gwenny told Aunty Alice, as if beside her my Mam was deaf. "There's something in it to make blood. Then when she's stronger her monthlies will come right."

She then turned to Mam. "When you go to the lavvy to open your bum-hole what comes away will be black. Don't be afraid, it's what's left over from making blood."

We left Gwenny Getbetter's with hearts uplifted. Mam looked as if she felt better simply from hearing Gwenny's words. She gave her a sixpenny piece.

When we got to the end of our street and dismounted the cart Aunty Alice gave three-pence to Dan. He took it and nodded his head.

"That's my last, Maud. You'll have to ask your Tom to pay me."

"He'll give you double when he hears Mam's going to get better," I told Aunty Alice. "I know he's got some money saved in a bacco tin in the cupboard."

My mother took Gwenny Getbetter's elixir as directed. Each time she vomited.

"I'm going to persevere with it," she told Aunty Hilda. "I want to be well for New Years' Eve when we all go to our Mam and Dad's."

"You better had," Aunty Alice advised, "or this'll be the last New Year you'll see."

If Aunty Alice had known the truth of her words, they would never have been said. My Mam died on 1st January, 1923; a week before her thirty-fourth birthday. God didn't allow her the privilege of growing old.'

Clarice's eyes were wet with tears as were mine; one or two trickled down my cheek. I broke the rule instilled by my first ward sister, many years before. "You may weep, Nurse Phillips, but ensure there are no witnesses." Clarice witnessed my sadness.

'Shirley, I didn't mean to upset you. I was one of many who lost their mothers in childhood. Things have changed now. We have a National Health Service to prevent young mother's dying, and indeed, fathers, sons and daughters. And we have nursing homes like this where people like me will end their days with dignity and in comfort.' She held up her hand and waved it around the four walls of Willow Lounge.

'I loved your story, Clarice, and if you won't mind, I would like to put it into writing.' This I did and I asked my grandchildren to read it. My intention was to make them realise how lucky they are.

Chapter 11

INDECENT BEHAVIOUR

Clarice's birthday was celebrated quietly. She insisted on there being no fuss but was delighted with the birthday cake the kitchen staff presented. It was a large round tier of pink and white icing with "Happy birthday 80 designed in icing on the top. It was a birthday surprise she had not experienced before.

'I've never had a birthday cake,' she said. 'It's so lovely. It's too lovely to cut. Thank you.' She was, obviously, touched; at a loss for words.

She had chosen a birthday present on our insistence.

'Well,' she had said. 'I'd like a bunch of flowers. It's a miracle that beautiful blooms are available at this time of the year. Perhaps they are not now, but I used to see them in florists' windows. Before he became ill, Gareth sometimes used to take me into town.'

Erika Powell, the head of housekeeping, and I had gone into town to select a voluminous bunch of the loveliest blooms the florist shop could produce. It was delivered on the morning of the twenty-third of December and presented to Clarice in the afternoon, after she'd cut into her birthday cake. Pleasure beamed from her lovely face.

The conglomeration of colours gave pleasure to everyone in Willow Lounge, already festooned with brilliant Christmas decorations from the week before. We all sang Happy Birthday; not very melodiously but the whole event touched her.

'How lovely,' Clarice gasped with surprise. 'And all for me.'

'Yes,' I explained, 'some for this table where you always sit and the rest for your room. We'll give them a little drink every day and they should last well into the New Year.

The Christmas and New Year celebrations came and went. As happened every year in The Nightingale Nursing Homes, the Christmas trees and festooned ceilings and walls remained longer than the tradition dictated.

Erika's role as head of housekeeping was more demanding than the title suggested. It was she who removed the decorations from the ceilings with me holding the ladder.

Her remit was, predominantly, to keep the homes running smoothly in all aspects other than nursing, though she was often called upon to be a nurse when the need arose. She was in charge of the kitchen and catering and maintaining the good look of the homes: soft and hard furnishings, laundry, disposal of waste and any other extraneous task which cropped up. That was often.

Erika had an assistant, Shaun, whose wife worked as a carer at night. He was a strong, healthy man in his thirties. Shaun and Alison had two young children, hence her having to be on permanent night duty. She was a carer in The Bedford Home.

Shaun was a handyman who could put his hand to anything. He did everything from mucking out the cellars to climbing onto the roof to repair loose tiles. He was paid a pittance but he enjoyed his work at The Nightingales and he lived a stone's throw from his place of work so didn't need a car. He couldn't have afforded one, anyway.

Shaun drove and maintained The Nightingale's bone-shaking mini-bus. He drove the residents on days' outings and to hospital appointments. He was a kind, gentle man; the residents thought well of him. He talked to them and made them laugh with his joking and teasing. When residents died I saw him cry at the funerals.

His DIY talents were endlessly versatile. There was very little broken that he couldn't repair. He enjoyed his job but one afternoon he happened upon a duty which he did not enjoy or would ever forget.

Erika had a check of the curtained windows of all the rooms. She found faults with the opening and shutting of some of the windows and curtains needed changing in rooms in all three homes.

One afternoon Shaun became involved in an unexpected event when he was working at The Bevan Home. He was repairing a window frame and replacing the cracked panes in a room at the same time as Erika and I were working further down the corridor. We were hanging fresh curtains to the windows of a room that a relative would view that evening for the possible residency of her mother.

I helped with all sorts of tasks when I had time from my own training commitments. I enjoyed it, but that afternoon Erika wasn't in a happy mood.

'This is robbing Peter to pay Paul,' she said. 'I'm taking curtains from one window to put on another when all the windows here need new curtains. Hajiv says there's not enough money in the pot.'

'That's daft,' I replied. 'When people come to view for placing relatives, the windows are the first things they see.'

Erika heard only half of my remark. 'Blast!' she tutted, 'I've bought the wrong type of hooks. This is what I need.' She held a curtain hook in her hand which she'd taken off the worn ragged ones we were replacing.

'Never mind,' I replied. 'I'll get on with as much as I can and you pop down to the DIY. You know the type we want.'

'Are you sure you don't mind? You have plenty of work of your own.'

'No,' I said, 'nothing that can't wait. These curtains must be up before we go home this afternoon.'

Off Erika went whilst I continued with needle and thread turning up hems on the curtains which were too long for the small window we were working on. I was reminded of an often said proverb of my grandmother. *"Trying to make a silk purse out of a pig's ear."* Life was hard then. Having to "make do and mend" was a necessity for survival. It was what Erika and I were doing, but in days of plenty compared with those long gone days.

She closed the door of the room as she went out and I was soon lost in my thoughts as I, spontaneously, stitched. She'd gone less than half an hour before my day-dreams were broken into by the click of the door opening.

I turned around to acknowledge her. 'Well, that was quick,' I said.

It wasn't Erika. It was Melvyn Baker, the rapist, leering at me with the eyes of an animal.

'On your own, are you, my lovely?'

I stiffened with fear and had difficulty disguising it, which I knew was the thing to do in the situation which I guessed was coming.

'No,' I replied, in as nonchalant a tone as I could muster. 'Erika will be here any minute now. Why, Melvyn? Have you come to help us with the curtains?'

'I will if you like, my lovely, but it's a fuck I want. I don' half fancy you. An' you fancy me, don' you?' He stepped in front of me. His tall bulk towered over me as I sat on a low foot-stool beside the bed.

I continued sewing the curtain hem and put on an attitude of indifference; needle-pricking my out-of-control shaking fingers.

'I might if you stop using foul language and get out of my way. Erika will be here at any minute now.'

'Ha! Ha! Ha!' he laughed loudly; there was no-one near enough to hear him. 'I's not daft. She jus' wen' off in 'er car.' He lowered his arm until his hand reached my bosom and fondled it. I inwardly cringed before stabbing the back of his hand with my sewing needle. He yelled and jumped away.

I took the opportunity to do as I was taught to do in such a situation – go for the door. "Do not let the attacker get between you and the exit".

I leapt up from the stool, rolled across the bed and bumped my back heavily against the closed door. I had my hand on the handle but not with enough leverage to open it.

'Wha' you do tha' for? Just a little bit I wan'. I 'ont hurt 'ou.' He rubbed the blood that had appeared on the back of his one hand with his other hand. He didn't seem perturbed.

His voice was gentle but madness seethed in his eyes. He began loosening his jogger bottoms from his waist, revealing an, already, erected penis. I tried desperately not to show fear.

'You touch me again, Melvyn, and I'll see that you go back to prison for rapists and you will never come out.'

He laughed again. 'Can't. I'm registered insane.' He came towards me, reached out his arm to the neck of my blouse, wrenched it and dragged me from the back of the door and threw me onto the bed. He fell upon me and grunted as he rubbed his spade-size hands up and down my legs.

In all my life, through hardships and many tight corners over the years of travel, in dangers of being shot and beaten, I had never felt the fear as I did that afternoon.

He moved off me and began taking off his jogger bottoms. In that second I leapt to the door again, managed to pull it ajar and screamed and screamed throat-bursting screams into the corridor until it slammed closed again.

Melvyn grabbed me, threw me back onto the bed and resumed his position on top of me. I continued screaming.

I heard heavy footsteps running up and down the corridor. They belonged to Shaun; he couldn't recognise at once from which of the thirty rooms my screams came from.

After some terrifying moments Shaun burst through the door and threw himself at Melvyn and pulled him off me.

Melvyn stood up and grabbed Shaun by neck with one hand and punched him with full-force into the face with the other. Melvyn towered over Shaun but between us both we managed to curb the raging madness.

Shaun was about to hit him over the head with a heavy glass vase which had decorated the bedroom dresser. I freed one hand which restrained Melvyn to push back the hand which would have cracked open his skull.

'No, no, Shaun!' I shouted. 'You'll kill him.'

Shaun stopped; he saw reason. 'Yes, I'll stop smashing your head open but that's what you deserve.'

Melvyn growled like a rabid dog.

At that moment Erika entered the room. The atmosphere was electric.

'God, almighty! What's gone on here?' She was aghast.

Melvyn pulled his jogger bottoms up to his waist as I attempted to make myself decently dressed. It was difficult because the straps of my bra had snapped and the front of my blouse had been torn open down to the waist. I was in a state of shock but I had to make the best of it by buttoning the few that hadn't been torn off.

Erika glanced at me and guessed what had happened. She pressed the emergency button. Before anyone arrived in the room I ran out of it and made for the bathroom across the corridor. I wanted no-one to see the state I was in. I wanted no-one to know what had happened. Attempted rape? What would Derek say and do if he found out?

What was wrong with me? I had been sexually abused as a little girl of eight and though my assaulter hadn't penetrated my body the event had a good deal to do with my unhappy childhood. I decided that Melvyn Baker wasn't going to tarnish my life in the way it had been when I was that little girl.

I returned to the room when I heard the voice of RMN Trevor Ellis, who was in charge at that time, shouting at Melvyn. It was Helen Young's off duty day. They were the two nurses who alternated their shifts to cover the unit.

'Stop shouting, Trevor,' I snapped. 'Let's discuss the situation rationally.'

'After what he's done to you? You know you shouldn't have been in this room on your own.'

I retaliated. 'Melvyn shouldn't have been allowed to snoop around the rooms. And anyway, what has he done? Tore my blouse, yes; but no-one's been hurt except Shaun.'

I looked at Shaun; his face was already swollen and his nose was trickling blood, to which he held a paper tissue.

'Thank you for coming to help me, Shaun. You prevented a small incident becoming a big one. I'm not hurt and I don't want this event to go outside this room.' I spoke with determination.

'I'm glad of that,' Shaun responded, 'but if you hadn't stopped me with that vase I would have smashed his thick skull open.'

'Melvyn shouldn't be allowed to get away with this, Shirley,' Erika said. She turned to Trevor. 'I'm as much to blame for her being left here on her own. I thought Melvyn would have been in the lounge having tea with all the others.'

Melvyn was crouched in the corner with his head in his hands, crying like a child. The wailing interfered with the discussion.

'Shut up, you animal,' Trevor snarled. 'You're not fit to be among decent people. You'll be put behind bars, where you belong.'

The sound of Melvyn's noisy self-pity became louder. Trevor went to him, grabbed him by the shoulders and hauled him to a stooped standing position. That took strength; Melvyn was a big man and his hands didn't leave his face to support himself.

'He's sick, Trevor. You should know that more than any of us. And I repeat, this event will go no further than this room. If it does, the reputation of The Nightingale Nursing Homes will be ruined and we can't afford that to happen. We need to attract residents or there'll be redundancies here.' I looked at each face in turn. They all nodded; even Erika.

'That's right, Shirley.' She turned to Melvyn. 'And if I hear that you have mentioned your behaviour today or touched or hurt anyone again, you will definitely be out. Being elderly won't help you next time.'

Melvyn vigorously nodded his agreement. 'No, no, no. Yes, yes, yes!' He was becoming increasingly deranged.

I shouted. 'And that includes Bill and Iris! Do you understand!'

'Yes, yes, yes. No, no, no.'

'Right, then. Erika, we must get these curtains up. Shaun, you stay with us. I want to swab that face of yours. Alison will think you've been in the ring with Mohammed Ali. I'm sorry you were hurt, but thank you. I'll not forget how you helped me today and put yourself at risk. For that you'll have a little black eye in the morning.'

'You mean a bloody big one, don't you, Shirl?' The atmosphere lightened. We were all amused by his remark, except Melvyn.

As I walked past through the main hall to make my way home, Trevor called me into the office and closed the door – something which rarely happened. I knew exactly what he would say.

'You know, Mrs Phillips, I have to report the incident. It would not only be unethical, but I wouldn't be doing my job. If you don't want to tell me the details, that's up to you. Then I will describe the incident in my own words but I will ask you to countersign the report.'

'All right, Trevor. We mustn't forget Melvyn is sick and it's our job to treat him as such. I'll read and sign your report on Tuesday. I'm away on Monday.' Trevor agreed with that. It would be difficult putting such a report into words.

Apart from discussing the incident with Erika and Carole I heard no more about that terrifying event. I was surprised when Erika told me I was lucky that Shaun was nearby.

'Others haven't been so lucky. You're not the first and, I have no doubt, you won't be the last.'

I couldn't understand. 'You mean mine was not an isolated case?'

'Not by a long chalk.'

Melvyn Baker's indecent behaviour affected me more than I would admit. I avoided going near him when I went to The Bevan Home but I was pleased to see that he didn't bother Bill and Iris; – at least, not for a while. After a week or so, I noticed he'd gone back to his usual lounge chair, next to them.

When I had to pass close by him, he leered at me as he had done before the unpleasant incident. It seemed as if he had forgotten all about it, but I hadn't, nor will I ever.

Trevor had agreed with me. 'He's severely psychotic, Shirley. He most probably doesn't remember the evil crimes he committed before going to prison. He wouldn't be with us if he didn't have a heart problem and his psychosis can be medically controlled.'

'I didn't know that,' I replied. 'He seems pretty fit to me.'

'Let's hope he stays like that then,' Trevor grinned. 'We need his residency. I hear we have too many empty beds. Empty beds to me means job losses.'

'And less money for training,' I pointed out. 'We must go on training. It's needed. And we need the place to look good if we want to attract more residents. The rooms are beginning to look shabby. Afterwards, I'll be popping up to see what we can do to make the place look worth coming to, if you don't mind.'

'Do that,' he nodded. 'We need to attract residency. But what about your training remit?'

'Yes, I hadn't forgotten. The training is my priority, though you wouldn't think it, would you?'

Trevor was amused. 'No, you seem to be doing anything but training.'

I wasn't sure how to take Trevor's remark. He might have been insinuating that I wasn't fulfilling my role but I enjoyed being involved in various matters, whatever he thought. Also, at that time The Nightingales were, indeed, low on residency. Consequently, low on carers to make my position tenable.

'Would you mind if I had a few words with Beth Hamer now, Trevor?'

'Not at all. Beth is a good little carer. She'll soon be joining the ranks of university nurse students. From what I've heard, she's learning more here than she will in a year in a university lecture theatre, though.'

I shrugged my shoulders. 'Yes, I know all about that and I'm not impressed. I agree with you; Beth is benefiting being here with you to guide and advise her.'

Twenty-two year old Beth was sitting between two residents. She must have passed a funny remark because they were laughing. That was the beginning of her assessment though she didn't know it.

Good communication skill is one objective of the test. It seemed wrong to take her away from the residents at that point but I know she was nervous about the assessment and would be glad when it was over.

Beth and I took chairs not too far away from the two elderly ladies she had been talking to. We sat close to Mrs Dora Bell. She smiled; she had been expecting us. Beth would not have known that I guessed she would have primed Mrs Bell earlier.

I had to confirm with Beth that she knew how the assessment would be conducted. She knew it well: "Maintain personal hygiene, ensure safety and comfort".

The assessment was to take place the following Tuesday. The resident, Mrs Dora Bell, whom Beth had chosen to be the subject, had to be asked, in case she objected to being "used". Mrs Bell smiled and nodded. Not only did she agree but was flattered that she had been selected.

Her mobility was poor but that would pose no problem; she was able to stand for short periods. Beth had arranged with one of the other carers to help her, if necessary.

Mrs Dora Bell was approaching her ninetieth birthday. She was a manic depressive and prone to severe mood swings. I hoped she would be co-operative throughout the assessment.

Beth would help Mrs Bell out of bed and cover her before wheel-chairing her to the bathroom. When undressed, Beth would be expected to, discretely, check Mrs Bell's body for broken skin, soreness or rash. She would then help her to bath, dress, check that her mouth was clean, rinse her dentures before handing them to Mrs Bell to put into in her mouth and groom her hair. Mrs Bell would be taken down to the dining room for breakfast.

Whilst Mrs Bell took her breakfast Beth would write a short report of the care given and the general condition of Mrs

Bell. Her relationship with Mrs Bell would be assessed as well as her attitude throughout the assessment.

Writing about it makes it sound an easy event but it is rare for an assessment in an EMI unit to take place without variables and hitches cropping up. The morning Beth Hamer's assessment took place a horrible event spoiled it, but she passed.

It took place on the following Tuesday morning, as arranged and I was early to work. My ten o'clock start became an half-past seven one. For morning assessments I had to make the effort to be on duty at the same time as everyone else.

Beth was to approach Mrs Dora Bell at eight o'clock – the time the residents were being prepared for the day. The needs of the residents varied. Some washed and dressed themselves, some needed help, others were totally dependent on carers.

It was before eight o'clock when I arrived on the floor of the private rooms, toilet and bathroom areas. I heard a disturbing squealing sound. It was eerie. My grandfather kept pigs when I was a girl and the sound reminded of the squealing of his pigs being made into pork on slaughtering days.

On that day, I assumed that the squealing sound I was hearing was someone squeezing air out of a vacuum or a window swinging open. It was a windy, wet day; it might well have been a broken window swinging on its hinges. Shaun must have missed it when he was looking for damaged windows.

The doors of the occupied rooms were closed. I was not sure which was Dora's so I first approached the left of the stairway. The rooms that were unoccupied had their doors wide open. As I passed the occupied ones I hear the sound of chat and activity.

I knocked on one of the doors, which after a few moments was open by Joyce, an experienced carer. 'Beth is checking the bathroom, Shirley. She's expecting you for the assessment. She's awful nervous.'

'Yes, I know. She's afraid I'll beat her soundly if she goes wrong.'

Joyce and her two carers chuckled.

'Thank you Joyce. I'm early so I'll let her be for a minute or two so she can get sorted.'

I decided to stroll to the right of the stairway and check the rooms. The squealing had become louder. Loud enough to be followed until I came upon its source from a half opened door. It was open wide enough for me to witness the evil treatment which was being inflicted upon Mr Arthur James. I didn't know his age but knew that he was approaching his ninetieth year and had had a stroke which rendered him partly paralysed.

He was stark naked on a bare mattress with all his soiled bed linen strewn across the floor. It was stood on by Stan Jones, leaning over Mr James with a large kitchen scissors in his right hand, his left hand gripping Mr James penis and stretching it towards the scissors.

'If you piss yourself again I'll cut this off and feed it to the cats,' Stan seethed through the gap where his front teeth should have been.

Mr James was stiff and could do nothing except squeal with pain and fear.

The carers in the occupied rooms on that side of the floor wouldn't have heard Stan's evil threat or the distressed sounds from Mr James.

Stan was so engrossed by his action, he didn't hear me as I pushed open the door. For a few seconds I stood and stared in disbelief; time enough for Stan to let go of his grip on Mr James's penis.

An irresistible force of anger surged through me; I lost control of myself. I snatched the scissors from Stan's hand and punched his face with as much strength as I could muster. I hadn't hit anyone before – not that I could remember; certainly not in the face.

He was flabbergasted as he put his hand to his smarting face allowing Mr James to cradled his penis with both hands. He cried like a child.

I had a mouthful of loud, foul words spat at me from Stan before I screamed at him. 'Get out, you evil beast!'

The loudness reached the ears of the carers working on that landing. Doors of the rooms opened and running footsteps arrived at the threshold of Mr James's room. The carers passed Stan going in the other direction toward the stairs. Blood from, what must have been his nose, leaked through his fingers as he held them to his face. He continued to cast foul aspersions upon my character.

The carers saw me embracing and comforting Mr James. One of the carers handed me a towel which I wrapped about his shoulders, covering part of his nakedness. Another carer gathered the fouled linen from the floor and put it into a black bag. No words were spoken.

Mr James was the first to speak. 'He was going to cut it off with those scissors,' he sobbed and cast his eyes across the room to where the scissors had slipped when I dropped them onto the floor. 'I can't help peeing myself. Oh, God. Why can't I die?'

Joyce, the senior carer, sat on the other side of the bed beside him and put a shawl about his knees. All expressions were pitiful.

'We know you can't help it, Arthur. You've had a stroke and we don't want you to die.' Joyce was on the brink of tears. 'I don't know how that evil Stan has been able to get away with the wicked things he's done. He's done awful things, Shirley. We know that Stan has frightened some of the women half to death but they've never spoke up about him.'

The other carers came further into the room to reassure Mr James. 'We won't let him come near you again, Arthur. We'll look after you.'

He looked up at her with relief. 'Will you? I'll try not to be a nuisance.'

Beth caught my attention. 'I'm sorry you had to see that, Mrs Phillips. It was because you came to see me. We'll do the assessment tomorrow, if you like.'

I was surprised at her being so naïve. At her age I was married, had Paul and lived and worked in Ghana, once known as "White Man's Grave". It crossed my mind that she'd assumed I'd had a sheltered existence; unused to and protected against the unpleasantness of life.

'Of course the assessment will go ahead today, Beth. And, of course, I'm upset, as we all are. But, I assure you, I've been involved in much worse than this. I've been caring for people for a long time. You must be aware that all carers aren't as good and as nice as ours. Neither are all nursing homes as good as The Nightingales.'

Joyce interrupted. 'Yes, that's right. We live and learn, but Shirley, it was a good thing you happened to be here at the right time. Beth, you go now and see to the bathroom for Dora. The rest of us had better get on. We're well behind. I'll see to Arthur.' She turned her eyes to him. 'Is that all right, Arthur?'

He nodded.

Beth cared for her resident, Mrs Dora Bell, as I would have myself; that has been one of my criteria of a learner passing an assessment.

We didn't see Stan Jones in The Bevan Home again or anywhere near The Nightingale Nursing Homes, although he lived locally. It was believed he didn't return to work because it was being rumoured that Marlene had claimed benefit for the baby. I didn't know if that was true or not or if she had been successful, but it was known that he couldn't have got away without giving support to Marlene by denying that he was the father of her baby.

Nothing was seen of him and it was believed that he'd gone somewhere far away from Bryncelyn, where he had lived with his widowed mother and sisters.

I found out that Stan Jones hadn't gone far. Or if he had, he'd returned. Some years after he escaped Bevan EMI unit, I came across him when he was working on a stall at the Abergavenny open market.

It is a popular market whatever the weather, but especially when the sun shines. People come from far and wide to enjoy the hustle-bustle and bartering, or searching for items of bankrupt stock going for half the normal price.

Market day is always on a Tuesday. When Derek and I retired we often went there. We enjoyed meandering between the crowds and wandering through the stalls, even when we weren't looking for something in particular to buy.

The day I saw Stan, I was on my own. Derek and I had planned a Mediterranean cruise and I was looking for something cheap and cheerful to wear on board The Aurora. I had worn uniforms for most of my working life and was clueless about what was fashionable. I was careful when choosing. I didn't want to dress like lamb when I was, certainly, more on the mutton side of my life.

I was wandering along one of the narrow strips of gangway between the double rows of stalls, when in the near distance I saw a head of shoulder-length greasy hair topped with a red base-ball cap. It was on the stocky body of Stan Jones wearing a bright T-shirt and a loose-fitting jogging trousers.

We caught sight of each other simultaneously. He was standing in the middle of the path gazing down to where I was walking towards him. I stopped in my tracks, he scuttled back into the stall. But too late. He knew I had spotted him.

I walked up to the stall which was overloaded with hardware: buckets, bowls, metal tubs, gardening tools of all shapes and sizes, with hardly an inch to spare on the wooden-planked counter and canvas sides. Ironware had spilled over the counter, restricting the already narrow pathway. I saw Stan duck under the counter.

I leant over the counter to ensure he knew I had seen him. 'Good after noon, Stan Jones. I'd like to buy a big, sharp, pair of scissors, please. You know the sort I mean.'

His bright, red peaked cap and face popped up. 'Who are you, my lovely? How d'you now my name, 'cause I don't know yours, nor want to. An' no, I don't sell scissors.'

'I'll go to Bevan EMI unit, then. They have one there. I expect you remember it.'

A torrent of disparaging words were spat from his dribbling lips which, in simple terms, told me to go. He would have been disappointed had he known that I was unaffected by his Anglo-Saxon terms, having heard them many times before.

He concluded by threatening me with getting his boss to move me.

'Get him then. I'll explain how I know you.' I spoke loudly as I walked away. I wouldn't have liked talking about that awful morning. It was a long time ago. I should have forgotten it. My old aunty Hilda's words crossed my mind: *"Come tomorrow, only the good times you'll remember"*. She was wise but I'm not sure her words can be related to life in general.

Chapter 12

FORGOTTEN

The upper floors of The Homes, where the residents' private rooms are, are normally deserted during the day. I realised I was lucky that Shaun was there when I was alone at The Bevan Home, trying to make the curtains look pretty.

During an afternoon two weeks later I visited the room again. I needed to check that those curtains were hanging straight and to check the soft furnishing of the other rooms. Erika had complained that some of the duvets were faded and looking tatty. I wondered if and how the covering materials could be turned to make them look brighter.

All the doors were closed, except one. The door to Laura Dutton's was half open. I went to shut it and would have done so had not an unpleasant smell waft out. It was the smell of death; something that was not new to me.

I gasped on entering the room. Laura was there but was dead. Her soiled, night-dressed body was slouched over the side of her bed. Her left arm was outstretched towards the bedside table as if she had been reaching for her glass of water. She must have just managed to touch it. It had spilled and the water, or whatever it was, had formed a pool which had dried around its edge.

Her top dentures had dropped from her mouth onto the floor and the plate of her bottom ones was half in half out of her mouth. I was shocked to inaction. For some strange reason, my brain focused on her dentures being contaminated on the floor and her bottom plate about to drop. I removed them before snatching the top set up from the floor and striding over to the wash-hand basin. I grabbed her denture pot from the glass shelf above it, dropped her dentures into it and replaced the pot tidily on the shelf before pressing the emergency button – the priority. My brain must have become numbed by shock. A principle of my early training came into force – "you may panic, Nurse, but you don't show it"

I noticed a tray with equipment for oral toilet on the bedside locker. It was messy and, obviously, hadn't been used since the day before. There was also a dish with, what appeared to be, the previous evening's soup.

I glanced over the observation and "turn" charts which were unprofessionally arranged on the shelf of the dressing-table. A "turn" chart is maintained to ensure the resident is moved at intervals to prevent pressure soreness and other complications of being bed-bound.

I cringed when I saw that the last time Laura had received care was at six o'clock that morning and it was then 3 o'clock in the afternoon. A nursing sin had been committed.

She had been cared for by the night staff. I knew there had been just five staff on duty – the nurse in charge and four carers. Not nearly enough to carry out the necessary tasks thoroughly and maintain the safety of the unit.

The two rooms on the ground floor, reserved for the terminally ill, were occupied, so Laura remained in her own room and was forgotten. The morning hand-over report didn't include Laura Dutton. Helen Young, the nurse in charge and her carers, who had arrived on day duty, knew they had their work cut out to carry out the many tasks throughout the day shift and to observe those particularly prone to accidentally injure themselves.

Helen had cared for Laura the day before, so should have remembered her and should have questioned the night staff about her. The stress of the pressure of the day before and the fatigue of being constantly overworked must have made her less alert.

After I had pressed the emergency buzzer it seemed like an age before someone came, yet two carers appeared almost immediately. While I was waiting for help I had folded my arms about Laura's stiff body and manoeuvred it as far back onto the bed as I could. I forgot about not having to strain my back.

'Oh, my God!' one of the carers gasped and, as if on an elastic pulley, sprang down the corridor on her way to let Helen know. She sprinted up the stairs and along the corridor to Laura's room to find me kneeling at the bedside with my arm across Laura's stiff, cold body.

When she saw that Laura was dead and lying in a fouled bed, rigor mortis already beginning to set in, she burst into tears. 'God forgive me,' she sobbed. 'I forgot about Laura. I just can't go on like this.'

'Helen, pull yourself,' I snapped, but didn't mean to. The staff were too over-worked; they weren't able to keep up. 'Let's work together to put Laura right.'

I looked to one of the two carers who stood stock-still in the doorway. 'Get a trolly with bowls, sheets, towels and all we will need .' The young carer leapt into action.

I took Helen's hand. 'You forgot about Laura because you had too many other things on your mind. Now go down and telephone her daughter, then call the doctor. We'll get Laura and this room in order before they arrive.'

'Yes, Shirley. Thank you.' She was glad that someone had taken the helm but I wasn't feeling so sprightly myself.

The two carers with me were in tears as they gently handled Laura, made her clean and look at peace between pristine bed-linen. They managed to put her dentures into her mouth though it had become stiff in death. We were pleased to find a fine, cotton nightdress in the dressing-table drawer. She had a loving family who ensured she had everything she needed.

When Gail, Laura's daughter arrived, she threw herself across her mother's body and sobbed. 'Mam, Mam, Mam. I'm sorry. I'm sorry I wasn't here. I didn't want you to die on your own. I'm sorry I couldn't have you home.'

Brian, Gail's husband, knelt beside the bed and took her hand. 'You couldn't look after her at home, Darling. You did all you could. She knew that.'

When Brian stood up his eyes turned to Helen. 'Why didn't you call us before she went? When did she die?'

'I'm sorry, Brian. I called as soon as we found her. I don't know the exact time she went. I wish you and Gail could have been with her.' I realised Helen was lying by omission. I knew she wasn't deliberately defending herself. She was feeling for them.

She was, also, concerned about the effect her sinful oversight would have on her staff. They respected her position and knew that she was concerned about how her neglect of forgetfulness would affect The Nightingale Nursing Homes

Helen was strict with her carers and wouldn't accept shoddy care. She was one of "the old school" and put her residents first. Her staff knew exactly where they were with her. She was the boss; not one of "the girls".

As well as that, she recognised good staff and respected their dedication. She knew how hard they worked but had no qualms about having to chastise a carer if she was seen to show frustration to someone who was emotionally disturbed and demanding. Elderly mentally infirm residents are difficult to console sometimes. It is one of the characteristics of the illnesses

Laura had suffered from Alzheimer's syndrome since she was in her sixties, so her disease was advanced. She also had a chronic heart condition.

I interrupted Helen's flimsy explanation of what had happened. 'We would have liked someone to have been with her all the time but it wasn't possible. We have a number of residents who, like Laura, are apt to injure themselves or fall.'

Gail moved from beside her mother and stood at the bedside. 'Never mind now. She's gone and she looks peaceful. I'm grateful to the carers here who have nursed my mother and for putting up with her difficult moods. At least, I know she was in the right place and she was kept clean and comfortable.

That was more than I was able to do. They have been understanding and kind.'

At that point the doctor arrived. Helen introduced him to Gail and Brian. It was Dr Field; a friend of Derek.

'Hello, Shirley,' he nodded as he looked at me. He gave his condolences to the relatives before they left the room. Helen suggested that Gail and Brian wait in the visitors' room while the doctor did his routine examination – a matter of form.

Helen beckoned Gail and Brian out of the room. 'Someone will bring a tray of tea. I'll join you after we've gone through the usual process. It won't take long.'

Dr Field leant over to examine Laura. 'She's stone cold,' he said with some surprise as he looked up at Helen and me. 'What happened? I'm usually called soon after death.'

I explained what happened in an apologetic tone. 'I think she leant over to get a drink and fell too far forward.'

'She could have had an acute heart attack. But this is not good,' he frowned, 'not good at all. This sort of thing is happening all too often.'

'And what are we expected to do, Donald?' I knew Dr Field socially. He and Derek frequently played golf together. I sounded angry. 'Do you think we don't know it's not good? Of course we do, and we punish ourselves for unsuitable circumstances which are beyond our control.'

He recognised I had been emotionally upset, as had others of the staff. 'Yes, I know. We can't do more than our best. I'll make out the certificate and go down and speak to the relatives.'

Helen and I were in the room alone with Laura. 'Helen, I'm in a difficult position. I know of the circumstances under which you work, but as you know I can't pass this off as if it were a normal occurrence. I have to report it and I cannot make excuses for the terrible thing that has happened.'

'I know what you must do, Shirley. And it's right that you should report exactly what happened. It's best that the circumstances in nursing homes are known. Don't concern yourself about offending me. It doesn't matter because tomorrow I'll be writing my letter of resignation. I've had enough of nursing. Especially when something like this happens.'

It shouldn't have happened but we both knew it wasn't an isolated event.

Chapter 13

COMPASSION IS THE KEY

It was some months before Marlene Phelps returned to her carer's job at the Bevan EMI unit of The Nightingale Nursing Homes. As planned, I helped her to continue studying for the NVQ.

There was some hard feeling among the staff when she returned. The homes were becoming dangerously low on residency and there had been the concomitant redundancies which had been predicted by Rajiv. I had to explain that we were committed to accept Marlene's return after maternity leave.

The reason for the low residency was considered to be, partly, the result of the NHS and Community Care Act, 1990 and others which followed in the nineties. The Acts were passed to provide more help to the elderly and debilitated who were residing in the community:

"The Local Authority has a duty to carry out an assessment of need for community care services where a person appears to be someone from whom community care services could be provided, AND a person's circumstances may need the provision of community care services."

When elderly people approach the end of their lives, it is a known fact they become concerned about a time when they are unable to care for themselves. An outdated stigma still exists: the black shadow of the dreaded, old workhouses looms over many. They choose to remain in their own lifetime homes and perish there rather than become a resident in a nursing home. The frightening predictions of the media have become strongly implanted in the world of the elderly and, indeed, those who are not of an advanced age.

When the choice is given to an elderly person to be maintained in his or her own home or to become a resident in a nursing home of choice, it is inevitable the choice will be to remain in one's home. Certainly, the nursing home for the elderly and infirm is, rarely, the first choice.

The residency of The Nightingale Nursing Homes had become the lowest since Rajiv and his co-directors became its owners.

'We have to do something to improve our residency. Our bankers are getting fidgety about our financial situation,' Rajiv frowned as he thumped the desk around which he, Carole, Erika, Pat, his secretary, and I sat.

'What?' Carole emphasised. 'We can't go out and drag people in.'

Knowing that Rajiv was a persistent pessimist didn't alter the fact that he was justifiably concerned. Bedford, the home for the elderly, was forty percent down on residency. A number of our carers had been made redundant with the promise of being called back when the situation improved. By that time, they had found other employment and chose not to return to The Nightingales.

'We still have Bevan and Nightingale EMI units. They shouldn't change,' I reminded him. 'When an elderly person becomes mentally deranged he or she, usually, has to be institutionalised.'

That was agreed but it meant that supplies and carers had to be reduced there to make up for the loss of The Bedford Home.

The atmosphere in the three homes became fractious. Not only were the staff poorly paid, but also over-worked. So over-worked that Rajiv didn't know that some of the carers were, already, seeking employment elsewhere. If the registered nurses – two for day duty and two for night duty – resigned, the problem would disastrously increase. Agency nurses would have to be called upon and they were, and still are, expensive to nursing home owners.

I was made partially redundant. I was allowed one day a week but continued to work three. Pat, the secretary was dismissed, Carole was employed for three days but continued to work five. She did her own work and Pat's.

Whether I was there or not, some of the carers that remained were NVQ candidates and relied on me to guide them through. Financing them was a difficult issue but posed no problem to them.

'If Rajiv can't pay, then I'll pay myself,' was said more than once.

Karen and Franny, were two carers who said they would finance themselves. It was the first time in their lives an opportunity had arisen which gave them a chance to achieve something academic. It gave them a sense of pride and added an importance to their work.

At the eleventh hour, when the financial circumstances of The Nightingale Nursing Homes was at its worse, it looked as if most of the carers doing the NVQs would have to be made redundant.

Being totally redundant would not have made a difference to my financially sound life-style, but I would have been disappointed. I enjoyed the companionship and the versatility of the work. Being the training manager was the priority but being part of the team to keep The Nightingale Nursing Home's reputation and its smooth day to day functioning enhanced the position.

Those carers who remained had to rely on their wage to keep their household afloat and to be in a position to provide their children with the essential items of schooldays.

However, running at a persistently low ebb didn't follow with a lighter work-load. We were busier than ever. The needs of our residents had to be met to the high standards that were always aimed at.

The circumstances of the social services following the Act of the early nineties saved The Nightingale Nursing Homes.

The 1990 Community Act wasn't the success it was expected to be. The work-load of the registered nurses and carers of the social service Community Care fell short of meeting the needs of the elderly and infirm who were striving to remain within their own homes.

The private sector was called on to help. An arrangement was made between the social services and the nursing homes. It was agreed that we would take the responsibilities to care for the overspill of people in the community who needed twenty-four hour care.

It involved experienced nurses, such as myself visiting, on invitation, the homes of the destitute. They would still have the choice of whether to remain in their homes but an important obstacle had to be overcome by people like myself.

The necessary objective was to empty the minds of the bad impression of hospitals and nursing homes that the media had instilled.

I have found that people are afraid of having to go into a hospital or nursing home, even if it be for life-saving treatment. We have lost their confidence.

Going into the houses of proud, respectable, elderly and infirm citizens who could no longer maintain their standards and attitudes, opened my mind to suffering that I could never have imagined; suffering that I understood, did not exist in our country.

When I lived and worked in developing countries at the time I travelled the world with Derek, I witnessed poverty and hardship in spite of millions of pounds of aid being received from other generous countries. The deprivation which remained was, and still is, said to be the fault of their corrupt leaders.

Why is it happening in our rich country, led by "honourable" leaders?

Before the period of low residency and low staff numbers recovered, an event occurred in Nightingale EMI unit that gave rise to guilt and despair. It was a shameful event of innocent neglect and forgetfulness; not a lack of compassion, but certainly an event which would deter attracting new residents. It happened on a night when an eighty-two year old resident, Emily Burgess, left the building and no-one noticed her absence.

She was a gentle lady with a pretty face and an easy smile. She was self-caring apart from the administration of her medication. Whenever my work took me to the Nightingale Home I made time to chat to her.

For much of the day she sat in the main entrance hall, watching people coming and going. She sat with the other residents in the dining area at meal times, but not often, in the comfortable lounge during the afternoons.

To leave the building an implement directly on the wall on the right of the door had to be digitally manipulated. Only the staff knew the code of numbers to press to get out. It closed automatically and opened from the outside as did all other doors. However, for a visitor to gain entry they were expected to press an impressive brass bell on the outside which clanged loudly on the inside.

Emily often tried to get out of the building when the door was opened.

'I want to go home,' she would pitifully plead. 'Let me out to go home.' She couldn't understand why she was at the nursing home when, she claimed, she had a nice home of her own.

'I want to go home, Shirley,' she often said. 'Will you arrange for someone to take me home? I've asked Myra and she says I'm not well enough yet. But I am.'

Myra Thompson was Emily's daughter. She visited her mother two or sometimes, three times a week. One afternoon when I happened to be at the Nightingale EMI unit she and I were surprised to meet. We had known each other from when we both worked at The Nevill Hall Hospital but our paths had rarely crossed during the past ten years or so.

Myra had been a staff nurse when I was the junior sister on an acute medical ward. She had begrudged me being offered the sister's position because, having been the staff nurse there for almost two years, she assumed she would be given the post.

She bore me a grudge which I tried to ignore. That was difficult on a hospital ward where good team work is essential.

Consequently, she didn't serve me to the best of her ability and we often had cross words. I had to chastise her for persistent lateness even though she always had a legitimate excuse. I felt I had to check her written reports to ensure important details weren't overlooked, as did the senior sister, Janet Morris. Janet was younger than I by ten years but had begun her training at eighteen and had quick promotion.

Myra created a bad atmosphere when she was on duty. It wasn't conducive to smooth running of the ward and I was always pleased when she wasn't on duty with me.

On the afternoon we caught sight of each other when I walked into The Nightingale Home, I immediately sensed Myra's guilt. I went across the room to where she was sitting next to her mother and greeted her. To my mind, the differences we had on Ward 4/1 were past and forgotten.

'How nice to see you again after all these years, Myra. I didn't realise Mrs Burgess is your mother.'

'Yes and I wish I could look after her at home but she'll get well here, won't you, Mum?' She questioned her mother as she looked at me. 'I knew you were the training manager. I've noticed you a few times but you've always been too busy for me to interrupt.'

'You should have. I like meeting people I knew from working at Nevill Hall.'

'I've wanted to talk to you. Could you spare me a few minutes today? I'd like to tell you about Mum.' She turned to her mother. 'Is that all right, Mum?'

'Yes,' Mrs Burgess replied. 'Ask Shirley if I can come home, won't you?' Myra didn't reply.

I suggested to Myra that we go into the visitor' room. 'There's no-one there at the moment.'

A few minutes of idle chatter passed between us. She thanked me for giving her time as we made ourselves comfortable in easy chairs, facing each other. She began by telling me she felt guilty and unhappy about her mother being in care.

'But I want you to know why I can't have her home and I can't see that I ever will. She's a danger to herself and others. After my father died she lived alone and on two occasions she tried to take her own life. We understood it was grief, of course, but she used to harm my father when he was alive. My mother swears that someone tells her to hurt people. That someone, of course, is invisible.

'When people visited her, she attacked them with a kitchen knife or anything near to hand. She wounded one lady quite badly. Eventually, no-one went to the house; even the neighbours were afraid of her.

'She attacked the postman and the milkman. She threatened the milkman with a kitchen meat-cleaver.. They stopped going to the house.

'I couldn't let it go on so we sold her bungalow and she came to live with us; Alison, my daughter, Dennis and me, because I was afraid to leave her on her own.

'She'd been seen by two consultants; she was diagnosed as being dangerously psychotic and they started her on a course of medication. It didn't seem to do much good. My mother insisted that someone talks to her and threatens her if she doesn't do what she is told.

'The last straw was when we were taking her to see a third consultant. Dennis was driving; Mum was in the passenger seat because it was easier for her than having to strain her back to get into the back seat, where I was. When we were going along, she grabbed the steering wheel and was screaming for Dennis to turn around and go back. She steered the car all over the road. It was swerving fast and Dennis managed to force the steering wheel hard left and we crashed into the bank.'

At that point, Myra stopped talking and put her hands to the sides of her head, trying to shut out frightening memories.

'Thank God it was on a quiet road and there was no on-coming traffic.'

I interrupted. 'You needn't be telling me all this, Myra. I know your mother is mentally disturbed and she will be looked after here. You know the nurse in charge is a very experienced psychiatric nurse, don't you?'

'Yes, I've known him for years. But it breaks my heart that my mother wants to come home but I don't think she will ever leave here. You must know she's attacked other residents.'

I did know but didn't admit to it. 'Do you want to go on?'

'Yes, I want you to know why my mother is not with me.'

Myra went on. 'We all had bumps and bruises but the thing is, if Dennis had been forced to steer to the right, the car would have rolled down a steep bank and landed at the bottom of the gorge. We all could have been maimed or even killed.'

Myra began to cry. I put my arms about her shoulders. I felt sorry for her.

'You must try not to torture yourself with guilt, Myra. Your mother must remain here for as long as is necessary.'

'I know, but for most of the time she is a loving, gentle person and I want you to know that.'

Myra dabbed her eyes and sniffed before going back to where her mother sat, happily sipping a cup of tea. She smiled at us.

'Now Myra,' she said, 'have a cup of tea and a piece of cake then we will both go home.'

Myra looked up at me with wet eyes and a face full of pity. 'I know it's hard for you to accept,, but try not to worry. Your mother is looked after here and kept safe.'

I was wrong.

The staff shortages continued well into the New Year. One freezing-cold, January night, The Nightingale Home, with a residency of twenty-nine, mentally disturbed people had four night staff on duty. Liam Drew, a registered psychiatric nurse, was in charge with three nursing aides, one a "bank nurse" from the nursing agency at Abergavenny.

The directors of the homes were averse to employing agency nurses because of the added expense but Liam insisted on employing one that night. He would have refused to take charge with only three carers and that would have been, not only illegally, but dangerous.

The agency nurse hadn't arrived for duty at the usual time. The frozen engine of her car took longer than she expected to start. She had contacted Liam to say she'd be along as soon as possible.

Being elderly and infirm, many of the residents needed care and strict observation. Many were incontinent so had to be washed and dressed before having their late night bedtime drinks. Physical care and constant observation to maintain the safety of a number of residents who were likely to wander off, fall and injure themselves was excessively demanding. Many of them were confused, irritable and disorientated.

Unless the day staff had managed to help a few of the residents early to bed, the first four hours of the night shift were frantically busy. The night Emily Burgess escaped was such a night.

As usual, Emily was in the main hall, sitting in the shadow of the staircase well. She was entertained by the scurrying and hurrying, the goings and comings of the active carers. No-one noticed her. No-one heard her whispering to herself that she was going home.

She was already dressed for bed. She had on her warm, winceyette nightdress, a cosy, thick woollen dressing gown, a shawl about her shoulders and quality, fur-lined carpet slippers. I had noticed that Myra ensured her mother had the best of everything.

The heat of the nursing homes was at the correct, suitable temperature for the elderly but overwhelmingly hot for the fast-moving staff. Emily was comfortable under all her clothing. A waft of cold air which reached her when the main door opened was refreshing. She thought it must be pleasantly cool outside and she wanted to get out to go home.

The agency nurse had arrived. She snatched open the main door and pushed it to close it. Thick ice which fringed the outer frame of the door prevented it from closing tight. It rebounded and remained open.

'How nice of the lady,' thought Emily as she made for the door.

She stepped out into the night's biting cold. Her first few steps on the slippery ground-frost were easy. It was lit up by the beams of light through the flimsy curtains of the front windows.

'How lovely,' she said to herself as she began the descent of the steep hill. She breathed deeply to fill her lungs with the fresh air.

It didn't stay fresh for long; it soon became too cold and she shivered. The soles of her fine, bedroom slippers were of a slip-free leather, designed specifically to prevent falls. Unfortunately they weren't secure against the thick ice patches on the tarmac forecourt of The Homes.

Emily slipped and landed on her buttocks. Her plumpness padded the fall from hurting her but it gave her a warning. She would have to be careful.

She managed to heave herself up with her hands and realised getting home might be more difficult than she had anticipated.

Her home, The Nightingale EMI unit, was at the bottom of the hill, so nearest to the wide metal gates which were always open and just a few yards from the road.

The palms of her soft hands were grazed and felt cold from her fall. She wrapped her warm, woollen shawl more tightly about her shoulders and tucked her hands beneath it. She stood outside the menacing gates looking to her right and left and wondered which direction she should take.

'It must be over there,' she said to herself. She was looking towards the light of the town centre which was glowing over the roof-tops. Her eyes and legs followed the glow. She strode towards it with big strides. In her demented mind, she was going home.

The thicknesses of her night-clothes retained the heat of the home for a while. It didn't take long for the icy chill of the night to penetrate the frailty of her ageing body.

On the way she passed a few people, no doubt hurrying to their own firesides. They walked past her and didn't take notice of her strange appearance in night-time clothes; it was too cold to loiter.

By the time she got to the main, brightly lit street, she was perishing cold and began to get frightened.

'I want to go home,' she wailed, but there was no-one to listen.

The town was quiet with just a few people here and there. Bryncelyn was always quiet, especially at night since the main road had become closed to through-traffic.

The savoury smell of a fish and chip shop entered her cold nostrils. She followed the wafting aroma and pushed her way through a group of teenagers which had gathered around the shop doorway. They were engrossed in eating their piping hot chips; blowing on each chip to cool it before putting it into their mouths. Emily loitered on the threshold to enjoy the warmth that lingered there.

The couple serving behind the counter looked at her before looking quizzically at each other. 'We got something funny here,' the man said in a hush to the woman.

'I want to go home,' Emily said pitifully. 'Please take me home.'

'Where do you live, my lovely?' the woman asked.

Emily had forgotten where she'd come from. She shivered, 'Home. I want to go home.'

The tall, heavily built man's face was partly hidden by a thick, black beard and moustache. He opened the half door between the steaming deep-fat chip fryer and the other side of the shop, slammed the half-door with a resounding bump and strode towards Emily.

The loudness of the bump startled Emily. She became terrified at the sight of the man, who she thought was going to harm her. She screamed and ran out of the shop onto the pavement. Giggles arose from the teenagers. They didn't seem to care about a strange old woman wandering about the street when she was dressed for bed.

Emily's hasty runaway footsteps were too near the edge of the curb. She tripped and fell onto the road as a cyclist was riding by. The cyclist had no time to stop to avoid pedalling into her. The front wheel twisted, the cyclist fell off his bike and landed beside Emily.

Two of the teenage girls ran to help her. 'Old woman, are you hurt?' one of them said.

'You shouldn't be out dressed as you are. It's too cold,' the other said.

Emily wailed quietly; she could hardly be heard. She was shocked and frightened. 'I want to go home,' was all she could say.

The man from the chip shop leant down close to her. His hairy face gave the appearance of fierceness, but he was gentle. 'Don't move, my lovely. My wife'll phone for the ambulance. Don't move in case you've broken a bone or something.'

The dazed cyclist, was sitting on his buttocks supporting himself with the flat of his hands on the rough surface of the road, his legs wide apart.

'I couldn't help it,' he said. 'She fell right in front of me. I hope my bike's not broke.'

'The bike's alright, lad. Are you hurt?'

'No, I don't think I am. Don't tell on me, will you? I know I shouldn't have been riding my bike without lights.'

'You shouldn't have been riding here at all,' the chip-shop man said. 'This is a no-through road now. But no. You go off before the police come.'

At that point a lot of loud talking and shouting came from the opposite side of the road. It was a group of people leaving The King George pub. Out of morbid curiosity, some of them crossed the road to see what had happened. They arrived at the same time as an ululating ambulance stopped at the scene.

A police car also arrived. The quiet street took on the character of a fairground.

The police took details before the paramedics carried Emily into the ambulance. They were gentle and reassuring with her. Her state of confusion must have been as it never had been before and she was physically hurt. The paramedic suspected a broken wrist. She was taken to the casualty department of The Nevill Hall Hospital.

One of the policemen guessed she must have wandered away from the nearby nursing home.

Back at The Nightingale EMI unit, it was well past midnight when the routine work had been done and the residents settled for the night. Most were abed, but a few chose to remain in the lounge to watch the television until they fell asleep there.

In their psychotic state, a few wandered back and forth between the two lounges, peering here and there, looking for something but not knowing what. They had to be kept constantly under observation in case they injured or disturbed other residents.

When Liam passed through the main hall he felt a draught and noticed it came from the front door, which was ajar. At first he thought he was imagining that it was open but he let go the hand of the resident he was leading from the toilet and went to close it. Liam was astounded and angry.

He shouted at the top of his voice. 'What idiot left the main door open?' Of course, no-one confessed.

It was the rule of the units to allow the residents to do as they pleased as long as safety was maintained. Keeping certain doors, especially the main door shut, was sacrosanct.

It was some time before the fatigued staff were able to draw breath and take a short break to drink tea and eat their packed sandwiches.

The agency nurse, Joan, had worked in The Nightingale Home before that night. She asked a question of those sitting beside her around the office desk which allowed a good view of the lounge on one side and the hallway on the other.

'What happened to that nice Emily Burgess?' she asked. 'She used to sit in the hall for hours before she'd be taken to her room.'

Liam sprang from his chair and dashed out to take a look in the recess under the stairway. He was disappointed; Emily wasn't sitting in the shadows as he had hoped. He pointed sharply to one of the carers. 'Quick! Go up and see if she's in her room!'

She dashed up the stairs two at a time; it was quicker than taking the lift. She was up and back in minutes.

'No, Liam, she's not in her room.'

'Oh, my God! She's gone! Right! Get searching,' he snapped. 'Look in all the rooms, in every nook and cranny. If we can't find her she must have got out when the door was open. Which of you was daft enough not to close the door?'

'No-one, Liam. We haven't stopped making sure that everyone has been seen to since we came on duty,' Alma, the more experienced carer, told him. Joan agreed; she didn't realise she was the guilty one.

They searched high and low. Of course, Emily had escaped.

'Oh, my God!' Liam repeated. 'She's gone out in her night clothes. She won't last half an hour out there in the perishing cold. I'll have to call the police.'

'Don't panic, Liam,' Alma said. 'If she's wandering about, someone is bound to see her and bring her back.'

'How would anyone realise she's from here? There's so many weirdos out there they wouldn't think anything about an old lady walking about in her nightdress. She wouldn't know to put on a heavy coat.'

'Someone is bound to, Liam, but you'd better get in touch with the bobbies for all our sakes and then you should call Carole and let her know.'

'Oh, God.' Liam despaired. 'Poor Emily. I hope she's all right, even though her escaping could lose me my job.'

'That won't happen. We'll see to that.' Alma glanced around at the other worried faces. They nodded.

'With how things have been around here lately I'm surprised something like this hasn't happened before. I wouldn't be surprised if it has and we haven't been told about it.' It was Joan the agency nurse who spoke up. 'It's the same in all the nursing homes. You are doing much better than most, I can tell you.' Being an agency carer she would have worked in several nursing homes.

Liam called the police, then afterwards, when he was calling Carole to tell her the worst, the front door-bell clanged. It was P.C. Probert.

Liam let him in. 'That was quick. I contacted the police just minutes ago.'

'Then I'll call the station to tell them I'm here before they send another officer. I think you called because you lost someone, didn't you?'

'You've found Emily Burgess. Thank God. I was worried to death,' Liam's shoulders dropped with a loosening of tension as he let the policeman into the hall. 'Is she all right?'

Jane, one of the carers was standing close by. 'It wasn't Liam's fault,' she said. 'We've all been rushed off out feet trying to keep everything in order. We've all been worried about Mrs Burgess. The hinges of the door couldn't have reacted right when someone closed the door. It's happened before but someone has always noticed in time.'

'Yes. She's not frozen to death but she was knocked over by a cyclist and an ambulance took her to Casualty at Nevill Hall.'

'Thank God,' Liam repeated. 'I'm Charge Nurse Liam Drew, but I won't be Charge Nurse for much longer; I am so ashamed of what's happened to Emily. I deserve to be whipped.'

'Indeed you don't, Mr Drew. We couldn't do without people like you.' His eyes included the carers standing behind Liam. 'Mrs Burgess is being looked after in Nevill Hall. She's not the first resident who's left the safety of these homes and I don't expect she'll be the last. I'll just take a short statement from you all then let you get on with your work.'

Which is what they did, surreptitiously opening the room doors to check that all the residents were in bed and safe. They cared for the few that wandered about in their confusion and encouraged those who had fallen asleep in front of the television to be taken to their beds.

When all routine checks were over, the staff tried again to have something to eat and drink. Liam looked down in the mouth.

'I wonder how Carole is getting on at the hospital??' he questioned himself rather than his staff.

'It was a good job she was in when you phoned her, Liam. I expect she'll have called Emily's daughter,' Jane said.

Liam's relief that Emily was safe was short-lived. He thought of how the relatives would accept the error which could have caused a fatality. Carole, too, was concerned about the repercussions. She cringed; of all people, it had to be Myra Thompson's mother. She was known to be over-anxious about her mother being at The Nightingale Home.

Carole arrived at the casualty department before Myra and her husband. Myra embraced her mother tightly. 'Oh, Mam, we could have lost you. Why did you leave the nursing home?'

'I wanted to go home, Myra. Can I go home now?'

'No, Mam. These good people here will look after you for tonight. We'll come for you tomorrow.' She turned her eyes to Carole whose normal, healthy pink had paled. She found it hard to form a suitable explanation to give to Myra. Myra recognised Carole's anguish.

'You needn't worry over this, Carole. I'm surprised it hasn't happened before. Mam hasn't fractured anything, thank goodness; just bumps and bruises which will be treated with painkillers. They're going to keep her here overnight and I'll pick her up tomorrow and take her back to The Nightingale, which I have to admit, **is** her home. You'll hear nothing more about this mishap; I'm grateful for the good care she's having.'

A few days later, what happened that night when Emily Burgess left The Nightingale Nursing Homes appeared in the press. The event was treated with extreme contempt. Reporters had questioned people who were at the fish and chip shop and a couple who had been drinking in the pub across the road from the shop. Their words were distorted and the reputation of The Nightingale Nursing Homes was unfairly tainted. The reporters didn't take the time to research the background of the event; to know how Mrs Emily Burgess "was allowed to walk out on a freezing night". They were not interested in discovering the care and compassion of the other side of their damning report.

Is it any wonder why the elderly and infirm fear the nursing homes?

I am reminded of the famous Griffiths Report, 1983: Mr Roy Griffiths was commissioned by the Rt Hon Norman Fowler, then Secretary of State for Social Services Department of Health and Social Security to investigate the dire failings of the NHS It was found the problem lay in the bad management within the Service.

A number of "experienced" "clever" people, from outside the health services, formed a team to "put it right". At the time it was being looked at, I was a clinical teacher at The Nevill Hall Hospital.

One of the selected heads of the inquiry and his entourage visited The Nevill Hall Hospital to carry out their observations. As I was walking along the corridor with a ward sister on her way to do afternoon and evening duty, they were sauntering down the corridor towards us. I guessed they were on their way to the dining room for a "working" lunch. Sister and I walked close to the wall to let them pass. I counted about ten smart suited, white-collared gentlemen and one tall, smartly dressed lady. They didn't seem to see us as they barged past.

Sister told me her ward was on emergency intake that day. They were seven staff, including herself, to deal with emergencies and the existing twenty or more acutely ill patients.

I remained to hear the take-over report. As a clinical teacher I needed to know the patients.

I heard Sister telling her staff that we'd seen a "herd" of the Griffiths' team on the ground floor corridor and she expressed her disdain of there being so many and they were only seven to do the most important job of caring.

I agreed with her and one of the students passed an apt remark: "Too many chiefs, not enough Indians".

I hadn't heard that saying before but I thought it quite apt. The enquiry achieved nothing except waste money.

Emily Burgess going missing was not because of lack of management, or of neglected care, but because there was insufficient staff. Some of the residents at The Nightingale EMI unit needed constant observation but they hardly ever got it.

Chapter 14

WITHOUT DIGNITY

Helen Young did not resign her post at Bevan Home after the event of Laura Dutton being forgotten and dying alone. She was chastised and the incident mentioned in her personal file. Her professional qualification was not affected by having a black mark on her personal report but her conscience was. She was among the best of our profession and will never forget the nursing sin with which she blamed herself. She considered that nothing could be more wicked than letting a woman die alone in a fouled bed.

Yet, she is aware that this disgraceful sort of event is happening throughout the country every day. The media is making the nation aware of our badly run nursing homes and failing national health. The stories are not exaggerated. I know because I have seen and experienced similar events. I have been sickened by some of the hateful nursing. The bad, cruel nurses are of the minority and when they are identified they should be taken out of the profession. Only then will there be a chance to regain the confidence and respect our profession once had.

No registered nurse of The Nightingale Nursing Homes resigned in spite of the unethical and dangerous conditions.

Circumstances began to slowly improve after the arrangement between the social services and the nursing homes in the private sector went into action. We accepted elderly and destitute people and so lightened the burden of the community nurses.

As a result of the horror stories published by the press, a fear of hospitals and nursing homes had arisen. People were dying alone, without heat, in filth and squalor, rather than accept the warmth, comfort and care which most nursing homes have to offer.

The extra issue which was added to my job description was put into practice: To visit people in the community, to assess the needs of the elderly and advise.

With the registered and experienced nurses of our nursing homes, I became involved in some of the assessments of the needs and quality of life of people living in their own homes. They were often people who didn't know their rights within our social system. There were those who had slipped through the nets of citizens who needed help and support to enjoy the basic necessities of life they were entitled to. The wicked suffering I witnessed is deeply notched on my memory. To this day I shudder when something happens to remind me of some of those assignments.

One morning I was given an assignment to visit Mrs Aggie Moore. I chose Carer Amanda Brown to accompany me. I wanted someone who was diligent but had no experience of the seedier side of life. She had been accepted for interview for professional training, so I considered the experience would be beneficial to her.

We were given no information of Aggie Moore's past history except that she lived alone in undesirable circumstances. She was of unsound mind, unsafe, unable to care for herself and had a criminal record. From those few sentences it was evident that she needed help and support.

The type of life a person had lived, whether saint or sinner, within or outside the law, meant nothing to me or my colleagues. My father's wise words rang true. This was one of those times – *"There's bad in the best of us and good in the worst of us."*

I drew up at the curb directly in front of Aggie Moore's house, one of a street of ten. It was a prefabricated bungalow, built after the last world war. They were built of shaped sections for rapid assembly and, at the time, were considered a temporary arrangement. They were expected to be habitable for ten to fifteen years. They turned out to be permanent; people were currently living in them.

Initially, when they began to become dilapidated, the local housing authority kept them going by patching, plumbing, roofing and mending. That arrangement petered out but people continued to make them their homes. The rent was low.

My assessment began as Amanda and I walked through the gateway onto a few yards of frontage. The gate was not there and the patch of ground, what might have been lawn, was dirt and covered with household waste. The four, small front windows were curtained by tattered rags and the panes, many of which were cracked, were diaphanous from years of dust clinging to them. Aggie Moore's prefab looked as if it should have been bulldozed and carted away a long time ago.

Amanda and I looked at each other in disbelief. 'Have we got the right house?' she asked me as she rapped with her knuckles on the paint-flaking door. A small slit in the middle of the door looked as if there had once been a knocker. The door was not answered.

'Of course we have. Anyway, you were navigating,' I replied as I, too, knocked on the door. No answer. 'She must be deaf,' I added.

We both knocked again and Amanda shouted through the slit. 'Mrs Moore. It's the nurses. Can we come in? We won't keep you.'

'There's an awful smell coming from that letter box,' Amanda said as I turned the knob and I let the door open to a slit. It wouldn't budge further. Anyway, it wouldn't have been right to open it and let ourselves in. We knocked and called again.

'We have to get in,' I said. 'She might have fallen and can't get to the door.' I pushed the door without the intention of being intrusive but we just couldn't walk away and admit defeat. The door wouldn't open even when I pushed hard.

'There's something blocking the door,' I said. 'She's put a door-stop or something because there's no lock to keep thieves out.'

'I'll go round the back. Perhaps there's a door open,' Amanda said as she made her way to the back of the house. She hadn't gone long. 'The back door's locked,' she said. 'We definitely won't get in that way but there's a window open. I'm going to climb through it.'

'I'm not sure you should do that,' I said reluctantly, 'but we have to get in somehow. I feel something's wrong.'

'Oh, well. You've taught me to take the initiative when needs be and it's needed now.' Off she went while I waited at the front door. I looked up and down the short street. It was deserted but I knew there were people living in the other houses because their rubbish bins were outside. From next door I saw flashes of lights from their front window. I assumed they were from a television screen.

I was startled by Amanda's scream from the other side of the door. She had, obviously, managed to make a forced entry.

'Ugh, it's horrible!' she yelled on the top of her voice. 'Shirley, come in quick! Push the door hard, hard, hard! She's dead!'

I realised it was Aggie Moore's body which was preventing the door from opening. I pushed with all my might and eventually managed to squeeze in. I stepped on her body and cringed. I felt I had sinned by stepping on her, but if I had tried to step over her I might have fallen – face first into the hall and landed at Amanda's feet. She was frozen stiff with shock.

The smell of death was putrid, made worse by four fat cats prowling like hungry, caged lions about Mrs Moore's body. The cats had made the narrow hallway their latrine and had fed well on rodents. Part of a carcass, of what I thought was a rat, was close to Mrs Moore's body. The mortifying stench of the half eaten rat added to the smell of Mrs Moore's body and the filth of the house was almost unbearable.

I knew it was a rat because I had seen rats about my father's chickens' cots when I was a girl. His cots were near the river and the river rats were attracted by the chicken feed my father put out for them.

Mrs Moore's one arm was stretched upwards. It looked as if she had been trying to reach the latch to open the door. She must have fallen somewhere in the house and crawled to the door. She wanted help; she wanted to live.

'Stay with her,' I instructed Amanda. 'I'm going next door to phone for an ambulance.' I felt like adding that there was little they could do for her apart from moving her body out of that dreadful house and taking her to a more dignified place, though the morgue in Nevill Hall Hospital wouldn't be much more of a dignified place. Having worked in that hospital for over twenty years I was familiar with its morgue and its lifeless occupants; some awaiting post-mortems.

'Don't be long, will you?' Amanda trembled. 'I'm off if you're not back soon.'

'Don't you dare go until I'm back,' I insisted. 'Now help me to drag Mrs Moore away from the door so that I can get through.'

Amanda moved stiffly but managed to bend her knees, as I did. She closed her eyes and looked away as we grabbed Mrs Moore's unrecognisable apparel in both our hands and pulled her body a few inches further into the hallway.

The action moved Amanda out of a stupor.

I rapped the knocker of the house next door and waited impatiently for someone to appear. I heard the television; it sounded as if it were on high volume. I knocked again – hard.

'All right, all right, I'm coming! Don't knock the bloody door down!'

A man appeared in a vest and shabby trousers held up with red bracers. He looked surprised; I didn't give him time to speak.

'Please let me use your telephone. It's for Mrs Moore.' My fingers were crossed behind my back hoping he had a phone and would allow me use it.

'What's the matter with her?'

'She's dead. Where's your phone?' I spoke as I walked past him into where the telephone stood on a hall table much too large for the small hall.

'Dead!' he shouted. 'Are you sure?'

Having heard what he said, his wife appeared, having torn herself away from their television set. 'Dead, is she? I thought you was the paper boy come for his money.'

'I dialled 999 and explained the circumstances. The voice on the other side of the phone went through the usual rigmarole of questions. 'Where are you?' Address? Is she conscious? Is she breathing? … Etcetera, etcetera …

'She's dead!' I yelled unnecessarily down the phone before repeating Mrs Moore address.

The wife didn't seem concerned. 'If she wasn't such a weird, miserable old witch we would have checked on her. But where are her kids? They hardly ever went there?'

'Thank you,' I called as I hurried back to Amanda. I found her standing stiffly in the same position as when I left.

'We'll have to move her further in or the paramedics won't get in,' I said.

We both went on our knees again, grabbed Mrs Moore's clothing and pulled her further away from the door. It wasn't easy. She must have been dead for many days because her body had stiffened into the position we found her.

The paramedics arrived within minutes. The first man who entered put the palm of his hand over his nose. 'Phew,' he sniffed. 'She's certainly dead.' When a second man came in he was told sharply to get rid of the cats.

He did that thoroughly with the heel of his heavy boots. The cats mewed and hissed as they scuttled away.

The third paramedic, who was the female ambulance driver, stepped over Mrs Moore and stood in front of Amanda and me.

'Are you all right, m'darlin's?'

'Yes. Thanks,' I frowned with distaste. I didn't like the way she addressed us, especially since I must have been twenty years her senior.

The paramedics worked together and moved Mrs Moore's grey-blue stiff body as easily as if she were a bag of rags. In life she must have been a tall, lean person. In death she looked like a witch with a skeleton covered with skin under the worn black, wool dress that covered her.

Hair pins were loose in her straggled, strands of white, straw-like, long hair, about her face and shoulders. She reminded me of a scarecrow.

The expression on her face held horror. I shuddered at the sight of her and the thought of her terror as she must have struggled for the door latch. She tried to get out for help. She wanted to live. Words of Dylan Thomas came to mind again. Aggie Moore followed the advice of those wise words but couldn't live up to them. *"Do not go gentle into that good night."* This was a nightmarish experience for Amanda and myself.

The paramedics questioned Amanda and me and recorded our answers in a dog-eared book. Amanda didn't do much answering. She was too horrified to think straight. She wasn't aware that such events occurred in her own community.

Later, it made her wonder if she was making the right move by entering the professional training course in the coming year. I refrained from telling her that she might experience worse situations than she had that day.

The terrible torture Aggie Moore must have suffered in her last hours was beyond comprehension. She should have been rescued months ago from her hellish life and admitted into a nursing home. She might have been just as lonely with many people around her, but at least, she would have died in comfort, instead of being in pain, alone, cold and starving hungry. She died without dignity.

Chapter 15

FULL HOUSE

The residency of The Bedford Home gradually approached its established number of residents. Elaine Kenwood or myself carried out assessments of prospective residents for the elderly care unit.

Helen Young, Trevor Ellis, Liam Drew and others in charge of the EMI units were involved in assessments of the possible residency of elderly mentally infirm people. Each of the three homes had the minimal number of three registered nurses and three SENs (State Enrolled Nurses). It became difficult to get SENs. They were being phased out since the introduction of Project 2000 Nurse Training. Registered Nurses were considered expensive to the nursing home owners but legislatively essential.

When there was a subtle difference between an elderly resident and an elderly mentally infirm resident, the choice of whether the person needed elderly care or psychiatric care had to be considered. Sons and daughter preferred to consider their parent to be elderly, rather than mentally infirm, so sometimes a difficult choice had to be made.

I was not asked to help with the assessments for a while because the staff number had increased. There was a predominance of young people taken on as carers, some of them not having had any experience of nursing. It was my responsibility to nurture them into becoming good carers. It was my priority.

I advised some bright carers to prepare themselves for entrance into professional training. Both that and involving them to undertake the NVQ. I would quote Amanda Brown as a motivator. She had been at The Bedford Home for three years and had been invited to be interviewed for professional training, though she hadn't yet been given a definite date.

In the meantime Amanda was happy at The Bedford Home with me as her mentor for the NVQ She avoided being involved in assessments of prospective residents after our experience of Mrs Aggie Moore's horrible death.

One morning Elaine asked a favour of me. I guessed what it would be. It was to carry out a home assessment. The son and daughter of Mr Leonard Anderson were worried about him living alone in a big house.

Elaine explained that her back up SEN hadn't turned up for duty.

'Shirley, I can't leave the unit without proper cover so will you take the hot seat until I get back or do the assessment for me?'

I chose the latter; it was easier. I was still unused to being in charge of a unit. I enjoyed the assessments and it was a reason for getting out for a while. It was a sunny autumn day.

Elaine went on. 'I'll release one of the new carers to go with you. It won't be nasty as Aggie Moore's was, at least, I hope not, and Avril Travers might be doing it herself one day.'

'That's good, I'll take Avril, then.'

Eighteen year old Avril Travers was a new carer whose intention was to enter professional training.

Mr Leonard Anderson, was a seventy-nine year old gentleman who was determined to remain in his own home though his son and daughter insisted he needed twenty-four hour care. The NHS community nurses called on him twice a day and he had a cleaning lady twice weekly.

He was an insulin dependent diabetic and had suffered a cerebral vascular accident (a stroke) which he had overcome and was mobile, though not fully. He used a Zimmer walking frame at home but when outside he sported a silver-topped walking cane. His daughter claimed that he was too proud to be seen among his friends using a Zimmer frame. He was of the misconception that only very incapacitated people relied on Zimmer frames.

Mr Anderson hated getting old, as many of us do. He fought hard to lead as normal a life as possible, in spite of his incapacities. His son and daughter hoped he wouldn't fight too hard to overcome the contingencies of aging and have a falling accident.

The notes Elaine handed to me didn't tell me much about his past, except that he was a widower living alone and the limited information his daughter had given her over the phone regarding her concern for her father's safety.

A community nurse visited for half an hour every morning and evening to ensure he took his medication, to administer his insulin and to check that he was well and safe. The family thought a cleaning lady calling for a couple of hours twice a week wasn't enough. They thought he needed someone to be there day and night to help him to wash and dress, to prepare regular meals and to maintain his safety.

Mr Anderson had been a successful business man and his son and daughter both lived too far away to help with his care. They worried about him living alone and would have preferred if he went to live with one of them, although their homes had not been fitted with the many invalid aids which helped him to exist in his own home. He adamantly refused to leave.

'When I die,' he explained with determination, 'I will be happier here in my own home; the home I and your dear mother built over many years. She died here and so will I.'

'Anyway,' he had said to his children, 'haven't you read the newspapers? These nursing homes are torture chambers. They let people die of dehydration in pain and filthy conditions, as do the hospitals. No thank you, that's not for me.'

Avril and I set off shortly after ten o'clock, when I had arrived for duty. Carole was already there doing something that she had done three years ago – liaise with the Foreign Office to recruit registered nurses from Nigeria. It was a stressful task with much administration and too much unnecessary telephoning. She was not in a good mood.

'Shirley, Elaine is taking advantage. You have plenty of your own work and Erika and I could do with your help here today. Erika is complaining about having to be in three places at the same time.'

I replied in an apologetic tone. 'It won't take long and getting a new resident is as important as getting new qualified staff, isn't it?

Avril and I made for 2, Alderton Crescent; it took about twenty minutes. I was able to park in the driveway of Mr Anderson's house.

I could understand why he was reluctant to leave it for The Nightingale Nursing Homes. It was an impressive, double-fronted bay-windowed house with well-kept lawns surrounded by trimmed hedges and a few copper beaches. I guessed he must have hired a gardener.

'Wow!' Avril gaped. 'Nice. No wonder he doesn't want to leave here. What a lovely house.'

I responded. 'That's just what I was thinking.'

We walked up the driveway to the porch which fronted a heavy wooden door with large, ornate glass panels each side. Avril pressed a gleaming brass door-bell and a loud clang could be heard coming from the inside. We had no reply.

She pressed again and we waited a while for a response. None came.

'I expect he's in the back of the house or in the lavatory,' Avril suggested. We waited.

'Elaine told me that his son and daughter told her that a spare door-key was left under the flower-pot in the porch. If he didn't answer the door we had permission to let ourselves in. He's hard of hearing, too.'

'Shall I go round to the back to see if he's in one of the rooms there?' Avril asked.

'Good idea, but don't be too long. I don't want it to look as if we're snooping.'

She'd gone a little more than five minutes, during which time I'd looked up at the windows. It seemed too quiet, though I didn't know what to expect.

'I don't think he's at the back of the house, Shirl, but I couldn't see much. There's a big veranda with lots of big flower-pots and creeper plants and I'm not tall enough to look in all the windows. We've got the right house, have we?' I remembered Amanda asking me that when we went to Aggie Moore's house.

'Of course we have,' I replied, but to be sure I took out the file to check.

'Well, we'll have to use the key under the pot. We can't just leave.'

There was only one pot in the porch so we didn't have to search around. It was Ali Baba size, nearly as tall as me, and heavy. Avril tilted the pot and I scraped the rusting key from underneath. I cleaned off most of the rust with a paper tissue before putting it into the brass-ringed keyhole. I found it stubborn to turn but Avril's young fingers succeeded.

The heavy door opened easily. We stepped into a huge, terrazzo--floored hall after wiping our feet vigorously on the door-mat. The hallway and wide staircase were elegant even though a mechanical chair-lift had been fitted on its left side. We stood for a few moments and looked around. The silence was telling me that all was not well.

'I have the feeling that no-one's here,' Avril said.

'I expect Mr Anderson has fallen asleep,' I suggested. 'He must be somewhere, because the social service community nurse must have called to give him his insulin this morning.'

'Mmm,' was Avril's response. 'It's a lovely house but a bit creepy, isn't it?'

I did not answer the question but I was beginning to be of the same opinion. 'Come on, we'd better get on. You go upstairs and look. He might be in bed but is more likely to be dozing somewhere down here.'

'But look, Shirley. The stair-lift seat is upstairs,' Avril spoke as she had already began to ascend so there was no point in her changing direction.

A stupid oversight on my part. If I had noticed that, I would have suggested I go upstairs and Avril search the downstairs rooms. I didn't want a repeat of the Aggie Moore's incident – a social sin. Amanda hadn't yet recovered from the shock of finding her stiff dead body. She had been off duty suffering acute anxiety. I didn't want Avril to experience a similar event. I intended to encouraged her into professional training, not frighten her off.

I searched in the spacious lounge. A large screen television set was there and newspapers were scattered on a low table in front of the settee. Mr Anderson could have fallen asleep in one of the comfortable velour-covered chairs. The soft furnishings were rich and the furniture the most luxurious I'd ever seen on a community call.

I had paused to admire my surroundings when a blood-curdling scream moved me. It was Avril and something frightening had happened to her.

I dodged in and out of the furniture, forgetting my sensitive back bone, and bounded up the stairs faster than I'd moved for a long time.

'In here! In here!' I followed Avril's fearful voice. She was in the large luxury bathroom. Mr Anderson was in the bath, up to his chest in water.

His one hand was on the device which closed and opened the bath door. It was an invalid walk-in bath; one with a door which allows the bather to step in and out with ease and safety. Something must have gone wrong with the mechanism. Mr Anderson didn't have his S.O.S. necklace near to his hand. When in trouble, this device would have called for help at the press of its button. For some reason he was unable to lift the plug which would have emptied the bath-water or click the bath-handle to get himself out of the bath.

His lean body had become a mottled blue colour, his fingernails were blue-black, as was much of his bearded face. His eyes and mouth were wide open. I shuddered as I thought the expression on his face must have stiffened when he had shouted for help. His death must have been agonisingly slow. I

178

was shocked and felt faint. I sat on a chair beside the bath for a few minutes to gather my senses.

I had sat on a chair which had on it his clean underwear and checked, woollen dressing gown. On a clothes horse close by was a well-pressed white shirt and a light, grey suit trousers and jacket. It appeared he had planned to dress smartly to go somewhere.

Avril's face was as grey as Mr Anderson's suit. She held her hand to her face to blot out the scene she had already witnessed.

'Pull yourself together, Avril. Go downstairs; the phone is on the hall table. Dial 999, wait until they've gone through the list of questions, then call Carole. I'll see what I can do up here.'

I didn't know what to do; where to start. Open the bath-door and get him out but let the water out first? I wasn't thinking straight and my old tutor's words came to mind, as they often did at such times. "You may panic, Nurse, but you may not show it". I wished I had someone to show it to.

I paused and took a deep breath; I felt I was about to vomit and if Mr Anderson couldn't let the water out how might I. I certainly didn't have the strength to get him out of the bath, whether the bath-door opened or not.

I took off my woollen Cardigan and rose the sleeve of the jumper underneath as far up my arm as I could. I closed my eyes as I leant over the bath-door, pushed Mr Andersons body out of my way to reach the bath plug. The plug had an extended arm attached to make the removing of it easy. I pulled it and it wouldn't budge. It was stuck fast. I snatched my arm away quickly before trying again. I huffed with relief to see that on my second attempt it functioned and the water began to drain away.

I hoped to be as successful with the latch of the bath-door but I was not. There was a special way (no doubt, an easy knack) to open the door and I didn't know it.

The ambulance arrived promptly as it always had. I heard heavy foot-steps stomp up the stairs.

'What do have here then?' came a thundering voice from a tall, smart uniformed, paramedic before he entered the bathroom. There were two paramedics.

Avril returned to the bathroom before the second one came in.

He said, 'Well, well, Jack. This is the second time for me to see this. There must be some manufacturing fault.'

'Never mind about a manufacturing fault', I snapped. 'Get Mr Anderson out and get him on a bed in one of the bedrooms.'

'All right, my lovely. Don't get all het up. You've had a bit of a shock.'

My shock was becoming anger as I laid a big bath towel onto the floor. I didn't like the thought of Mr Anderson's body being put on the cold tiles. 'I'll go and see which bed to put him on.'

The paramedic put his hand on the latch of the bath-door. It clicked open immediately.

I felt stupid. 'I've been struggling to open that until my fingers are raw. What was I doing wrong?'

'There's a special little lever under the handle. Never mind, now. Do as you said you would and lead us into the bedroom.'

That activity didn't go smoothly. The paramedics had to straighten Mr Anderson's arms, legs and body to get him out of the bath. He was stiff in death.

I had turned back the bed-sheets and as soon as Mr Anderson was on the bed I folded a warm blanket over him before covering him with the bedclothes. In retrospect I realised I had nursed him as if her were alive.

Avril waited in the porch until Carole arrived. She comforted Avril.

'It's a pity you had to see this, Avril. But if your working life is going to be as a nurse, you'll have to get used to seeing awful and sad things.'

Avril sobbed. 'I was hopeless. I couldn't do anything to help. Shirley did everything.'

'It's all right. She can manage instances like this, no trouble.' Carole, it seemed, had some false confidence in me. Yes, I think I managed the unfortunate, unexpected event correctly, but not easily. My emotions were in as much of a whirl as were Avril's.

I remember the look on Mr Anderson's face as if I had seen it yesterday. I was sad and angry that he died the way he did. He wanted to live and chose to die in his own home. At least, he was allowed that privilege. The suffering he must have endured before he breathed for the last time must have been beyond endurance. If there is a devil, he must have been responsible.

Carole had the more difficult part to play. She had to contact the close relatives and deal with the authorities. Avril and I had a few simple questions to answer.

I was pleased my main remit was training. I hoped I wouldn't be asked to conduct a home assessment again. However, I was and accepted with annoyance. I had fallen behind with the work I was employed to do but care of the residents always had to take priority.

Elaine apologised for having to ask me to carry out an assessment on an elderly man who had refused help from the social services or anyone except his daughter-in-law. I began to think Elaine didn't enjoy home assessments although I know there were one or two she couldn't avoid doing.

The man's condition had become beyond his daughter-in-law's ability to carry out the little care he allowed her to. He was known to be a cantankerous old nuisance, living in a filthy house.

On the day Elaine asked me to make the short visit to a Mr David Owen at Number 11, Cardiff Road, Nanty Bryn she had no qualified nurse on duty to stand-in to free her to do it herself. I was told it would be a short visit because up to that day the elderly man I was to visit had refused all interference with the way he lived.

'He'll see you, Shirley, because he has a painful toe which is interfering with him getting about. You'd better take your chiropody " tools".'

Since I had undertaken a short chiropody course some years before, I was considered an authority on foot-care, which was wrong. Treating corns, callouses and in-growing toenails was the limit of my knowledge and ability.

Elaine went on, feeling guilty for having to ask me. 'The coordinator of the social services told me they despair of Mr David Owen, but the neighbours have been complaining for months, so please go and see. Try to entice him to come here. We have a few empty rooms. His daughter-in-law called us and warned us that his house is filthy and you need to watch where you step or put your hands.'

'Sounds nice,' I smirked, 'but I want someone with me. Not Avril. She's not ready to see anything unpleasant after the last time she came with me. Can you spare Jim Craig?'

'If I must, because he's my senior carer. But yes. I don't think you'll be long and the house is close by, in Nanty Bryn.'

Jim Craig was a retired soldier and did a few days a week caring at The Nightingales to boost his pension. He was approaching middle age and seemed the right person to deal with Mr David Owen.

After the visit I knew of no-one else who would have been the right person. The degradation Jim and I witnessed that day will not be forgotten by either of us.

Chapter 16

NO PYJAMAS

I drew up directly outside Mr Owen's small terraced house. I was surprised to see it was opposite a health centre. I thought it would have been more convenient for someone from there to see him. I guessed there must be a reason.

The front room window of number eleven was boarded up from the inside, as are derelict houses. The stone door-step and flaking, rotting, yellow-painted door looked as if it hadn't been touched with a paint brush since the house was built, not much less than a hundred years ago. The door-step was a narrow stone, parallel with the pavement. The buttercup-yellow door must have been startling bright when it was painted.

'Well, Jim. You know the drill; begin your assessment as you approach the house. So what do you think about the yellow door?'

'I think Mr Owen must have a taste for pretty colours.' I grinned at his dry wit as he knuckle-knocked the door. We waited a few minutes; there was no answer. There was no knocker and the letter-box was a slit at the bottom of the door.

Jim knocked again; no response. 'Blow this,' he said as he turned the knob to open the door. 'He must be in.'

As soon as the door was ajar we heard a voice telling us to go in.

That was easier said than done. Jim had to shoulder-butt the door open. A waft of foul air made us both wince.

'That gives us the first clue of why he doesn't want anyone interfering with him,' Jim said, as he massaged his shoulder.

The door was jammed by the contents of the passage which led to the door of the living room and the bottom of the stairs. Behind the door was a large, bulging, cardboard box, dangerously overflowing with bicycle and motor-cycle parts. The end of a protruding bicycle wheel-guard sprang up and hit Jim's face, missing his eye by a blink.

'I'll be putting in for danger money after this,' he moaned with his hand covering his left eye.

'Let me have a look,' I said as I moved his hand from his face. 'It hasn't touched your eye, but nearly. It's just a small nick. Keep your dirty hands off it.'

The passage wall was behind layers of old, rusting bicycles, precariously fitted one behind and on top of the other, up to the stairs and up the stairway itself. It appeared to me that no-one had been to the bedrooms for a long time. It would have been dangerous, if it were possible, to have mounted the stairs.

'I wondered who pinched my old bike,' Jim whispered under puckered nostrils. 'Now I know, but I don't want it back.'

'Shush,' I quickly added. 'He's old, not deaf.'

We squeezed through, avoiding stepping in dog-muck and small mounds of other unidentifiable filth. There was a worn path between the rubbish and the wall.

We went into the middle room where Mr Owen was sitting in an upright chair beside a roaring coal fire. It was in a large well of an old black-leaded grate but it hadn't seen black-lead polish for a long time. I remembered how my mother took pride in her gleaming black-leaded grate when I was young. She riddled out the dead ash every morning and scooped it into a zinc bucket with a shovel. She then black-leaded the grate until it shone.

A large chest of drawers stood against the wall opposite to where Mr Owen sat. A number of bikes, intermingled, one on top of the other were stacked to the ceiling. The drawers overflowed with rags, papers, bicycle chains and other unrecognisable greasy bicycle parts.

Mr Owen was not a big man, neither was he small. It was difficult to tell from his position in the chair. His sparse, grey hair, looked overdue for a wash and a visit to the barber, as did his beard, which scraggily wilted down to his chest. It looked to me as if he had trimmed it himself.

His clothes were putrid; the front of, what was, a waste-coat and pin-striped trousers, were shining with slime.

'How be, Mr Owen,' Jim said. 'We've come to see how you're doing, living on your own like this.'

Mr Owen was smoking a sagging cigarette which he had rolled himself. On the table within his reach was a tin of rough-shag, tobacco, a packet of roll-your-own papers and an enamel kitchen bowl. The bowl was nearly full of fag-ends and burned tobacco. Mr Owen coughed and spluttered and before he spoke he stubbed out his cigarette on the pile in the bowl.

'No' on my own, Butty,' he said. 'Go' my telly and Boyo, here. Enough company for me.' The mention of the dog's name roused the animal from under Mr Owen's chair. It slid out and rubbed its head against its master's knee.

'Goo' boy,' Mr Owen said as, with coal-engrained hands with which he must have kept the fire banked up, he stroked Boyo; a mangy, scraggy greyhound. Coal-ash filled the hearth and spilled over on to where, once upon a time, a homely hearth-rug must have been. The ash and dross crunched under our feet with every step we took.

I noticed that Mr Owen's coal-cwtch (coal shed) was where the scullery usually is. He must have had a recent delivery of coal because slack, or small coal as I knew it, spilled into the living room.

In the corner of the room, the door of a walk-in-pantry, was blocked by a wide plank of wood on which was a small portable television.

'How do you turn your television on and off with all this stuff about, Dai?' Jim asked. 'Got a remote, have you?'

'Wha's tha'? Dai asked. 'I goes and presses the switch, o' course.' Jim decided not to go into an explanation about a remote control.

Parts of bikes were piled under the window on the right of the "scullery" door. They covered the sill and part upon part of bicycles were balanced precariously to the top. Any light which tried to penetrate the unwashed, cracked panes was shut out. The darkness was broken by a naked light bulb suspended from the ceiling in the middle of the room.

The stench of grease, filth, animal and human excreta was almost unbearable. I tried not to breath in unless I had to.

He must have noticed the look of disgust on my face which I thought I was hiding. There was a zinc bucket near his chair which he, obviously, used as a lavatory.

'Can't go to the lav see, gel,' he said. 'Bad toe.'

'Why don't you go across to the surgery, Mr Owen?' Jim asked.

'What! Go across to that rotten lot! They should be put behind bars, the lot of 'em!'

'Righto,' Jim frowned. 'I've got the gist of how you feel about the Services.' I couldn't but grin.

I was born and lived in a poor, rough valley until I married Derek. I travelled with him and lived and worked in developing countries where there was no sanitation or clean water on tap but I had never entered such a filthy home as poor David Owen lived in. I felt pity for this proud old man.

'Dai's my name, Gel,' he said. 'Worked down the pits until they shut up shop.' (Dai – Welsh colloquialism for David)

'Talking of shop, how do you get your food?' Jim asked. The top of the kitchen table in the middle of the room was hidden beneath stale food, half-eaten sandwiches, empty packs of fish and chips and a plate of bacon, swarming with maggots. I struggled not to retch. Again Mr Owen must have noticed my expression of distaste.

'Boyo'll eat tha',' he said. 'I gives 'im a bit now and again. It 'on't go to waste; he enjoys the maggots. I haves meals on

186

wheels and Cissy, my daughter-'n-law gets the rest. I pays her well, mind, but good as gold she is.'

'What do you intend doing with all these bike parts, Dai?' Jim asked.

'Make whole bikes like them up there and sell 'em.' Dai pointed to the top of the chest. They looked outdated bikes compared with my own second-hand lady's bike which I had when a teenager.

I remembered taking it to Old Mr Tamplin's bike shop when I had a puncture or the chain came off. His work-shop was in the front room of his house. It was always a greasy mess, too, but pristine compared with Dai's. Mr Tamplin lived with his family in a terraced house which was opposite my grandparent's.

Dai went on. 'Tha's what my old dad did. I helped him when I was made 'duntant from the pit. Work-shop's in there.' He pointed to the wall behind him to where the front room of the house was. I was born and lived in a terraced house similar to Mr Owen's. My mother looked upon her front room as her parlour, where the fire was lit on special occasions.

'Tha's why the winder's boarded up.' Dai looked sharply at Jim. 'It is boarded up isn' it?'

'Yes, Dai, the window is boarded up,' Jim answered. 'But it'll take years to make bikes out of this lot.'

Dai shook his head with determination. 'Not when this ol' leg's better.' Cissie's boy'll help me. I pays him good money, though.'

I interrupted. 'What's wrong with this foot of yours, Dai?'

'I don' kno'. You tell me and put it right. I's giving me bloody jip.'

"Jip" was a word I'd heard only from my miner father. He used it when he felt pain.

I looked down at Mr Owen's feet and recognised blue checked house-shoes similar to which my father used to wear. Old man's slippers, Derek called them.

'I needs my nails cut, I 'spect. In-growin' toe-nail. Used to have 'em wi' pit boots.'

The slippers were putrid; black and slimy. I had to hide my reluctance from dealing with them but deal with them I had to.

I took out two white plastic aprons from my carrier-bag which I kept in my arm-pit, having decided not to put it down anywhere. I laid one apron on the floor to kneel on and one on the front of myself. As I knelt down I had to tell Mr Owen to get the dog out of the way. He growled the dog's name as he punched him and Boyo slinked under the chair from whence he had come.

What I saw I had not seen before but had heard of such, otherwise I would not have thought it possible. Dai's toe-nails had grown through the front of his slippers. The smell was almost beyond bearing and I recognised mortification – dead flesh.

'Dai, I'll have to cut your slipper off. I think your foot is infected,' I spoke as I breathed out.

'Will 'ou? Haven't been off for long time. Can' bend down see.'

'It will be less painful if I cut it off. Is that alright?'

'If 'ou have to 'en. Go on. Cissie'll get some from the charity shop for me. Cissie, my daughter-'n-law. Good as gold to me,' he repeated.

Jim was holding my chiropody case. He kept it in one hand and unzipped it with the other. 'Pass me those big scissors, Jim.' As he did so he spoke to Dai.

'Dai, why don't you come into our nursing home. You'd be more comfortable there.'

I was putting on a pair of latex gloves which I'd kept in my tunic pocket.

'What! Go to the workhouse. Not likely. An' what about Boyo, here. Who'd look after him? Don' talk to me about them holes of Hell.'

I had managed to slice the front of the stiff, tough material down to the end of his toes. He winced with pain. I was surprised he didn't yell out because the pain must have been excruciating. As I slipped it from his foot a stream of yellowy-green puss poured out. A clump of maggots wriggled in a space behind the heel of his foot. I eased off the slipper. The foot was black and gangrenous; infected to above his ankle and creeping towards his calf.

Jim made a quick exit. He couldn't get to the front door quick enough because of the junk. He picked up a metal bowl from the pile and vomited into it.

'Sorry, Shirl,' he kecked. I didn't comment; I knew how he was feeling.

'Jim, take that bowl to the tap in the scullery, swill it out and bring in some water. I'll have to wash this but there's nothing much more I can do.' I looked up at Dai. 'Dai, you'll have to go to hospital.'

'Not likely,' he responded angrily. 'Once you in one o'them 'ou don' come out.'

Jim had difficulty getting to the tap and even more difficulty getting the bowl of water back without spilling some.

Dai put his foot slowly and gradually into the water. He winced all of the time. 'Bloody cold, this water,' was his only comment. His pain threshold was high or he didn't wish to show weakness.

I swished the water over the foot and calf with a sterile pad which I always kept in my case, until the water was too foul to be effective. I asked Jim to take it out the back. He didn't step off the back step to thrown the water away. The yard was under a mound of household rubbish.

I waited until he was in the room to hear what I had to say. 'Mr Owen,' I said. 'I am not a doctor but I can tell you, if you don't get this foot seen to in hospital as soon as possible, you'll lose it.'

Dai looked worried. 'Can' you do it? I can' go to 'ospital? Got no pyjamas.'

'That won't matter. Many people go into hospital without pyjamas or anything else. They won't care about that; it's your foot they'll be concerned with and I can tell you it's not good.'

He paused and scratched his balding head. 'I don' think I'll go to 'ospital. I'll stay here and wait for it to get better.'

I guessed that Dai knew exactly how bad his foot was but he was afraid. He knew it wouldn't get better but not that it

189

could kill him. I decided to go deeper into the possibilities of the outcome.

'You must do as you wish, Dai, but not only could you lose your foot if you don't go into the hospital, you could lose your leg up to the knee.

If I'd spoken truthfully I would have told him he would lose his life if he didn't have his leg treated as an emergency.; Septicaemia would kill him.

'Jim and I will go back now and get in touch with your daughter-in-law and tell her what I've told you. You must think seriously about it and if you decide to go into the hospital some-one will arrange an ambulance to take you. Dai, they'll do everything they can to get your leg better: You ought to give them a chance.'

Dai burst into tears. 'Oh, Boyo. Wha' am I to do?' I felt like embracing him but I was repulsed. I couldn't put by body onto his slimy clothes.

I asked Jim to pass me a couple of sterile pads and a bandage from my case. I poured at least, half a dozen sachets of saline over the mortifying foot before I dressed it with the pads and bandages before I rose from my knees, leaving the plastic apron under his foot.

'I's feeling better already,' he smiled revealing a mouthful of black dentures.

Jim had been watching closely. 'It's not better, Dai. Now think of what Nurse has told you. I promise you, you will be well looked after.'

He looked beaten. 'But I go' no pyjamas.'

'A lot of people don't have pyjamas, Dai. We have to go now. I'll see what can be done to get you into hospital today. Is that all right? Jim is right and before you come back here the house will have to have a cleaning. Ask Cissie or your grandson to look after your dog.'

Mr David Owen was ill, though he played down the extent of his condition. 'Aye, I suppose you're right. Go' to get this foot right.' He looked up at me. 'Will 'ou be in the 'ospital, Nurse?'

'No, Dai. I used to work there but I work in The Nightingale Nursing Homes now. I'll see you there when you come out of hospital.'

He looked disappointed and worried. 'Ay, all right, then.'

'So-long Dai, and good luck.' Jim sounded cheerful. You'll do better after a spell in our nursing home when you come out of hospital. You can't come back here until it's tidied up a bit.'

'Tidied up!' Jim sounded surprised. 'I's good enough as it is for the bikes I sell. There's one in the work-shop ready to go. Tha's a motor-bike, though. Cissie's boy's been working on it. You can have a look if you like. Give the door a good kick to open it.'

As we sidled our way through the passage, making our way to the front door Jim decided to do as Dai suggested. He kicked open the front room door, dislodging a protruding piece of metal which jumped up and nicked the calf of my leg. I knew without looking that my leg had been cut. A small blob of blood pushed itself through my tights. I knew they had been ruined.

'Sorry, Shirl. Is your leg hurt?' Jim sounded furtive.

'Yes, and my tights are a goner. Good thing my tetanus jab is up to date. Is yours?' He didn't answer my question; he wasn't concerned about my cut or my tights.

'Good God, look at this!'

I looked further into the room with only a faint light beaming in through the dim passage. All I could see was a motor-cycle and the slight sparkle of its chrome fittings.

'A brand new motor bike?' I wondered.

'As good as new and better if this is an old BSA. It was the tops in the sixties and is now sought after by biker enthusiasts as far as I know. I think it's worth a lot.'

'Never mind that now, Jim. Let's get him into Nevill Hall. And this place has to be ransacked and fumigated whether he likes it or not. It's a health hazard.'

We made our way to the front door carefully. The passage was just wide enough for us to squeeze out. This must be the way Cissie comes in and out,' he suggested. 'God help her.

She's a saint to put up with it. Aye, bu' I pays her well.' He mimicked Mr Owen. I couldn't but grin.

When outside on the narrow pavement Jim and I gasped in the damp, nectar-like cold air.

'I can't understand why his daughter-in-law let it get so bad,' I said. 'She liked his payment, I expect, but didn't think much of him.'

I went straight up to the office Carole and I shared before calling Elaine from the duty-room office. I wanted her to hear what I had to say about my visit to the infamous Mr David Owen. I described the state of his leg and that if he didn't get prompt treatment he could die, and we should avoid having that on our consciences. I gave my view that he wasn't mentally infirm. He understood it was a Hobson's choice he had to make.

I was aware of a strong, unpleasant smell of 11, Cardiff Road about me as I explained the events of the assessment. Carole intermittently sprayed the air with air freshener. Unpleasant or not, it was important that I gave an account of mine and Jim Craig's afternoon's visit when it was fresh in my mind.

I admitted, that in my opinion, Mr Owen should be admitted to the hospital as soon as possible and it would be advisable to contact his daughter-in-law and have the situation explained to her. Elaine interrupted at that point.

'I think she knows how bad he is. That's why she called for help.' I agreed with Elaine.

I felt my knowledge of community politics lacking. I didn't know at this stage whether Mr David Owen was our responsibility or the social services' or The Homes' I didn't think anyone did, but informed Elaine and Carole that I would write a report and explain the situation as I saw it, but I hoped that one day we would see Dai in The Nightingale Homes. He was an old miner; I've always had a bit of special respect for them. My father was a miner for nearly fifty years.

I hoped Mr David Lewis would accept admission to the hospital where the doctors would do the best for him and try to save his limb; or at least part of it. I hoped he would receive the nursing care he deserved. I thought he could be in their hands for a long period. The stories we were hearing of bad hospital care went through my mind and I wasn't sure he would be.

That indiscriminate indictment of my profession is, perhaps, unfair. But it was a thought that sprung to my mind which, less than ten years ago, wouldn't have.

Chapter 17

WHATEVER ROWS YOUR BOAT

On the afternoon of Mr David Lewis's assessment, followed by the information I had given to Carole, I left work early. She understood why: I was smelling of filth. However, before I left I put my report in writing.

When I arrived home I let myself in, only to snatch a towel from the downstairs toilet. I wanted to avoid the stench lingering in the house. I undressed down to my bra and pants in the garage and wrapped the towel about me to sneak into the house unseen. Then I took a long, long shower.

That night, gangrenous feet, maggots and dirty dogs haunted my sleep.

I wondered if our honourable leaders knew that people were living in the conditions Jim and I had witnessed. I assume they must have informants so I think it might remain either beyond their comprehension, or they considered other national issues on their agenda to be more important. I wondered how far down the list care of the elderly and infirm was. Notwithstanding Mr David Lewis's low social standing choice of life-style, I hoped he would be treated with the respect he deserved, as all others did. The bad reports of nursing care have made it clear that patients in hospitals are not always treated as they should be, no matter what their social stranding might be.

The media had strongly made the nation aware of the cruelty and wickedness of how the elderly were being treated. I hear and read nothing about how the problem is being dealt with.

"There is none so blind as he who does not wish to see."

My work at The Nightingale Nursing Homes made me aware of the fact that there are millions "passing through the net". The care is no better in 2014 as it was then, in 1998.

Francis Hardy's report in *The Daily Mail* (Saturday, May 31, 2014) of the cruel treatment of Laura Lamberty's 45 year old mother is indicative of how the sick and debilitated continue to be cared for.

"Acute pain had reduced Margaret Lambert to almost animalistic desperation. The nurses' sole concern, as she writhed in agony, was that she was disturbing other patients."

Laura Lamberty, the daughter of the "victim" of the University Hospital of North Staffordshire, took a photograph of her mother when she was suffering treatment from which she died. The photograph takes up a large section of the article:

"In a photo that's horrified Britain, a dying woman crawls in agony on a hospital floor as nurses laugh and joke nearby. Here, her daughter tells a story of cold-blooded neglect that'll appall you".

These words were said by Francis Hardy, a reporter of that newspaper. She reported: Laura was admitted to the hospital with agonising stomach pain after a 999 call. She was forced to prostrate herself – literally to crawl on her hands and knees like a stricken animal in her attempt to get help …

When Margaret's condition deteriorated, some nine hours after she was taken to the hospital, Laura, her daughter, had tried to summon a nurse by pressing the buzzer at her mother's bedside.

When no-one arrived after half an hour, Laura went to the nurses' station to find the nurses were laughing and joking and drinking tea. When Laura asked one of the nurses if she could give her mother some pain relief she was told she "would have to wait her turn".

Francis Hardy's long article about this one incident puts our national health system into shameful disgrace. It must have appalled all who read it. The care within our system hasn't changed since earlier articles in the late nineties.

Margaret Lamberty's treatment is not unique. I have witnessed such treatment and I cringed when I read the excuses of Mark Hacket, the hospital's chief executive. He claimed that the situation is not as clear cut as it seems since Mrs Lamberty was very ill with a number of serious conditions when she came into hospital and the clinicians "sought to deal with those".

Laura Lamberty claims that any interest taken in her mother's condition came too late. She died when she might have lived if she had been treated with skill, compassion and professionalism

When I read this *Daily Mail* article, I had no doubt of the truth of it: it happens.

Some months after the visit to the home of Mr David Owen at Cardiff Street, Jim beckoned me to join him across the lounge. He was playing draughts with one of our residents. He left his resident and prompted me aside so he could speak to me out of the earshot of others.

I sat opposite him. 'What juicy secret have you to tell me, Jim? Bit of hush-hush gossip. I don't take much notice of gossip, but go on.' I lied; I was all agog to hear what he had to tell me.

'You remember us going to old Dai Owen's house?'

'Will I ever forget? Poor old thing. What about him?'

'He put up a good fight to carry on his life but sadly lost. He must have let himself get too low. But poor, you said! Poor! He left a small fortune! He could have lived in comfort for the rest of his life. No wonder Cissie looked after him. She must have known he was well off.'

I was amazed. 'You're saying he could have lived in the best home in the country, wherever that is, and he chose to life in that filth?'

'Yes. Pity, isn't it,' Jim said. 'He could have enjoyed a life of luxury.'

'Jim,' I said sharply. 'What makes you think he didn't consider he didn't enjoy his life?'

'Yes, you're right. It depends on what rows your boat, as they say.'

Chapter 18

BEST IN COMFORT

Two months after my assessment of Mr David Lewis I was asked to carry out a home assessment on an elderly lady who was ill. She was living in undesirable circumstances and chose to remain in her own home but was not capable of caring for herself. Her name was Mrs Lilian Hutton.

'Can I have Amanda to come with me,' I asked. 'It's quite a while since we had the shock of Mrs Moore and Amanda must get used to the community side of nursing. She must know that it's not all sweetness.'

Amanda displayed some reluctance but agreed to come with me.

We arrived at Mrs Hutton's house just before eleven o'clock. Her house was one in a row of prefabricated houses, similar to the house Mrs Moore had lived in, but less dilapidated.

I watched a smile become a frown. 'I hope she's alive and kicking,' Amanda said, as she stared with a doubtful expression.

'Of course, she is,' I replied, with less confidence than I displayed. Amanda's thought was going through my mind. 'Every home and every person living in it is unique. I hope you've learned that much since being a carer.'

I drew up at the curb directly outside Mrs Hutton's door. There were a few other cars parked in the street but it was quiet. I couldn't imagine a traffic policeman strolling down it, even if there had been double yellow lines.

The front gate squeaked on it hinges as I opened it and the small patch of greenery in front of the house hadn't been cultured, but it was neat.

'At least the gate is in place,' Amanda said. 'And the windows don't have rags for curtains.'

As I locked the car Amanda rapped the knocker. 'And it has …' she was about to say, "a knocker." but instead, said with surprise, 'Oh, the door is open.'

As I knocked the Perspex door I pushed it more ajar and called out, "Mrs Hutton, we're the nurses. Can we come in?'

I heard a bell ringing followed by a weak voice which called out, 'Yes, please come in.' It was similar to the old bell I remembered of my early school days, which rang loudly and persistently to call for morning assembly and at home time.

The sound of that bell, I've thought since, must have been as welcome to our teachers as it was to us pupils.

The air in the small hallway was stale and smelled of grease; cooking lard, I guessed. The bell clanged again and I followed the sound. Mrs Hutton was only a few yards away, sitting in a big, upright armchair.

We greeted her and I introduced Amanda and myself. Mrs Dutton gasped and smiled. My first observation was that she was suffering from acute breathlessness.

'Sorry,' she gasped. 'Can't talk much.'

'That's all right, Mrs Hutton. Amanda and I will do most of the talking and not enough to tire you. You look tired enough.'

She nodded. 'Haven't taken my pills yet.' The short sentence was said with difficulty.

'Would you like Amanda to make us a cup of tea and I'll help you to take them?' She nodded a little more vigorously.

Amanda disappeared into the tiny kitchen. She was there for a longer time than I expected. She told me afterwards that the tea-pot and kettle were easily found but not the tea, sugar and milk. There was no fresh milk; she found a tin of powdered milk.

The kitchen was unclean, cluttered and smelled of mould and dampness. The work-tops were hidden under all things which should have been in the cupboards. There was a grease-engrained gas cooker with a black iron frying pan containing a pork chop. It was half burned and half undercooked, smothered with congealed cooking lard. Mrs Hutton must have tried to cook herself a meal yesterday, or even the day before, and didn't succeed.

While we waited for Amanda to bring the tea I, discreetly, questioned Mrs Hutton. She was ill and if she felt as I do when I'm just off-colour, she wouldn't want to chat, and certainly not be questioned.

I gathered she was seventy-five but she looked older. Her face wasn't wrinkled but puffed out from, what I guessed to be, steroid medication. It has side effects which are known to include weight gain and sometimes gives the face a "moon shape" appearance. She appeared overweight, but I guessed that she was, adversely, retaining fluid because of her poor physical condition. Acute Oedema is a condition which, in my days as an RGN, was treated in a hospital medical ward.

She told me that she had difficulty in walking, even to the kitchen, toilet or bedroom. I happened to look to the back of me, seeming as though I was looking for Amanda to bring the tea. I caught a glimpse of Mrs Hutton's bedroom. I couldn't see her bed but I guessed it hadn't been slept in.

'Do you sleep in your chair at night?' I asked her.

She gasped before nodding. 'Can't get to bed and lie down. I want to be nearer the commode.'

She thought she wasn't making herself clear because of her breathlessness. I felt cruel questioning her but I decided that this lady needed twenty-four hour care near an oxygen cylinder and the only place she could get that was in a long stay NHS bed, which was unlikely, or a good nursing home. In some instances it is possible to receive oxygen therapy at home but there are dangers to be considered, especially that of fire. Mrs Dutton had been suffering with chronic heart failure for some time and didn't want to leave her home in case her children came back. She'd had four children; two had died and the other two were abroad.

I pointed to the scores of framed snaps, photographs and pictures of happy scenes scattered throughout the room on shelves, ledges and the window sills. I told her I understood the sentimentality and why she wanted to remain in her own home. I pointed to them and nodded to prevent her having to tell me about them, which I knew she wanted to. She told me her son and daughter were in Australia; she'd visited them twice and they had come home a few times.

'Can't go again,' she said. 'Too far and …' she put her hand on her chest and gasped. 'Can't breathe.'

'And you think they might want to come home at sometime?'

She nodded.

'You can't walk very far, can you?' She shook her head.

I spoke as I looked down at her ankles. She raised her skirt to reveal her cold, blue-mottled legs. They were swollen up to her thighs. I gently pressed her foot and ankle and as I guessed, my fingerprints remained deeply pitted.

Amanda arrived with a tray laden with a teapot, three mugs, milk and sugar. 'You'll feel better after you've taken your pills, I expect,' Amanda said, as she fumbled to find a safe space on a nearby bedside table.

The table was cluttered with a dish of porridge which looked as if it were there the day before, two mugs half full of some sort of fluid and cartons with the remains of fish and chip meals.

'Who gets the fish and chips for you, Mrs Hutton?' I asked.

She gasped. 'Little girl in end house' She pointed to the left.

Amanda put a mug of tea within Mrs Hutton's reach and pointed to the sugar and milk with a questioning expression. Mrs Hutton nodded and smiled. 'Thank you. You're very nice.'

I asked where her medication was kept. She pointed over her shoulder to the dresser against the front wall of the house.

An ice cream carton containing the medication was on the shelf of the dresser. I detected that she'd not been taking her regular doses. A wave of pity washed through me. I guessed she was suffering too much to get the carton or administer her own medication. I considered she was acutely ill and needed to be hospitalised.

The regime of medication was clearly arranged in a plastic strip. It was designed to ensure the correct pills and capsules are taken at the prescribed times. Beside the carton was a familiar type of inhaler which, when used correctly, assisted breathing. It was empty of inhalant. She hadn't taken any of yesterday's doses and I was of the opinion the community nurses had been calling on her to ensure she had them. Anger flared up inside me which I couldn't reveal to Mrs Hutton. The last thing she needed was for me to ask for an explanation of what had gone wrong. She needed twenty-four hour care but was receiving nowhere near that.

I selected the medication which Mrs Hutton was due for. Amanda helped her to take them and I excused myself to go to the toilet. It gave me an opportunity to look around. The house needed a good cleaning throughout. I saw her bed and as I guessed, it hadn't been slept in and I understood why. The room smelled of dampness. Mrs Hutton couldn't get to it as ill as she was at that time and the bed wasn't designed to allow her to sleep in an upright position to aid her breathing.

I knelt on the floor beside her and waited until she'd had her medication. One was a diuretic, the effect of which would help to relieve the fluid retention of her body. Opposite her chair, at the side of a gas fireplace, was a commode. Someone had acquired it, realising that Mrs Hutton's urgent need to pass urine wouldn't allow her to get to the toilet in time. The pungent ammoniac smell of stale urine wafting from where she sat told me that she didn't have time to get to the commode, either.

A television set was on the other side of the fireplace. Amanda and I talked quietly to Mrs Hutton, avoiding any questions which would cause her to become more breathless. She gasped between every word and I recognised she felt bad.

'Do you watch a lot of television?' Amanda asked.

Mrs Hutton nodded and held up a remote control which had slipped down the side of her chair.

Amanda and I had been with Mrs Hutton for longer than we had anticipated. My fault; I prolonged the suggestion of her coming into The Nightingale Nursing Homes.

'You are finding it difficult to look after yourself, Mrs Hutton. I can see how bad you feel. Would you like me to call a doctor and arrange for you to go into the hospital for treatment?'

She rigorously shook her head. The loose flesh of her chins wobbled with determination. 'Never,' she replied.

'No, and I can understand why. How about coming into The Nightingales. Your children will know where to come, if they come home, and it's not far from here.'

We got the same response. Amanda came up with a good suggestion.

'Why not come to The Nightingales for, what is called, respite care? It will be for a week or a fortnight – just until you are back on your feet.'

'Amanda is right, Mrs Hutton. You'll have a lovely room of your own, the carers will see that you have your pills at the right time, they'll help you to wash and dress and they'll help you to the commode, which will be put in your room. There'll be plenty of pillows on your bed so you can sleep sitting up, if you want to.'

Mrs Hutton accepted. 'Just for a week,' she didn't gasp so heavily. The thought of comfort relieved the stress and eased the difficulty of breathing in.

She had a telephone which she wouldn't have been able to use even if she wanted to; she was too breathless to speak on it. I rang her GP surgery, explained the situation and asked the receptionist to arrange an ambulance.

Within an hour an ambulance came. The paramedics chatted cheerfully as they wrapped her in warm blankets and transported her to The Nightingale Nursing Homes. She was admitted to the care of the elderly unit; The Bedford Home. They put an oxygen mask to her face from which she took large gulps. She was soon washed, dressed in comfortable clean clothes and placed between crisp, pristine bed sheets.

It was lunch time. Amanda had joined the team to help with the meals and Elaine, the nurse in charge, did as I suggested; she called Mrs Hutton's G.P.

The G.P. was a lady doctor. She changed Mrs Hutton's medication and said she'd call the next day. If Mrs Hutton's condition hadn't improved, then admission to a medical ward at The Nevill Hall Hospital would be arranged.

Mrs Hutton didn't want that to happen. She was feeling much better by the following morning and remained at the nursing home.

In fact, Mrs Hutton was happy and became better in health. She didn't leave The Bedford Home. Her prefabricated house remained vacant.

Amanda was delighted with the outcome. She had helped and told me the experience was a good learning exercise: A happy ending.

I continued nurse training at The Nightingale Nursing Homes for the next four months. The term "carer" had taken the place of "nurse" and to this day I do not understand why. But I've got used to it. I look upon it as "nursing" as did Florence Nightingale, although she had her Ladies and Probationers.

I was retiring from Nursing. I did no more assessments; the homes were satisfactorily established. It was a good time to leave. My mind was on retirement so I concentrated on seeing as many as possible of my NVQ candidates complete the course. I told those who needed help that they could contact me at home.

It was in September 1999 I resigned from The Nightingale Nursing Homes. I had far overstayed my intended time there. I had put off leaving.

The Chief Executive asked me to remain with them as a training consultant but during the time I was making up my mind whether to accept that commitment I decided it was time for a clean break. I was approaching my 66th birthday.

PART 2

Chapter 19

EXCEL COMMUNITY CARE

I enjoyed being a full-time housewife for a while. I busied myself doing a hundred and one jobs that had been waiting for my retirement.

The first thing I did was to clear my wardrobe of clothes I hadn't worn since the 1950s and 60s and black-bagged them for OXFAM. I cleared out a score or more of untidy drawers and cupboards and ransacked our shared study. Derek looked worried when he arrived home and found three black bags in the porch awaiting the refuse truck.

'I hope there's nothing of importance in those bags, Shirley. You should have waited for me to check.' I had a moment of panic.

'Well, the bags haven't gone yet; you can still check.' I was glad he didn't take me up on that because, for security reasons, I'd torn most of the papers to bits before discarding them. I should have shred them but that would have taken too long

For some hours each day I spent going over short stories I had written over the past years and had stored them in box-files in our "glory hole". Until I had my computer and got the hang of its rudiments I had typed on a honky-tonk old Jones portable which I'd bought for Derek's Christmas present some years ago. He had discarded it for a sophisticated computer.

After about two months I was beginning to get used to life without routine: time tables, marking NVQ exercises, home assessments and having to get smartly dressed to leave the house by ten o'clock. However, I missed the company.

I had just about mastered the basic complexities of my new personal computer and was getting stuck in to all the stories I wanted to proof read, when I had a phone call. It put my creative writing on "hold" yet again.

The call was from the director of a private community care company in Abergavenny, about four miles from where I live. Eileen Hunter had heard about me from my close friend, Erika Powell, who, like myself, had been in a managerial position at The Nightingale Nursing Homes. She had left there and was already working for the company, Excel Community Care.

Erika had left The Nightingale Homes after having a disagreement with the Chief Executive, as I had. He had agreed to meet the NVQ cost of three carers on night duty but changed his mind when the invoices arrived. I was disappointed by his changed principles; he had always budgeted for a generous training allowance.

Eileen Hunter asked if I would call in to see her at the headquarters in Abergavenny. She and I were acquaintances so I had no qualms in asking her why she wanted to see me.

'If I tell you, you won't come,' she said.

My curiosity was well roused. 'Yes I will, but give me a clue as to what you want me for.'

'We are desperate for a nurse-training manager,' she said. 'I know you are enjoying a well-deserved retirement, but I need someone now, to formulate an induction programme for community carers and to teach the basic nursing care yourself. Training for community carers has become legalised. I don't have the time to spend on advertising and I want someone who I know is right for this job. Just for a couple of months, honest.'

'Well now, this retirement isn't what it's cracked up to be, so I'll come and have a natter. Shall I come tomorrow?'

'What are you doing this afternoon?' she asked.

I laughed. 'My goodness, you do sound desperate. I have to go to the bank later so how about three o'clock.'

I arrived at Monmouth House, the headquarters of the company, a little after three. At half-past four I left there having committed myself to three days a week as Training Manager.

Monmouth House was old but tastefully decorated and furnished. Eileen saw me down the stairs from her office on the second floor to the reception area, which was a large conservatory that had been constructed at the back of the building. There was a smart young lady, partly hidden by a computer screen and the company's switchboard. She stood up and smiled a greeting.

I was impressed by the many tropical plants filling the wide sills. They threw a pleasant pale green light throughout the glass structure. The general atmosphere was pleasant.

'Derek won't be pleased when I tell him about this, Eileen,' I said.

She smiled broadly, relieved that I had agreed to work out a training programme for the Excel Community Care Company.

'Call in at the butchers and get a couple of nice steaks, get a bottle of wine and light some candles. Get him in a good mood before you tell him.'

I laughed; I felt happy to be getting back to work for a few months. Those few months extended to three exciting and happy years.

Eileen Hunter had a strong but approachable personality; she knew how to manage people. She was caring, fair and shrewd. She was one of three directors of the successful private care company. In fact, it was she who got it off the ground. It had become a thriving and well established business. It seemed there was a good relationship between herself and her two partners, who were man and wife. They had the money to start the business, Eileen had the managerial and administrative skills.

A strong link existed between Excel Community Care Company and the social services throughout the county and beyond. Care of the elderly and infirm on our community was the aim of both organisations.

Excel Community Care had in the region of a hundred and fifty community carers working for them. I didn't know the number of community carers that were with the social services but it wasn't enough to meet the demand of the elderly who were struggling to cope in their own homes. I was aware of that as a result of my work at The Nightingale Nursing Homes. Hence, carers employed by Excel Community Care bridged the gap.

My remit was to formulate aims and objectives for an induction course in basic nursing care, organise it into an eight week course and teach and assess the abilities of the carers.

Many who attended the course were already community carers but had had no formal training. Some had been doing the work for a long time and had been known as Home Helps. I would be training them to become official personal carers. There was a difference and I was now faced with a challenge that was new to me.

I was given the reigns of organising the training programme in my own way – the "old fashioned way" – before Project 2000.

I was allocated a large room on the third floor of the building. In the glorious days of Monmouth House, it must have been the servants' rooms but the dividing walls had been knocked down to make three large rooms. They were too cold for comfort in the winter, stifling hot in the summer.

The last family that had lived there left a few pieces behind which I made use of. Fitted bookshelves, a fitted wardrobe and a single bed with a hard mattress. There was a cupboard attached to the wall under the sloping roof which was useful for storing all learning equipment: toiletries, towels and spare linen, though there was little of that. I provided a pair of bed sheets and pillows. Laura Jane, Mrs Hunter's daughter provided a well-worn duvet cover and a few more pillows.

Laura Jane and one of the other administrators were given money out of Eileen's petty cash to go into town to buy bits and pieces from a list I had provided to equip the room as near as possible to a sick room of a small house.

I was reminded of the practical room in what we had called "the chicken cot" when I began my training at The New Nevill Hall Hospital, but which is no longer "new". My practical room wasn't as sophisticated as that. It wasn't as big, it didn't have a skeleton hanging in the corner of the room, or a variety of equipment in its cupboards, but it had what I needed for teaching basic nursing care, including Mrs Bedford, a life-size doll patient.

I was surprised to find a commode-chair among the pieces that were left by the previous tenants. It was antiquated but would serve its purpose. It must have been used for someone who had been nursed in the old days of Monmouth House, when it was a home. All proved very useful teaching aids, though old and worn. The commode didn't have wheels, nor did the bed have the mechanism to higher or lower it which we had in the old "chicken cot" at The New Nevill Hall Hospital. There was a bed there which was identical to the beds that had been on the wards at that time.

One of the carers raised her arm to let me know she had something to tell me. 'Mrs Phillips,' she said, 'do you think the rooms of the people we look after have commodes and soft towels and the beds are covered with fine sheets? They should be so lucky. And duvets? Many of them haven't heard of them. In some homes with the lav out the back they don't even have a toilet roll. Luxury that would be.'

'Do you think I don't know that?' I replied sharply. 'I didn't start nursing yesterday. Not only have I seen what you are seeing these days, I was born and raised in similar circumstances. In fact, the lavatory, where I was born and lived, was out in the back yard, up a flight of rough stone steps. It was next to the coal-cwtch. The lavatory wasn't very comfortable during the day, let alone in the middle of a cold, wet night. We were lucky, the people living in the nearby streets had to share lavatories.

'And those poor people you look after in the future **will** have toilet rolls and many other things for their comfort because you are going to tell them how to get them. And I will tell you how to go about it. That's one of the reasons I'm here.' I spoke with determination in my tone, as I meant to.

I knew there were elderly people living in bad conditions because they didn't know how to acquire help or even know what was available to them.

I didn't go into my experiences of the poverty I had been made aware of when I was a voluntary worker in Ghana, Aden and Nigeria. The conditions of the poor there have to be seen to be believed.

I managed to get what I wanted to make our practical room equipped well enough for teaching purposes but, initially, the most important piece of equipment was missing – Mrs Bedford, the adult-size doll. However, with some ingenuity and underhandedness, I managed to get a life-size doll to make the practical room complete.

With help, I retrieved it from The Nightingale Nursing Homes. It belonged to me. It was given to me by Age Concern as a teaching aid of First Aid. They didn't want it themselves; it was falling apart.

I decided to retrieve it and involved Carole and Erika, my two friends and colleagues in the plot. It would have been no use asking the Chief Executive to hand it over; he considered it belonged to him since it was on his premises.

'After all, it was given to you,' Erika said. 'We'll go and get it when it's quiet there.'

And that's what we did, one late evening in September, just as it was getting dark. We were like thieves in the night as Erika and I, carried the heavy coffin-like case from The Nightingale Nursing Homes' small lecture room, in which the "dummy patient" was stored. We carried it to my open car boot directly outside the main door. Carole carried an arm and a leg which had fallen off when we put Mrs Bedford from a chair into her case.

The exercise was sneaky and smacked of dishonesty but we had lots of laughs when we later talked about it. Erika pointed out an issue that hadn't entered my mind.

'If anyone had pinched your car that night he would have had a hell of a shock finding a body in a coffin in your boot!'

We called her Mrs Bedford which was the name of the male or female-size doll in the practical room where I began nurse training.

During the last of my teaching sessions, her head continually fell away from her body in spite of string, layers of cello-tape and sticking plaster. One of her glass eyes was missing; I think it must have been thrown out with the rubbish. When I left Excel Community Care I left Mrs Bedford behind. I didn't have the heart to throw her away. She had served me well as a teaching aid and gave us lots of laughs.

The induction programme consisted of two three-hour teaching sessions a week, on the afternoons of Tuesdays and Thursdays. The number of carers that attended varied between twelve and fifteen.

Forty per cent of carers in each training session were middle-aged women who had had no "learning stuff" since they'd left school at fifteen. They had been "home helps". Some hadn't read a book since leaving school. On being told that attending the course was compulsory, they weren't pleased. I think they were afraid. On training days there was a rush for seats at the back and corners of the room. However, that fear was overcome. They were surprised to find themselves enjoying the lessons.

At the end of the course everyone had to sit a written test. I wasn't surprised by the apprehension of this. Some of the older carers could barely write. It was a multi-choice question paper on which a tick had to be made at the side of, what was thought, the correct answer. Having this explained to them and shown an example of the question paper, the feelings of unease dissipated. It was compulsory for them and myself, as proof of the course being in existence and that learning had taken place.

I had an excellent rapport with my learners. They reminded me of women like my mother and her friends and neighbours. Literacy was a stranger to them but their caring for the needy was as compassionate as I'd ever encountered.

Some of those in the younger groups, eighteen to twenty-five, were with the company for experience of caring for the sick and elderly as they waited for invitation to be interviewed for professional training at the University of Glamorgan.

Some of the older ones had already been carrying out personal care for years and, no doubt, could have taught me. They had learned as they went along, from each other and from their own experiences. Being on an educational project was foreign to them, yet I found them a captive audience.

Coming to the classroom for an afternoon's learning turned out to be enjoyed and looked forward to. It was, also, an opportunity for them to be together. The nature of their work made this a rare occasion.

We had a ten minute break halfway through each session during which gossip and chats about good times and bad were exchanged.

The people I taught didn't do the work solely for the salary. The financial remuneration was at the legal basic rate. They could have earned more in the factories and supermarkets. They did it because they enjoyed caring for the sick and elderly in their homes and they could arrange their hours conveniently to fit in with their own domestic responsibilities.

One mature, experienced carer, Cheryl Morgan worked every hour she could, aiming to earn enough money to take her two daughters to New York in the autumn. Her thirty plus year old bachelor brother was going with them. None of them had ever flown before or been out of the UK.

Cheryl's age was past forty. She told me and the others in the classroom that her husband abandoned her when her daughters were little.

'He changed me for a younger model,' she laughingly said. 'No loss to me but it was for my girls; their father not loving them enough to stay with us. I missed his financial support more than I missed him. He sent me five pounds a week until his floozy had a baby. I don't suppose she'd let him give to us then, not that five pounds did much towards our keep. I managed to squeeze a few quid out of him, from time to time, when the girls needed something I couldn't afford, but I gave up trying in the end.

'I couldn't pay the rent on our house and was kicked out, but I had good parents. Me and my kids moved in with them and my brother. I nursed them until, first my mother passed on then only months later my father died. The house was their own and they passed it on to me and my brother. Things worked out great, and now, America, here we come!'

We all cheered when she ended the short story of that part of her life. Her colleagues in her training group admired her. They knew she worked every hour God and Excel Care could give her, until she nearly dropped with fatigue. Whenever anyone wanted help or an extra pair of hands, they knew Cheryl's would be available.

We all knew she had been saving for two years to take her daughters to America. Her brother had been saving for the holiday, too. It was going to be the holiday of a lifetime.

Myself and the others on the basic training course at Excel Care Education Centre had collected between us to get her a special gift for the trip – a glamorous swim-suit. I was chosen to be the one to buy it. Cheryl wasn't a glamorous person though she tried to be, so my task wasn't easy.

She had lean facial features and was pretty but for one of the front teeth of her dentures being broken. It looked unsightly when she smiled but she didn't seem to be bothered. Her hair was thin, over-permed and dyed to a bright reddish-pink. She was too thin and nothing fitted. Her uniform tunic sagged on her.

On the last day of Cheryl's basic care course with me, something memorable happened – she had a message brought up from the switchboard.

I had insisted that all mobile phones were to be switched off during the training session and arranged that anything urgent would be in writing and brought up from the switchboard. I insisted on that, as I did that there would be no lateness and no leaving early, except in emergencies.

This one particular Thursday, a gentle knock on the door was preceded by a head peeping through. It was one of the rota supervisors from downstairs.

'I'm sorry, Mrs Phillips, but could Cheryl Thomas please switch on her mobile, there's an urgent message?'

We all looked at Cheryl as the colour beneath her fake tan make-up paled. She snatched her mobile phone from a large canvas equipment bag which lay on the floor under her chair.

'Oh, God, something's happened to one of the kids!' she muttered to herself, but most of us heard what she'd said as she reached for her mobile phone.

All eyes watched Cheryl as her thumb played a private medley on the buttons of her mobile phone with a workaday hand. She read the message so we could all hear.

'*All flights to America are cancelled until further notice. All essential messages to New York are to be through local embassies until further notice.*'

'Something bad has happened,' Cheryl said slowly, with her mind not with us. 'Something bad has happened. I can tell.' She stared at the phone on her palm as if it would give further information.

There was an ominous silence in the room until her friend and colleague sitting next to her snatched the phone from her hand.

'Don't be daft, Cheryl. One of those downstairs is having you on. I'll let them know what for when I go down there.'

'That's right, Cheryl,' I said. 'And I'll have something to say to whoever is at the bottom of this. Someone is trying to be funny. Take no notice and let's get on. Some people don't understand the importance of these training sessions.'

Cheryl retrieved her phone and put it on the desk in front of her.

'No, Shirley, that was no hoax. Somehow I feel we won't be going to New York on Saturday. Would you mind if I go. I feel a bit sick.'

There was no more teaching and learning that day. So I began packing up my acetates. I closed the portable overhead projector and put it safely flat on its stand before gathering up the odd sheets of paper that were scattered about the room. I wiped the white-board of – *"Everyone wants to go to Heaven but no-one want to die."* The subject of our session that day was caring for the terminally ill.

I checked the register and began putting the chairs away. It was usually the learners who did that before leaving.

I checked the register and wrote a few words on the participation of everyone who had attended.

That Thursday afternoon was the last of sixteen weekly sessions. The following week two new group would begin the course.

I checked the shelves of the practical side of the room and checked what would be needed to restock before the following Tuesday. A list of items was forming in my mind as I went down to the stairs to the exit, passing all the other offices on the way out. I knocked on Eileen's door, opened it and peeked in. She was putting on her smart, leather jacket and was about to leave. She looked worried.

'Why so glum?' I asked.

'Something awful has happened in New York, she replied, 'but I don't know what. I'm hurrying to get to my car radio. Apparently there's news flooding through continually. I don't suppose you've heard anything, have you?'

I told her of the message Cheryl Morgan had received which had a bearing on her daughters and brother leaving for America on Saturday; in two days' time.

'Poor Cheryl,' Eileen said, 'I hope nothing's happened to spoil their holiday. That woman doesn't have much luck, bless her.'

We went down the stairs together towards the exit of the building then separated as we went to our cars, parked closely together on the VIP spots.

I switched on the radio immediately, as Eileen said she would. The news from New York dominated. I got the gist of what had happened. Large jets had crashed into two tower blocks in the business centre of New York, believed to be the work of Muslim extremists. It didn't make sense. I was tired and confused, thinking that the message Cheryl had received, after all, might not have been a hoax. I switched off the radio and concentrated on the traffic; it was rush hour.

When I got home and opened the front door, Derek appeared at the top of the stairs, peering down into the hall. He'd been working at home that day, writing up his psychological reports.

'Have you heard the news?' He looked and sounded shocked.

'A bit,' I replied. 'What on earth has happened?'

'Muslim suicide bombers have flown large jets into the twin towers of New York's business centre. A third plane is implicated but I don't know the details. New York is in chaos. Thousands of people must have been killed. This could lead to a war.'

I shuddered. 'Paul is due to go to New York on company business, isn't he? Thank God it wasn't this week.'

'Come up and change. I'll put the kettle on,' Derek said. 'We'll have a cup of tea and listen to the news.'

The date was 11th September, 2001, when the whole world shuddered at the horrible attack on New York created by al-Qaida.

After Paul, our son, the next person who came to my mind was Cheryl Morgan. I remembered her expression on hearing that all flights to America were cancelled until further notice. I guessed she would be choked with disappointment, but then, I hoped she would give a thought to the fact that if her holiday had been a week earlier she might have been there to witness the devastation. She and her family could have been involved.

I shared my thoughts with Derek. 'Her holiday will be postponed, I should think,' he said. 'She won't lose her money. She'll be reimbursed, but of course, there's no saying when. Anyway, never mind about Cheryl Morgan. The thought of thousands being killed or maimed out of hatred turns my gut as it does to everyone else, except those who are the killers and their followers.'

I nodded. 'I wish I were about twenty years younger, I'd volunteer to go; I could help. But then, I expect they've been offered help from everywhere. From what I've learned from my visits there, the Americans won't need help from any country to do what they have to.'

I heard nothing of Cheryl Morgan and her family until the following March, when I met her at a seminar in Prince Charles Hospital in Merthyr. She lived and worked in the Merthyr branch of Excel Community Care so no-one on our Abergavenny team had contact with her. One of the good points of my training course was that it brought the carers together. It was good learning: hearing about the experiences of others, having the opportunity to air views and hear the complaints and compliments.

During the time I worked for Excel Care, a programme of seminars was organised by the social service in the light of the rapid spread of the Methicillin Resistant Staphylococcus Aureus micro-organism, (MRSA).

A measure to eradicate it was given by the nurses of the area's Infection Control Department. Thorough hand washing was one issue which was emphasised and the correct use of protective, disposable gloves and aprons.

I attended the seminar with a dozen of our Abergavenny carers.

The lecture room at the hospital was bigger than ours at Abergavenny so it was more cost effective for us to go there where a large number of carers could be accommodated. It was compulsory for all carers to attend.

Administrators and other employees were expected to attend the seminars so that everyone would understand the prevalence of MRSA, its dangers and what could be done to prevent its spread.

It had become a problem and an embarrassment. Nothing that was being done seemed to stop the scourge.

It was at the Infection Control seminar, in March 2002, when I met Cheryl Morgan again, as well as others who had been on my induction course at Monmouth House in Abergavenny. She was in the front row of the gathering which was in the lecture room of the educational wing of the hospital.

'Mrs Phillips, Mrs Phillips!' I heard someone calling my name and I looked in the direction of where it came. I was surprised that anyone, except those from Abergavenny, would know me. Cheryl Morgan did. She called and waved. I waved back.

'We had our trip to America,' she called across the crowded room. I'll tell you before you leave. Don't go before I see you!'

I was delighted, but had to take my mind off her to be shuffled along a row of chairs until I was able to take one.

At that time the wide use of latex gloves became extensive.

At the end of the seminar we were given tea and biscuits and opportunity to talk about the subject. It was then Cheryl found me to tell me about her holiday in America.

She began by telling me she would always think of me on September 11th and associate me with the terrible attack on New York. I didn't feel flattered.

'We had our holiday, Shirley, and it was absolutely fabulous. We went at the beginning of November and we had an upgrade on the plane. We were treated like VIPs when we got to New York; I felt like a princess. And the hotel ...well, we all went daft; it was like in a film.

'We saw the devastation, mind. And though it had been cleared a lot by the time we were there, it still felt awful.

'I got lost, would you believe? Yes, I expect you would ....' Cheryl's chatter couldn't keep up with her brain. 'It was a good job we had decided to meet somewhere if one of us got lost, but I forgot the name of the place. That very tall building. What's it called, now...'

'The Empire State Building?' I suggested.

'Yes, that's right. Frightened half to death, I was, but we're all saving like mad to go to California next year. I wish I had time to tell you more.'

Someone shouted from across the room. 'Come on, Cheryl, we've still got more calls. We won't finish tonight since we have to spend half an hour washing our hands before and after every one.' The cynical remark was found amusing to those who heard it.

I enjoyed that day and learned a few useful points, though I had taught social and clinical hand hygiene more times than I could remember. I was satisfied to know about Cheryl's trip to America, otherwise I would always have wondered whether she got there.

Chapter 20

ASSESSMENTS

As an assessor of NVQ candidates I was often involved in looking at carers' abilities as they worked with our clients. A number of criteria had to be met to obtain a Pass. When the carer felt she was competent and ready to be judged as being worthy of trust to care competently for whomever was in her hands, she made the decision herself to be assessed.

She would approach myself or Erika Powell who had qualified as an NVQ assessor. Erika also worked as a go-between and would fill-in for the supervisors of the weekly rotas. This meant that she would make a visit to care for a client when no-one else was available. That often happened.

When prepared, the NVQ candidate would suggest a convenient time for an assessment to be carried out. It was similar to the NVQ assessments that were carried out in The Nightingale Nursing Homes except the selected resident was within the unit rather that in a private house in the community. Permission had to be granted by the chosen client to ensure he or she would accept being the object of training in his or her own home. Rarely were there objections. They were usually flattered and impressed that training was taking place.

I enjoyed doing assessments but the induction course teaching was my priority. I worked three days a week: two days for teaching, one day for preparing. When my teaching sessions and timetables were prepared I had one day for other duties since the same programme was used for every intake of carers.

One late afternoon I cared for a client without being attached to a learner. Joyce Wilson, one of our supervisors of the weekly rotas had forgotten she had allocated a Mr Jack Drake to herself. He was new and the details of his needs happened to appear on Joyce's paper-littered desk. The social services had asked for our help.

The rule was that, if the rota-supervisor didn't have a carer available to attend a home, she herself or Erika would do it. The supervisors were ex-carers who had achieved the NVQ and were known to be competent before being promoted.

Joyce was proud of her position. However, to keep herself skillful at caring for the elderly and disabled she put herself on the rota to cover a few calls during each month. She was always the first to volunteer to be the carer when one was needed urgently. She volunteered to visit Mr Jack Drake.

Normally she would call her home to let her family know she would be late to carry out the needs of the client herself. This time she had forgotten she had an essential GP appointment. She cleared her desk as usual and off she went to keep her GP appointment, forgetting she had allocated Mr Jack Drake to herself.

A few days before, Joyce had called me on my classroom phone. It was after an afternoon's teaching session when I was checking the register and writing up my notes. Joyce asked me if I were on my own and could she come across and discuss a personal matter with me. Hers was an office which she shared with four other supervisors. It was a structure which had been added to the main building as the business had expanded.

'Of course you can, Joyce. Yes, I'm on my own. I'm surprised you're still here. Your Emma will be wondering where you are.' She had a little girl of three and was planning to have another baby. She, her husband and Emma lived comfortably with Joyce's parents in a big, fine house on one of the prestigious side-streets of the town. Her family was well known in the town, her father being a councillor.

Before she arrived I placed a chair beside me rather than the other side of the desk; I wanted her to feel on an equal bearing.

'What is it, Joyce?' I started the conversation. 'You don't sound yourself.'

'Well, you know I told you Malcolm and I are trying for another baby? Well, now I think there's something wrong.'

'Yes, you did tell me and I think that will be lovely, especially if she'll be like Emma and I expect she will unless it'll be a boy.' I smiled as I spoke even though I had the feeling that Joyce didn't agree. She became tearful and fiddled in her handbag for a tissue. I handed her one from a box which I always had on my desk. She nodded a thank you and sniffed into it.

'I know what I'm here for won't go out of these walls and you're the only one who will be able to help me. I'm so worried I can't think straight.'

'Well, whatever is troubling you I'm sure can be put right. What is it?'

I began to have the feeling that I was getting into deep water and Joyce's problem would be too big for me to handle. My intuition was correct.

'I'm having an awful, smelly, vaginal discharge,' Joyce began. 'And it's not now and then but a lot. I'm having to change my pants three or four times a day and that's with using one of those panty-liners. I'm so afraid I'll be smelly in the office.'

My gut somersaulted as it always did when I heard something which shocked or frightened me.

'Joyce, I'm sorry. No wonder you're worried but, honestly, whatever it is I'm sure can be put right.'

In those days a nurse did not diagnose; she observed the symptoms the patient presented with and reported to the doctor involved. I had no idea what was causing her vaginal discharge but I knew it wasn't right. However, I decided to help, if I could.

'Do you want me to ask you about it and give advice?' I said. 'The questions will be very personal.'

'Yes, I do want you to ask me and tell me what to do.'

'I can put your mind at rest on one point,' I replied. 'You are close to me now and I can smell something sweet, and that's you. I'm close to you several times a day and have had the sense of nothing but freshness about you.'

I assured her that she had no unpleasant body odour, quite the opposite, but even with my limited knowledge I knew that there was something physically wrong and Joyce needed professional help which I was not qualified to give.

'Does Malcolm know?' I asked. He was her husband.

'I told him and he said he thought all women had that sort of thing. But he did mention an unpleasant smell under the sheets one night. He laughed it off and said it was him passing wind, or something. He knew he was wrong and I was worried. He just shrugged it off.'

'Is the discharge thick and sticky or watery?' I asked.

'Sometimes watery and I have to run to the loo in case it flows down my legs but mostly it's yellow, thick and sticky and as I said, it smells awful.'

'I'm going to ask you another very personal question but you needn't answer if you don't want to. Do you have a condition which is called, dyspareunia, which is pain when you have intercourse or afterwards?'

'No, I don't.' There was a sound of relief in her answer.

'I think, then, that indicates that there's no lump or broken areas of any kind there. But I'm not a doctor, Joyce, and I'm telling you things that should be said by your doctor. And if you don't mind me saying so, before you see your doctor, do you think you had better take precautions not to conceive until you are clear of all worries. You might have a bit of infection.'

At that, Joyce began to cry again. 'Yes, I'll make an appointment to see the doctor. I'll ask to see the lady doctor in the practice.'

'Right, then, there's the phone. Do it now.' I pointed to the phone and she realised I was ensuring she did, in fact, make an appointment to see her GP. She asked for an evening appointment because of having to be at work and she was given half-past five on the coming Friday. It was then Tuesday so we had a few days to wait.

Friday came and she kept her appointment with her GP forgetting she had been scheduled to make a house call on Mr Jack Drake.

I happened to be in the office of the supervisors. 'Where's Joyce?' one of them said. 'She's rushed away. She's forgotten about Mr Drake in Winston Terrace. One of us will have to go.'

I volunteered to do the house call. All four supervisors looked surprised. 'Are you sure, Shirley? You haven't done hands-on for a long time.'

'But I haven't forgotten how,' I replied. 'It's only because I have to be careful with my back.'

'The notes from the social service say Mr Drake is mobile,' someone else said. 'There'll be no lifting.'

Obviously, none of the supervisors there were keen on taking a house call. Their minds had settled on leaving at the end of a day's work.

'Then I'll enjoy the change,and you can all go home.'

I hurried off wondering about Joyce. Her appointment with her GP must have been uppermost in her mind. She was so worried she had forgotten about her house call.

The thoughts of her having contracted a sexually transmitted disease crossed my mind. There had been gossip about Malcolm, Joyce's husband. Apparently he had the reputation of cheating on her. He played football for one of the local teams and that involved playing away games. He was often away on Saturday nights.

There was talk about him "messing around" with women who were known to be "none too fussy" and other terms which were unknown to me, but I was in no doubt of their opinion of Malcolm. The supervisors, Joyce's colleagues and friends, knew about his infidelity. Joyce didn't. She loved him and considered him a paragon, agreeing and hoping to have a second child.

I was disheartened by the gossip as I went into the store room to help myself to some white plastic aprons, latex gloves, jay clothes and a few other bits of equipment which I might need at Mr Drake's.

I read the limited available information given by social services and noted that our carer had been correct about Mr Drake being mobile, so I would be in no danger of having to help him to move or stand. He suffered with breathlessness, so movement would be slow. He was an ex-miner so without meeting him he had my admiration. My father was a miner for nearly fifty years and I have memories of his breathlessness and gasping periods.

I had reached a stage in my working life when I had to be particularly careful when having to lift anything, even slightly: a box file, a couple of lever arches, a heavy shopping bag. Also, against the rules were small tasks, such as putting the weekly wash into the washing machine, ironing, cleaning windows or vacuum cleaning. I found it nigh impossible to stick to the rules and, inevitably, all too often I didn't.

The spinal surgery of six years before hadn't been a panacea but it had helped and would remain that way if I obeyed the rules. I try, but find it difficult. Over the years there have been times when I have found it impossible not to break the rules.

I get pain for which I take analgesics and antidepressants. The more I get the blues the more I get back pain and vice versa. When I worked at Excel Care no-one knew about my clinical depression. To me, rightly or wrongly, it bears the stigma of being weak.

I had to tell the director, Eileen Hunter, that I was arthritic and had a serious back problem. She had a compassionate nature. It didn't matter to her as long as I remained her training manager. Also, that I was able to get up the narrow staircase to the third floor of Monmouth House to reach the training room. I was the oldest person working there and managed the stairs easily. It became a joke – a geriatric getting up the stairs faster than some of the young ones.

Mr Drake posed no problem. He was able to stand and walk. However, he was feeble and breathless when exerted and needed more care than he would admit to.

Chapter 21

TO HAVE AND TO HOLD

As I drove towards 4, Winston Terrace where Mr Jack Drake lived, I felt strangely at ease to be doing a house call on my own; not being in a teaching and learning situation with a pupil or student beside me. I'd cleared my mind of Joyce's problem.

I felt in fine fettle as I rapped the knocker of Mr Dale's front door. I expected him to be surprised to see me, rather than a young carer in her twenties or early thirties. I wasn't young but I decided to prove to him that I wasn't new to the job.

I'd worked on the community for a short time after my year at university studying for the Certificate in Education. It was a good way of getting back into the swing of basic care and being involved in the different physical and psychological conditions. That was over fifteen years ago. I didn't consider then that the elderly were cared for as they should have been. It has worsened. The media has revealed that.

Working at Excel Care I learned more about how people were being cared for in the community and from what I witnessed when working at The Nightingale nursing Homes. I hoped, as a result of the bad press nursing had been having, the care would have improved.

Most of the homes of our elderly clients are clean and pleasant, too many are not; usually through no fault of their own.

Mr Jack Drake was an elderly man living alone, who should have asked for help from the services long before, but didn't know how to go about it. Or he didn't want the interference.

His house smelled rancid as I entered the door and though not putrid, it showed signs of becoming so. It was above average size, semi-detached, giving evidence of once being a home of comfort and good taste; possibly cared for by a house-proud wife.

Mr Drake made no remark about me being older than he expected. At his age, eighty-four, he most probably saw me as being young.

After introducing myself and exchanging pleasantries I donned the ubiquitous white plastic apron and gloves, preparing to attack the kitchen sink.

'Would you like me to make you a cup of tea before I start, Mr Drake? You can tell me what you would like me to do. I might miss something important.' He looked surprised.

'Well, that would be very nice, Nurse. Yes, I'd like that. Make one for yourself at the same time.'

The electric kettle looked overworked. I hoped it would function. It did and as I waited for it to boil I sussed out the tea, milk and sugar. The milk was where I expected it to be – in the fridge, which didn't have much else in it except for a tub of butter, a jar of marmalade and a fresh packet of sausages. I couldn't find a tea pot so I put each tea bag into the two cleanest mugs I could find.

I started at the sink until the kettle boiled. It was piled high with used dishes, scummy pots and pans, the work-tops having disappeared beneath an assortment of items which hadn't been put away into the cupboards. Yet, the wall and floor cupboards weren't empty, but crammed with items which should have been stored in a tool-box, garden shed, or as in my own house, in the attic.

I ran hot water into the sink, before pouring a liberal amount of dishwashing liquid onto it to soak its contents whilst Mr Drake and I sipped our tea.

He talked about his wife who had died a long time ago. He told me about his children and his day to day way of life. He was lonely and pity deeply touched me.

I couldn't spend as much time talking to him as I would have liked because I had already gathered there was a lot to do. I wondered what to tackle first; the sink or Mr Drake. He looked as if he hadn't had a bath for some time. He smelled of stale sweat and urine and his clothes were food-stained and shabby.

He had a small nick in three places on his face where dabs of newspaper had been stuck to stem the bleeding of a poor attempt at shaving before I arrived. He seemed to have forgotten they were there.

I started at the piled-up sink. I was glad the hot water tap actually *did* run with hot water and there was a container of detergent on the kitchen sill. I was surprised. Mr Drake didn't seem the type of man to think of putting washing-up liquid on his shopping list. It must have been brought in by a previous community worker; a social service care-worker, perhaps.

I wondered if he realised his hot water supply was switched on. I assumed not, because it was piping hot coming from the tap. I decided to remind him before I left and to switch it off before he went to bed. He didn't seem the sort of person to run up the electricity bill unnecessarily.

The washing-up liquid had soaked away most of the grime and grease. I washed them and let them drain while I looked around for the correct place to store them

On some of the shelves there were newspapers and journals, dating back years. There were empty biscuit tins galore, kept I thought, because of the pictures on them of royal coronations, anniversaries and weddings.

I found a plastic bowl under the sink. After the dishes I poured warm water into it and carried it into the room to wash Mr Drake where he sat on a settee in front of an electric fire. I had brought a cake of soap and a few Jay-cloths with me but I didn't expect to be using them.

'Take your dentures out, Mr Drake, while I'm washing you, is it?' I hoped I sounded tactful.

There was no Steradent in the house and I didn't think there would be. A jar of bi-carbonate of soda happened to be on the kitchen sill. I scooped a spoonful into a cracked mug marked "Dad's gnashers" so I guessed I was using the correct container. I directed him to let his dentures drop into the mug. They were green and slimy. It seemed as though he treated them as a permanent fixture but never to be cleaned.

I pride myself on having a strong stomach for dealing with unpleasant bodily secretions but I had to swallow hard to disguise my revulsion as they slurped out of his mouth into the mug. I was surprised at myself; I was out of practice. Nothing had nauseated me before, except the removing of bits and pieces in the operating theatres and observing a post-mortem taking place when I was working in the NHS. It wasn't the blood and gore that upset me but more the sorrow and pity from whom they oozed.

I helped Mr Drake off with his shirt and pullover, washed his face and top half before drying him with a small towel I'd found on a hook in the kitchen. The pieces of newspaper fell from his shaving nicks; he still didn't seem to notice.

I didn't ask him to remove his trousers and to stand in the bowl; it was too small. He could have done with a bath but that would have taken too much time. I rolled up the legs of his trousers to his knees and washed one foot at a time in the bowl. I put on the socks I had taken off; I had no time to search the house for clean ones but I would have felt happier if there were clean clothes.

I poured away the water into the kitchen sink, rinsed out the bowl and replaced it under it.

I thought Mr Drake must have few visitors because he had talked incessantly all the time I was washing him.

'Forty-six years in the pits, ended up colliery under-manager I did. Got miner's lung from it but never asked for a penny from anyone, always paid my way, never lost a day's work, except for a couple when I had boils on the back of my neck.

'Brought up three children, paid up front for everything, no questions asked and now I expect to have a bit back you're asking me to pay something in the region of eight pounds an hour for a bit of looking after for myself out of the bit of money I've scraped and saved for the future. Good job Martha Dew from up the road calls in now and then to give me a hand. Good as gold she is. Rids it up a bit here and does a bit of shopping for me as well, when my old legs won't get me to the shop. Does a bit of washing for me an' all but not much. I don't go far so don't have need to change my clothes all that much.'

I'd guessed that Mr Drake's clothes were well overdue for a change.

He gasped for air as he spoke, having to take pauses between words. He needn't have told me he'd been a miner. I recognised the symptoms of the damaged lungs of pneumoconiosis and the blue scars of old coal-cuts on his face.

It seemed he was glad of my company to air some grievances, including the fact he had been told he'd have to pay for my services out of the small amount he had saved for a rainy day. I felt like reminding him that he had reached that future time he had scraped and saved for and there were no pockets in shrouds. That wasn't for me to say, though. I would have destroyed the sense of security he had with the thought of having money in the bank; something for a rainy day. He couldn't recognise that at his stage of life it poured every day, even when the sun shone. I've thought that about other elderly people I've cared for. However, I had to explain to him that he wasn't paying **me** for my services.

'It's not me you'll be paying, Mr Drake. After the life and work you have given to your family and the prosperity of the country, I agree with you; you shouldn't have to pay for the little looking after which you need. You've already paid.'

I felt as if I were giving a speech and being over-reactive, but I didn't mean to be. I was speaking with sincerity. I hoped Mr Drake realised that. He seemed to, though his expression was hidden behind forlornness.

Toothlessly spluttering, he went on complaining, lisping and stammering but I managed to get the gist of what he was saying. I had rinsed his dentures under the kitchen tap and handed the mug to him. He stopped talking as he took them out of the pot and shook off the wetness before putting them into his mouth.

It gave me the opportunity to change the direction of our conversation which, I felt, was becoming too intense.

'I don't think I'll be able to do all your cleaning today. If you like, I'll do what I can, then make you a bit of supper.'

'I suppose so.' He sounded uncertain. 'I wouldn't mind a couple of meat sandwiches for supper,' he said with a smile. I liked seeing his face brighten.

'There's a tin of something in the pantry, I think. An' a fresh loaf.'

Having washed the mound of pots, pans and dishes in the sink and on the draining boards each side of it, I squeezed them into the cupboards where I thought they had originally come from.

I went into the walk-in pantry which was attached to the scullery. There I saw the tin of meat and a loaf of sliced bread, though it didn't look fresh.

I hurriedly made the sandwiches and took them to him.

'I'll keep them until later, if you don't mind, Nurse.'

'No, of course, not. I'll cover them and put them in the fridge.'

He went on talking. 'A woman came the other day. From the Social, she said she was. She said she would take me to see one or two of them homes where they keep old folk who sit around the walls from daylight to dark, looking like zombies.

'I showed her the door and quick. I end my days here.' He spoke with anger and determination in his tone as he pointed to the grease-ingrained carpet.

'And I'd be grateful if you see that the likes of her don't come here again. Tell her, what I have I intend to hold on to.'

'I'll try to, Mr Drake. I agree with you; you have every right to stay in your own home. That's what people like myself and the other community carers who've called on you are here for. But I think you need a little more help than you've been getting. I'll try to arrange that, too.

'But what we hear of the horrible treatment from the television and newspapers is sometimes exaggerated and frightening off people who would be best in a nursing home. You are right, though, your own home's best. I wouldn't want to leave my home.'

I felt anger against whoever suggested to this proud old man that he should give up his home, whether he wanted to or not. I wrote information to this effect in the report about my visit and that his needs should be reassessed.

Mr Drake went on. 'David, my youngest, calls in about once a week when he can, to see how I am. He lives a good way away up in Tredegar. He don't work anymore. His wife left him with four youngsters, one just a year old. He got to look after them. Enough I'd say, without having to do for me. But I know he gives Martha a few pounds a week to keep looking in on me.'

I wondered if Mr Drake knew he qualified for the state attendance allowance to help meet the cost of his care. I'm amazed at the oversight sometimes made of the home-care system. Many people don't know their rights and aren't enlightened about what help is available to them.

'Ask your son to make enquiries about what is allowed to you from the State to help pay for people like me coming in to help you, Mr Drake.'

He shook his head. 'Oh, no thank you. I'll not accept charity.'

'It's not asking for charity; it's your right,' I replied without sounding insistent. 'You've worked for it. Anyway, it's time I went. I've overstayed my welcome.'

As I was about to leave I reminded him about the hot water heater being on. 'Mr Drake, when you turn on your hot water tap for anything, you ought to remember about the immersion heater being on. It's very hot, you could scald yourself.'

'What!' he shouted. 'Immersion still on! It's been on since that last girl called here! Stupid girl! She told me she'd put it on for me to bath when she'd gone. I can't get into the bath!'

He approached the stairs as if he were about to bound up but couldn't, so shook an angry fist in the air. I went up and found the airing cupboard, where the switch was, and shouted down that I had switched it off.

'Thank you, Nurse Phillips. That girl will have a piece of my mind if she shows her face here again. They just have no thought for others!'

'I'm sorry about that, Mr Drake. At least it's kept the water pipes warm.'

I understood his anger. Derek was always having to remind me to switch off our immersion heater; we reminded each other. It was added cost to the electricity bill, but easily forgotten when it means only the press of a switch.

'You've been a blessing, Nurse Phillips. You've got that special something that is needed to watch out for old relics like me. And don't think I'd say that to anyone who comes here.' He had his dentures in but his words weren't formed as they should have been. I guessed he'd lost the fullness from his face since having the teeth out and now the dentures were loose on his gums. But he managed quite well to express his gratitude.

'I feel clean and comfortable. You've made me feel human. I hope it will be you coming next time. I won't mind paying extra.'

'I don't think it will be me, Mr Drake, but I'm sure it will be someone nice and you won't be asked to pay extra.'

I'll never forget Mr Drake's parting words; "you've got that something special". I knew what he meant and it pleased me. I wished, I wished, I could go back to near the beginning of my nursing life. I felt I had wasted time; there was so much I would like to have done and, indeed, change. But, here I am. Too late...

I stepped into my smart Peugeot; a far cry from the old bangers of long ago, and made my way home to Derek.

I knew he would be wondering where I was; it was past seven o'clock. I wondered if he'd remembered the fish and chips I rang and asked him to get.

On Friday nights we defied the rules of healthy eating. He'd be on his first glass of wine, waiting for me. I hoped so; I had a lot to talk to him about when I was on my first glass.

There was something relaxing about the Friday night feeling, with the weekend to look forward to.

But first, a soak of my arthritic bones in a warm bubble bath. I was aching and utterly exhausted after well over two hours at Mr Dale's house, but I had no regrets. Quite the contrary; I had that good feeling within me that went along almost permanently when I was nursing at the bedside; within touching distance of whoever needed me.

Mr Drake's caring problem, I thought, could be resolved. But what of Joyce Wilson, who had rushed away to her GP a few hours before. I couldn't push the thought of her pretty face out of my mind. I hoped she hadn't contracted a venereal disease from her husband. She loved him; how would she deal with her problem? I wondered if she would ask my advice, again. I hoped not. I would have to remain professional and not tell her what I would like to say to such a man as Malcolm. I am not the rough, tough girl of early youth, in those rough, tough streets where I had to struggle to be on top of the hardships and heartbreaks. Through my profession I am not allowed to judge.

The care of Mr Drake would most probably be the last time I would practice on my own. It had taken a lot out of me, both physically and emotionally. I was at the end of my professional life and I felt it; yet Mr Drake's care took no more than normal physical effort.

I was sixty-eight. I feared a day when my mind would be affected. I felt my memory was weakening and frequently told Derek.

'Don't be daft,' or some such remark he made. 'Your mind is as sharp as ever it was. All of us at our age feel the rot beginning to set in.'

I remember my father saying that the older one gets the faster the days come and go and the memory gets flustered by trying to keep up. He was right.

When I got home after bidding Mr Drake a good night, Derek hadn't even yet opened the bottle of Friday night wine. He had been late home, too. However, the house was filled with the delicious aroma of the grease of fish and chips from the village chippie. He hadn't forgotten them.

He was in the shower pretending to be Pavarotti so he didn't hear me come in. I shouted up the stairs to let him know.

'Righto, love. Won't be long,' he shouted back.

I set the kitchen table, put a couple of plates in the oven to warm and checked that the wine was in the fridge before I went up for my bath.

It was bliss. I lay back in the bubbles and thought of the events of the day, as I always do when in the bath. I thought of Mr Drake's bathroom and how lucky I was to be in my beautiful, modern suite. I saw his when I went upstairs to switch off the immersion heater. The room was grimy and obviously not in use any more, though I thought it must have been beautiful in its time.

I imagined his wife going through the same movements as myself – getting out of the bath and drying herself on a big, fluffy bath-towel. I expect she put something glamorous on but I didn't. I put on a well-worn leisure suit. All the same to Derek if I had put on my best frock.

When I got to our sitting room he threw back the last of his first glass of wine. He got up and made for the kitchen.

'Same for you, love. Lovely Chardonnay, this. The nine o'clock programme is about to start but I can't tell you what rubbish is on after it.'

We smiled at each other as he spoke; the first proper glances we'd had of each other since the night before.

'Shirley, love. You look all in. Are you feeling all right?'

'I will after a couple of glasses and a plate of fish and chips. It's been a funny old day. I took a house call on my own and did what I could to make an old gentleman comfortable.'

Derek spoke from the kitchen. 'You're getting too involved in work, Shirl. You shouldn't be working at all now.'

When he came back into the sitting room he put my over-filled glass in front of me and continued what he started to say when in the kitchen.

'We're both well past our sell-by dates. I'd like you to stop now and I will at the end of the year. Think of what the great Dylan Thomas said; *"Do not go gentle into that good night".*

'All right, Love, I agree. We both finish and get on with our writing. One of us is bound to turn out a best seller in no time.'

Derek laughed, 'In your dreams.'

I felt so weary I would have agreed with anything. The wine and the pleasant, warm atmosphere relaxed me, yet I didn't think I'd sleep well. The thoughts of Joyce Wilson were difficult to shake off.

'Oh, I nearly forgot; you had a phone call,' Derek said sharply. 'A Joyce Wilson told me to tell you she'd had her appointment with the GP and things could be put right. What did she mean? I hope you haven't let yourself get drawn into to something that you shouldn't have.'

'No, Derek Love, I haven't let myself get drawn into anything I didn't want to. What else did she say?'

'Nothing else, except to tell you not to ring back.'
'Bless her. She knows I don't like to be bothered at home.'
Derek sensed I wanted to avoid the subject of Joyce Wilson.

'Mmm. Naughty supper this, but we don't do it often, do we? Must think of the blasted cholesterol levels' he said.

I chuckled and nodded. 'No, we're very good, really. We stick to the rules of not having too much of what is nice, don't we? You don't deserve to have a heart problem.'

I fell asleep that night wondering how Joyce Wilson felt and if the doctor had diagnosed what I thought she would. Joyce's condition, I thought was serious, physically and emotionally. I think she guessed what was causing the vaginal discharge. She spoke to me hoping I would give a diagnosis which would suggest something other than a sexually transmitted disease. I wondered how her doctor had handled the situation. She certainly must have come across similar situations a number of times, as I had myself, but not under such difficult circumstances. I often have to remind myself that I am a nurse and it isn't for me to diagnose.

Chapter 22

THE POOR OLD RICH

On the following Monday I was in my office preparing a six week induction programme. Normally I began my working days on a Tuesday but I had extra work to do. Eileen explained that the training budget had been reduced and asked my advice on how best to arrange the programme. I suggested the only step I could see possible, which was to reduce the number of training weeks. The carers were paid the hourly rate when on the course. Therefore, a six week programme would cost less than the eight weeks. Eileen would have known this and that I would be disappointed, so she decided for the suggestion to come from me. I was disappointed but I had expected it.

During last year's summer months the request for home carers was less, so the company suffered a financial deficit. It was January as I was working on the new programme. She wanted it to begin before the coming summer months.

I waited for a call from Joyce. During the afternoon I heard that she had called in sick. I couldn't concentrate fully on what I was trying to achieve; I was anxious to know how she got on with her GP. She didn't call. I didn't see or hear from her all that week. Several times I was tempted to call her, but I resisted. It would have been the wrong thing to do.

The following day, when I was clearing up after Tuesday afternoon's training session, Eileen rapped her knuckles on the open door as she came into the room. She took a chair at my big desk – an indication that it wasn't about to be a quick in and out chat, so I sat opposite her.

'I expect you've been wondering about Joyce Wilson. I'm afraid she won't be coming again,' she said. 'She's ill and her parents have taken her and Lucy to a relative living by the sea. Her marriage is over, apparently. I don't know the whole story but her parents have sent Malcolm packing. They never did want Joyce to marry him. I don't know the details but I told her mother that Joyce can come back when she's ready. She's very competent and liked being here. I have the feeling that something has gone horribly wrong. I don't think we'll hear from her again. That's a pity. Her mother asked me to tell you and to say thank you.'

'Yes, that is a pity.' I didn't want Eileen to know that Joyce had confided in me.

'But it's not only Joyce I wanted to talk about, Shirley. I have a favour to ask.'

'Well now, and what might this be, I wonder?' I know my attitude intimated that I guessed Eileen was about to ask me to do something that was not my responsibility.

She chuckled. 'You're right, it's not on your job description but I have something unpleasant to do and I think you could do it better than me. In fact, this little job is right up your street.'

'Go on, then, ask me and get it over with,' I replied.

'I would like you to deal with two elderly ladies living in Raglan who need a lot of care and have been on our books for six months. A number of our carers have been out there and although they, the Llewellyns, are one of the richest families we deal with, they haven't settled their invoices. Trouble is, they think the invoices have been settled. That's what one of them told me on the phone and she didn't sound too pleased.'

'Well, what do you want me to do? Pay the bill for them?'

My facetiousness amused Eileen. 'Not quite, but I'd like you to go out there with one of our carers. You won't have any hands-on, certainly no heavy stuff, and get through to them that they have to settle their invoices. If they see me getting out of my car in front of their house they'll know exactly what I'm there for and I don't want any upset. The carers who've already been there say they're weird old women and refuse to go again.'

'I'll have Nicola Day to come with me, then. She's tall and strong if it does get a bit heavy, and I hope she'll learn something.' My response told Eileen that I would do it. It sounded interesting.

'I'd be ever so grateful if you do this before the next course starts, otherwise you mightn't have the time.'

'Yes, all right, but don't say I don't do anything for you. Let me have their notes or any information you have on them.'

'Here they are.' She handed the usual brown folder over the desk to me. She'd had it in her hand. She knew I would agree to go, but the clients' notes were on one page. Little information, not much more than the names, address, ages; nothing about their general health or living conditions.

'Is this all I have to go on?' I asked with some irritation in my tone.

'Sorry. Not very professional, is it? I'm glad you're in the picture now. The carers that have been there didn't stop long enough to write notes. I wasn't pleased with them. At some time I'll ask you do a training session to explain the importance of the notes they write when they leave a client.'

'I thought you have to cut down on training costs,' I said

'Yes, but they have to know the importance of writing a report on the clients when they leave. I don't think a lot of them do and I could be in big legal trouble.'

'Some of our carers can't write well enough,' I reminded her. 'I'll have to show them how to simply list things.'

I visited the Llewellyns' the following Friday. Nicola Day agreed to accompany me, even though she'd heard other carers call the sisters old witches and that they wouldn't go there again.

As I drove to Raglan, about ten miles away, I wondered what to expect. From what Eileen had said, it wasn't one of the usual run of the mill cases. Nicola, beside me, looked smart in her Excel Company's tunic, but I sensed more than a little apprehension. She and I had worked together twice before, during a period between induction courses. She was tall and shapely, a little on the plump side but a pretty girl with beautiful, long hair. It dropped down her back in a thick plait. She was to enter professional nurse training in the near future; she would be expected to keep it just as neat then if the policy about hair being back off the face and up from the neck, is as strict as when I was training. I didn't think so. From what I had seen of the appearance of many nurses in hospitals these days, when I've had to take Derek for his out-patients' appointments, the scruffy appearance of some of the nurses has made me cringe.

Raglan, a pretty area of the county of Monmouth, like many other affluent areas, is veneered by its prosperous village main street. I had visited clients there in the past, so knew there were elderly people, even in Raglan, who were poor, lonely and uncared for. I didn't expect similar circumstances on visiting the Llewellyn's because Eileen had said they were wealthy.

We were late getting there. The map I was given was wrong. I had to stop and ask a man walking his dog where the Llewellyns' house was.

On getting to its impressive, though rusting, wide, gate entrance I was surprised to find myself steering around bends of a long, beech tree-lined drive. I guessed the trees were beech though their branches were denude of leaves and were dripping thawed frost.

The drive widened into a large forecourt of an impressive, Georgian house; a mansion.

I parked my car near the main entrance on the forecourt which was surrounded by spacious, uncared for lawns, beyond which was an orchard and vegetable gardens. I wondered why a humble carer would be needed where, it seemed, there would be a team of servants.

I mounted widely-paved steps to an enclosed porch supported by heavy pillars above which, was a veranda of, what must have been, the master bedroom

On closer observation of the property, I realised it wasn't as grandiose as I first perceived. The steps were cracked and uneven, the paintwork of the entrance doors was flaked and the wood was rotten. The veranda which was being held up by the stout pillars was warped and threatened collapse. I hoped it wouldn't do so before we were well in or out of the house

Nicola pressed a large bulbous doorbell but heard no ding-dong or any other door-bell sound coming from within. She knocked the knocker hard. No response. I began to think we must have come to the wrong place and was angry with myself for getting lost.

I shouted through the ornate metal letter box, 'Hello, is anybody in?' 'All right, all right,' an angry voice replied. 'If you'd come on time there'd be someone about to let you in'.

A tall, stooped, thin lady, leaning on a Zimmer frame opened the tall, wide, heavy door. She was well clad with layers of woollen sweaters, the top one used to be of a Fair Isle pattern, I thought. She wore a felt hat topped with a bunch of feathers, snow boots on big feet and a long scarf which, even wrapped at least three times about her neck, still dropped to the top of her boots. She had jet black, shoulder length hair which was over-dyed and straw-like. Under her hat I guessed there would be white-haired roots.

The gaunt features of her face were exaggerated by too much pale-coloured make-up. Scarlet red lipstick was smudged around her thin lips. She had long hands which were tipped by scarlet-painted, talon-like finger nails.

'It's a mile from the kitchen to this frontage, you know,' the woman snapped. 'Two miles when you have to rely on a metal frame for legs.' She stamped the floor with the Zimmer.

'Don't mind her.' An obese woman in a wheelchair behind her interrupted. 'She's impatient; always has been. We've been waiting hours for you. Where've you been until now? Excellent and professional care was what the brochure said we'd have to pay for. Come inside now so we can shut the damned door.'

In appearance the Llewellyn sisters were as chalk and cheese. As well as being twice as wide as her sister, the obese lady's hair was short and white from the roots to its tips. Contrary to trying to enhance it with hair-dye it appeared not to have been given a thought for a long time. The sallow skin of her round face was dry and wrinkled.

I guessed they were both in their eighties but couldn't be sure. They were strange. Or perhaps, unusual, would be a kinder and more apt a description

The woman in the wheelchair wasn't dressed against the cold, as was her sister. She had a shawl about her shoulders and a heavy, woollen, tartan blanket covering her knees. Socks on her feet appeared to be bed-socks in a pair of man's black, lace-up shoes which looked as if they had never been touched by a brush and polish. They were stained with food and other mucky droppings.

There was a pregnant pause as the two women scrutinised Nicola and me; I could almost see their thoughts ticking over.

'You poor little things. You look frozen,' the thin woman said. 'Come into the kitchen. It's the only bloody place here with a bit of warmth.' She looked Nicola up and down again. 'Though you're not so little, are you?' Nicola didn't respond to the "lady" as she would have liked.

'Yes, come on in, my dears,' the lady in the wheelchair added. 'I'm Amy and she's my sister, Millie.' Amy pointed first to herself then to Millie.

Their attitudes changed. 'And since you must be wondering why I have to rely on this to get me from A to B, it is because God has smitten me with multiple sclerosis.' She slapped the arms of the wheelchair as if it were to blame. 'I don't know what I did to deserve it but it's stopped me riding in the hunt. I'm waiting for a magic potion to put me right because if He were to strike me with a miracle so that I could get up and walk he would have done so by now, wouldn't He? I don't know what I did to deserve it so I don't know what to do to put me right.' Her admission was meant to be amusing but neither hers nor her sister's expressions changed.

They both spoke with articulate, cut-glass accents. The result of ex-public and ladies' finishing schools, I thought.

'You look tidier than the last carers they sent, anyway.' Amy spoke as she manually directed her wheelchair through a hall bigger than the whole of my house. Its wide staircase bifurcated, about fifteen stairs up, into a balustraded corridor on either side of the house. The ceiling was high with an enormous chandelier hanging from a central domed roof down to the level of the top of the ground floor. It reminded me of the homes I'd admired in Town and Country magazines, films and television programmes portraying the domains of the titled rich.

However, there was a difference. The overall appearance was of a time of passed splendour. There was widespread signs of dilapidation and neglect.

The colours of the large oriental rugs on the cracked and loose tiles on the hall floor were faded to an all-over drab brown and the beautiful patterns were obliterated. The visible part of the stair carpet was threadbare, the stair-treads crooked, some spindle-posts of the winding banister were missing. The temperature of the building, I thought, must be near freezing.

On the wall parallel with the banister there were a number of four-cornered squares of a lighter colour than the rest of the wall where, obviously, man-sized paintings must have once been placed. The pale spaces exaggerated the drabness of the building.

The few pieces of furniture in the hall were handsome antiques. My knowledge of antiques was next to nothing but a couple of our wealthy friends had an avid interest and enjoyed visiting grand houses open to the public, especially when the contents were being auctioned. They managed to acquire a number of choice pieces but nothing like those I'd spotted in the hall that had been sadly neglected. I could smell the dry rot and most of the woodwork visible was paint-flaking and rotting.

What a waste, I thought. What a pity that a beautiful house and its contents are being left to crumble.

The large kitchen was warm. There were wood-burning stoves at each end and one at about its centre. It felt as if the stoves had been burning forever. The large room appeared to serve as what it was originally meant to be – a kitchen. However, it now seemed to be serving as a lounge, dining room, bedroom, library and glory-hole.

Four mullioned paned windows overlooked the side lawns of the house. The opposite inner and side walls were installed with the original upper and lower cupboards, divided by three kitchen work-tops. A large Twyford sink commanded two big, brass water taps. Only the sink and water taps could be seen. The work tops, tables, chairs, dressers, book shelves and window sills were under piles of clothes, papers, magazines, and household implements of all sorts. I tried not to scan the room and appear discourteous but from a quick glance my opinion was that I had never seen, or could have imagined, such a mish-mash of an all-purpose room.

Nicola didn't mind appearing discourteous. Agog with wide-staring eyes, she stalked closely on my heels. I think she was wondering what would be expected of her – as did I.

Most of the elderly people she cared for lived in houses with a middle-room which served as a sitting and dining room but there was always, at least, two other rooms in the downstairs part of the house: a scullery at the back and a "parlour" which was hardly ever used, at the front. When she and other carers went to houses where the rooms were cluttered and unclean the clients usually showed embarrassment and were apologetic. Millie and Amy didn't seem to be aware of their unwholesome living conditions.

The room had a dirty toilet smell throughout, mingled with the smell of blocked drains, grease and mould. The room looked as if it had never been cleaned

I had talked to other carers who had been out to the Misses Llewellyns. 'You ought to see that stinking house,' one said. 'It looks like a tumbled down mansion from the outside and those two women talk as if they've got plumbs in their mouths. They sound like royalty. They looked down their noses at me, a lowly carer, but our chickens' cot is cleaner than what they live in.'

'Who does the cleaning for you?' I asked the sisters. They looked at each other as if they were wondering what I meant.

'We do it ourselves when no one comes from the home care agencies, of course,' Amy volunteered, 'but as you see I can't do much. Someone comes nearly every day but not one of them stays long enough to do any cleaning.' It sounded, then, that carers from agencies other than Excel Care had been calling there. I wondered if they had been paid.

Amy went on, 'Our commode gets emptied down the toilet across the hall; I'm glad of that. I'm got out of bed for it to be tidied up and I get my hands, face and feet washed but nowhere else is touched with soap and water. Millie does what she can for me. She does most of the cleaning, too, and I try to do a bit of cooking

'Mrs Phipps, who lives in the lodge down the lane, comes in every other day to do our laundering and to do the washing up. Most of our groceries are delivered and what isn't, is got by Jonathan, our nephew. He looks after our finances, what's left of them, so he pays the bills.

'When Millie's got us some tea and biscuits we can sit down and I'll tell you what we want you to do for us.'

It seemed as if Amy did the talking and Millie did the nodding and the getting and carrying, to the limit of her ability.

Amy had wheeled herself to the sitting area of the big, rectangular room. She remained in her wheelchair and beckoned Nicola and I sit down somewhere. There was an enormous leather lounge chair; its seat under a mound of papers and magazines and there were two other similar lounge chairs and a Chesterfield settee. All the furniture was dilapidated to a point of being fit for a rubbish dump.

With a smile I tried to disguise my apprehension of sinking onto the chair. Nicola precariously sat on the edge of its wide arm.

'Throw all that on the floor before you sit down or it will hide you,' Amy said. I inwardly chuckled as a picture conjured up in my mind of myself appearing like Alice in Wonderland in that big chair. It was too near the wood-burning fire for my liking, too. I moved as far as I could from the direct heat. Nicola copied me.

'Who keeps your fires going, Amy?' I asked. 'Surely Millie doesn't.'

Amy sneered. 'What! Millie chop and carry wood. She just about manages to carry herself about. She's older than I, you know, bless her. Simon, the lad living down the lane with his mother, Mrs Phipps, does the fires. The wood used to come from our own trees but that got too much, even for young Simon, so now Jonathan arranges for the coal and logs to be delivered. Simon gets it in for us and he keeps the fires in this room going. I think Jonathan gives him a few pounds to keep him sweet. His name isn't Simon, by the way. It's Jeremiah, but we call him Simon because he's simple.'

'Jonathan pays him and his mother every week. Simon does other things about here as well but don't ask me what.'

Amy wanted to continue describing the existence of herself and Millie, ignoring the fact that the time was increasing her commitment to pay Excel Care with Nicola and I having yet achieved nothing.

'Miss Llewellyn,' I interrupted, 'you'd better start telling me what I can do for you now because I'm only to be here an hour.'

Millie had joined us and was pouring the tea. I didn't fancy drinking out of their cups and I had my fingers crossed, hoping we wouldn't be asked to do any cleaning. That one room would need an army of carers to get it anywhere near normal. I had been instructed to carry out personal care for Amy; washing and dressing her. Millie it seemed, was able to care for herself.

'An hour! An hour! What the hell are you expected to accomplish in an hour? If it's a matter of paying then we'll have to pay more, won't we?' Amy's face wobbled as she shouted at me. I wondered if the old lady realised that the last five or six invoices hadn't been settled.

I'd explained to Nicola that our employees considered me to be diplomatic enough to get the business settled amicably.

'Rather you than me,' Nicola had frowned. 'Other carers said they thought the old women are witches.'

I had to stick to the objective of why we were there. 'I'm afraid your care is charged for by the hour, Miss Llewellyn. It may seem unfair that our Government hasn't arranged care for the elderly to be free, but that's how it is. The company I work for, Excel Community Care, relies on staying in business by people like you asking to be cared for by them. I understand you haven't settled the charge of recent visits.' I quickly changed the subject, hoping to ease the embarrassment. 'May I call you Amy? My name is Shirley and that's Nicola.'

'Named after Shirley Temple I'll wager. The lovely child star? Of course, we have to pay, but we haven't any ready cash or access to any of our bonds. We have money bonds I think and some land to sell. What the hell do they think we know about selling land or anything, even if we were young and fit? It's all in the hands of our nephew, Jonathan, our brother's boy. We looked after him after his parents, our brother and his wife were killed when on holiday abroad somewhere. I've told them who sent you here, whoever they might be, that the bill will be settled when our nephew sells that bit of land beyond the orchard.'

Millie manoeuvred a huge wheel-squeaking, two-tiered tea -trolley up to where we were sitting. She did it skilfully, I thought, considering the clutter of the room. However, I noticed tracks on the worn, grimy carpet; the tea trolley must be used often. Were tea or coffee and biscuits Millie's and Amy's survival diet, I wondered?

Four cups and saucers, matching jug and basin of fine china on a large, heavy-looking, silver tray were on the top tier of the tea-trolley. The bottom one was hidden under cracked saucers, cups without handles, a pile of tea plates with moulding crusts of bread, jam pots, empty tins of processed milk and yet more magazines. It were as if they were loath to throw anything away

The silver and fine china must have been impressive in their time, but I didn't like the grain of the presentation. The cups looked as if they'd been used several times before and not washed afterwards. There was a lipstick stain on the rims of two of the cups; Millie's lipstick, no doubt.

Millie spoke as she put down the cups and plate of biscuits on a nearby occasional table. Under its thick coating of years of dust and water marks it must have been quite beautiful, and valuable, too.

'I need help to wash and dress Amy,' Millie dictated for the first time since we had come into the house. She sounded apologetic. 'The carers who come here only wash her hands, face and feet. They avoid the more important bits that I can't manage myself. She needs to be washed underneath and I can't manage to lift her to wash and dress her anymore. She can stand up but just for a few seconds at a time.'

Judging from the appearance of Millie, I thought she needed help to wash and dress, too.

I stood up rather abruptly. 'Look,' I said sharply, 'time is passing. I suggest that Nicola and I get a couple of bowls of warm water, wash and dress Amy and see how we get on. I will explain at the main office that you are waiting for your nephew to sort out your business.'

Nicola didn't wait for a response but approached the sink, looked for and found a large, enamel bowl, then ran water into it from the hot water tap. She dreaded the thought of how many days excrement Amy must be sitting in. The foul smell of the shawl draped across her knees in an effort to hide it was evidence enough.

As Nicola and I gathered the equipment together, the sisters enjoyed watching us dashing from place to place as they sipped their tea and nibbled their Garibaldis.

'Where are your clothes, Amy?' I called out. 'Would you mind if I went and got them?' I chose my words carefully so as not to be considered intrusive or stepping out of line. Amy and Millie looked at each other questioningly, appearing to have ignored my request. Amy gave instructions to Millie.

'You go and get my clothes, Millie dear. Vest, bloomers, stays, stockings and some jumpers and a skirt and other things to go on top, will you? You should know where everything is. I don't. How can I, stuck to this bloody thing.' Amy hammered the arms of her wheelchair again. I thought it a harmless way of the paralysed victim to vent her spleen.

Millie took a quick sip of her tea and a nibble of her biscuit before she grabbed her Zimmer and rose from her chair to obey Amy's instructions.

'And there's a box over there,' Amy pointed into the corner of the room as she looked at Nicola. 'That's where those awful pads are. They go in my knickers like a baby-napkin. Dreadful what comes to one isn't it?' She glanced at the floor; hiding her expression of despair and indignity.

'They're easier than having to change your knickers all the time, though.' Nicola tried to comfort. 'You'd be surprised at the number of people who rely on them; people a lot younger than you, too.'

'Really?' Amy sounded pleased.

I noticed a king-size unmade bed on the far wall of the kitchen. The room served as a bedroom as well as every other purpose of living. Since it was, obviously, the only warm room in the house, it made sense. I decided not to mention a change of sheets on this visit, remembering Amy saying that previous carers made the bed. I decided not to check the bed for fear of the state I might find it in. Since time was precious I hoped they were clean enough to last another night. They'd have to.

'While Millie is getting your clothes and Nicola gets a couple of bowls of water I'll get soap and towels from the cloakroom across the hall, shall I? And I'd better empty the commode there.' The door of the downstairs cloakroom had been open when we were guided through the hall.

'You can go and have a look,' Amy looked doubtful. 'You may find something in the cupboard – if it's still there. Haven't been across there for years. The furthest I've been is to the front door and that, not often.

I couldn't believe my luck. There was a towel a face cloth and a partly used bar of soap in the toilet-cum-wash room. Nothing smelled sweet but it would have to do. However, the sink and toilet were in a better state than I expected. It must have been the result of previous carers or Mrs Phipps using the room to empty the sisters' commode and the attempt to get it as clean as possible with the limited resources.

I decided to empty and clean the commode before washing Amy. I did this wishing I had brought a bottle of disinfectant with me when I left the car. It would now be too time consuming to go to the car to get it. Swishing the pot clean with water and a wipe around with a slimy cloth which was on the rim of the sink had to suffice. I was glad I'd brought plenty of disposable gloves.

Having done so I needed to dispose of the gloves and the cloth I used to wipe the inside of the heavily stained commode.

In the corner of the toilet room was a wooden kitchen chair covered with magazines and old newspapers. I took one of the newspapers to wrap in my used gloves and the filthy cloth. I tucked the wrapped newspaper under my arm with the intention of putting it into the nearest waste bin. That was near the sink in the kitchen. Not the most hygienic, but the only thing I could do under the circumstances.

I returned to the kitchen to find Nicola, garbed in rubber gloves and a white plastic apron prepared to begin washing Amy. She was surprised to find the water warm enough. She, like myself, needed to get the care done to move on.

Nicola pushed Amy's wheelchair close to a small table near the fire. She didn't bother to clear the table of debris; the bowl was put on top of it.

'Shall I start by helping you to take off your top clothes, Amy. I'll wash your top half, cover that up, then wash your bottom half with Nicola and Millie to help me. They'll support you when you stand up whilst I do the washing. Is that all right?'

'Sounds fine to me,' Amy replied. I sensed that she felt apprehensive. 'I'm rather manky, I'm afraid; haven't had a good wash in yonks. Haven't always been like this, you know. As I told you, the others who have come here only washed my face and neck. They would soak my feet in the bowl, as well, but wouldn't cut my toenails. Didn't even comb my hair. I did tell you, didn't I?'

It were as if she was warning me. 'I do know you haven't always been like this,' I emphasised, 'and I know you'll feel better for a wash and a change of clothes.'

'And here they are.' Millie Zimmered into the room sounding excited. 'You'll be surprised what I've found in those old drawers upstairs, Amy.'

A pile of clothes were draped over the crossbar of her Zimmer frame. "And look at this lovely wool frock of yours. I've brought other things down in case the frock is too small for you. Do you know, there are vests and bloomers galore up there?'

I smiled. 'Well done, Millie. Now we're getting somewhere.'

Millie found it strenuous helping Nicola to stand Amy on her diseased legs whilst I washed her lower half. It was done in fits and starts. Nicola had to change the water three times during the procedure. Amy's personal hygiene had been neglected to a point of disgust. I hoped my expression didn't disclose my revulsion. Nicola wasn't so polite. I saw her trying to hide a retch.

'Don't you dare vomit,' I whispered from the corner of my lips.

'What was that you said?' Amy asked loudly.

'Nothing important,' I lied.

With washing and dressing accomplished both sisters looked pleased and comfortable.

'I'm glad you've had a good wash, Amy,' Millie said. 'You smell nice. I'll have a good wash myself later. I'll bring the bowl near you so you can wash my back.'

The two women had chatted all the time the washing and dressing was in progress but were silent as I wrote my report in the Misses Llewellyn's file. I had to start a new one because they didn't know where the original file could be found in the ton of other magazines and papers that littered the whole area. I certainly didn't have time to search. The sisters weren't even sure that one existed and I wondered if previous carers managed to find it. Perhaps one hadn't been started.

They both trailed behind Nicola and me when we made haste through the hall to the front door.

'Thank you, Shirley. We will put you entirely in the picture of our poor circumstances and the part Jonathan is taking in our welfare. I'll tell him to settle up immediately. I do hope you and you dear assistant will come again. If you can't come you can tell your supervisor, or whatever she's called, we don't want anyone else.'

They stood in the porch to wave us off, ignoring the coldness which could have easily chilled their old bones. I couldn't look back to respond; I concentrated on driving as the car skidded and zoomed off the worn-out flag-stones and gravel chippings of the front courtyard. I reached the T-junction to the left of which was the main road, two miles away.

Nicola looked back and waved as she passed comment. 'I'll bet those two are stinking rich; "stinking" being the right word. Poor old things, though. Fancy being rich and living like that.'

'Yes', I replied, as I steered towards the main highway, that must have been very grand some fifty years ago. What a come down. They seem happy enough, though.'

Had I been able to describe the big house and its residents to anyone, I doubted I would be believed. I had suspicions that Jonathan had something to do with the Misses Llewellyn's sorry lot. I decided to try to find out on a next visit – should there be another one.

Finding the Llewellyns' house, hidden away in the countryside, had taken longer than getting back to Abergavenny.

As I drove into the forecourt of Monmouth House I told Nicola that after I'd reported to Mrs Hunter, I intended going home to get a shower. I know I smelled of the Llewellyn's house. I wrinkled up my nose.

'I think the car smells of the Llewellyn's, doesn't it, Nicola? I couldn't sit and work for the rest of the day feeling like this,'

'Nor me, either. I have house calls to make before the end of the day. I'll have a quick wash in the staff toilet room, change my tunic and use plenty of body spray. I'll shower off Amy and Millie when I've finished for the day.'

I told Nicola how invaluable her help had been. For someone who, I know, had had a sheltered life and came from a beautiful home not far out of town, I thought she coped well. I know she'd seen unclean homes but nothing to be compared with the poor rich Llewellyn's. No doubt she would, if her ambition remained to become a professional nurse. I doubted she would see the like of the Llewellyn's mansion again.

Chapter 23

A DANGEROUS CALL

As I drove down Duke Street one damp, cold Wednesday afternoon in March, I happened to see Nicola Day's red Ford Ka parked outside Mrs Edith Pritchard's house at number six.

Duke Street is a double row of terraced houses, two houses a mirror image of each other, similar to the house I was born and grew up in. There were twenty houses each side of Duke Street, ending with a T-junction before the beginning of the next street. Going through Duke Street was a short cut to the town's main car park.

I usually worked on Wednesdays, but I had a dental appointment and decided to take back a few of the many days I'd given to Excel Community Care. I was up to date with my work so I intended to take the opportunity to keep my dental appointment and do my shopping afterwards.

I honked on my horn as I passed Nicola's car knowing she would recognise it. Since we had worked together at the Llewellyn's home in Raglan we had become more than colleagues. I had become her friend and confidante.

Her distinctive Ka car was a birthday present from her parents. She would need her own transport when she began professional nurse training, if she got through the interview in about six months' time.

I was surprised to see her car outside the Pritchards'. I thought Mrs Pritchard was in the hospital recovering from major surgery: a hip replacement. I assumed she must have been discharged earlier than expected and Nicola had had a change of rota to carry out her care. Mrs Pritchard would certainly need help so soon after the operation; she was in her seventies. Knowing her, I thought she might have plagued the ward sister for an early discharge. She didn't like leaving her son, Terrence, on his own for too long, though he was no child.

Being well into his forties he should have been quite capable of taking care of himself. Mrs Pritchard didn't think so and she knew best.

Terrence was jobless and had a history of psychosis. He was known to have severe temper tantrums. He became aggressive and used strong language speaking to people when he suffered a particular type of mood.

Since carers, as a rule, were not aware of the client's personal background or of anyone with whom the client lived, most of them didn't know about Terrence's personality deficiency. For the carers to be informed was considered a breach of confidentiality.

Carers had a minimum of training to deal with aggression but all who went to Mrs Pritchard liked Terrence and had no objection to going to his home to care for his mother. His sickness was controlled by medication which his mother ensured he took. Mrs Pritchard had shared this secret with Nicola so she guessed it was why she would have requested an early discharge from the hospital. Nicola had told me, though I reminded her she shouldn't have divulged what information Mrs Pritchard had given to her.

'But you are my mentor,' Nicola had said. 'I tell you everything. Anyway, I'm not the only one who knows.'

Mrs Pritchard must have mentioned Terrence's illness to other carers or Terrence had himself discussed it. Certainly, it wasn't a best kept secret.

It didn't deter carers going to Mrs Pritchard. They liked Terrence and some felt sorry for him. So, as long as Terrence remained shy and gentle, no one held anything against him.

They recognised that he adored his mother and was good to her.

Terrence was his mother's main carer and he looked after her as well as he could. He did the shopping, cooked her meals, did the housework and kept the fire going. He did the laundry and ironing. He was a good son.

Few people, except those who had lived in Duke Street for a long time, knew that he was once married and had a little girl. They lived with Mrs Pritchard, until his wife one day, packed her bags and left, taking their little girl of three with her. She left Terrence to live with a soldier, hoping for a more exciting life. Living with Terrence and his mother was dull. He bored his ex-wife.

He was contented living with his mother in Duke Street. He was familiar with it. He couldn't deal with new experiences and felt inadequate. There was something strange about his personality and so he had no close friends. He got bored himself and at times he would undergo a change of personality. The symptoms of his sickness became apparent to the psychiatrists who treated him.

At first, his mother tried to keep the fact to herself that Terrence had a psychological problem. She hadn't shared her secret with her husband when he was alive. She let him think that Terrence was, simply, a little different to others. She found it easier to share her problem and had often bent Nicola's ear.

Terrence was respectful and grateful for all that was done for his mother. All the carers who went to Mrs Pritchard found him welcoming and gentle.

He didn't look gentle. He appeared aggressive, as was his intention, though he felt weak and unassertive when with people. He had a facial tic and had the reputation of being quiet and shy. He was generally considered, "not quite right".

He shaved his head until it looked like an egg. He had several rings in each ear, one in his right eyebrow and one on his chin. He wore heavy bracelets and necklaces and cheap metal rings on most of his fingers. His arms were excessively tattooed; dragons with fire throwing tongues and snakes with long fangs and forked tongues.

I wondered if he had tattoos on his body. Little did I think I would soon see for myself.

He dressed with battle-field camouflaged shirts and trousers. I knew that some of the younger carers liked the way he dressed. It certainly didn't change their favourable opinion of him. He amused them; it seemed he wasn't shy with the carers who went to his home. His lack of confidence and poor self-image only occurred when he was among adults, especially if they were strangers to him.

However, I was surprised to see Nicola's car outside 6, Duke Street. Mrs Pritchard wasn't due to be discharged from the orthopaedic ward, at least, until the end of the week. I knew it was a general rule for the occupational therapist to call on the house of elderly patients after major surgery, to ensure the house was safe and suitable for rehabilitation.

I knew no-one had been to look at Mrs Pritchard's home conditions, otherwise Vanessa, Nicola's supervisor, would have mentioned it. A raised toilet seat, a board for the bath and wooden pieces to raise the fireside chair Mrs Pritchard usually sat in, would be needed. It was usually supplied before, or on discharge.

Terrence would be instructed on how to help his mother to become fully mobile and this would include taking her for daily walks up and down the street. Anyway, I thought, everything must be in order. Since Mrs Pritchard would have requested an early discharge, someone might have called to see the home yesterday, or even today.

I didn't know Terrence had contacted Vanessa to request that Nicola went to the house that day to help him to make his mother comfortable. It meant more business for Excel Care, the fee being covered by the social services.

Consequently, Vanessa had contacted Nicola and changed her rota so that she could go to the Pritchards' that afternoon. Terrence had specifically asked for Nicola as his mother was used to her. Vanessa, as did I, assumed that Mrs Pritchard had been discharged from the hospital earlier than expected. In fact, it went through her mind to complain to the hospital authority that Excel Community Care should have been informed.

Nicola was the visiting carer most familiar with Mrs Pritchard's needs and the extent to which Terrence was able to look after her. Though, he did the shopping and most other household chores, Mrs Pritchard needed help with her personal hygiene and dressing. Not only were her hips severely diseased by osteoarthritis but she was also plagued with rheumatoid arthritis.

Nicola and Mrs Pritchard had a good relationship and she got on well with Terrence. At least, she had until one day of horror.

Over two hours later, when I drove back down the road on my way home, Nicola's car was still parked outside 6, Duke Street. I couldn't understand why. Terrence did the shopping so Nicola hadn't returned for any reason that I could think of.

I tried to convince myself that there must be some reason for Nicola to have returned. She certainly wouldn't have been working there for more than two hours. If that much attention was needed by Mrs Pritchard, Nicola would have called for help.

I drove to the first corner and turned; back to 6, Duke Street. Something wasn't right.

I stopped behind Nicola's red Ka. As I got out of my car I cast my eyes over the front of the house and noticed that all the curtains were closed. That was strange; Mrs Pritchard liked the daylight in her rooms. The curtains were always open. Sometime she found it was easier to leave the down-stairs curtains open at night when her arthritis had given her a bad day.

I slammed shut the door of my car, not bothering to lock it. It might appear to Nicola that I was overreacting but I wouldn't have felt right if I didn't check.

I walked to the door of number six and turned the knob to open it. It didn't budge. It was locked in two places; at a Yale lock and at the "bobby's lock" at the top of the door which was an extra safeguard against break-ins.

I bent my knees and stooped low enough to peer through the letter box. I saw nothing, so I put my mouth to the letter box and called out.

'Hello! Will someone open the door, please? Nicola, are you still in there?'

The response was a most horrifying, blood curdling, desperate scream. It was followed by my name being called.

'Help! Shirley, help me! Help! Help!' The scream vibrated through the house. I recognised it came from Nicola.

Puppet-like, I sprung up off my knees and stared down at the letter box as if it would open up and let me in. Adrenaline must have pumped around my body in full force. What was I to do with only the letter box as an entry into the house?

In the seconds I stood there the screams were repeated; I burst into action.

'Shirley! Help me! Help me!' Nicola continued to scream. 'He's going to kill me.'

I stepped onto the doorstep of number five, the adjacent door of number six, the home of Ivor and Betty Green. I banged with my fists on the door with hysteria; it could have fallen off its hinges, had someone not opened it in time. I banged on the door until it was answered. It seemed an age, not just a few minutes.

Ivor answered the door. 'What in the name of Christ ...?' He was about to chastise me in no uncertain terms for my demanding manner. He held a shaving brush in the hand which hadn't opened the door. His face was partly hidden beneath the white foam of shaving cream.

I ignored him and pushed him aside. His back bumped against the wall and he dropped the shaving brush. I darted, like a bat out of hell, through the living-room of his house to the back door of their built-on scullery.

His wife was standing at the kitchen table with her hands in a bowl of pastry. This explained the delay in the answering of the front door. The couple must have argued as to whose hands were the more available.

Betty stopped mixing the pastry and stood with her hands in the air dripping flour over the bowl. Her eyes widened as if they were about to pop. She was aghast and adjusted her spectacles, ensuring it wasn't her vision was at fault, as I tugged open the back door. She forgot her hands were covered with sticky pastry.

'If I'm not back in five minutes, call the police,' I ordered Betty, as I disappeared out onto the back yard. The back yards of number 5 and 6, Duke Street, as all the other blocks of detached, three up, three down houses, were divided by a five-feet high, rough, stone wall. Over the years, the mortar between the stones had crumbled, leaving gaps to form foot-treads which allowed for climbing over from one yard to the next.

I leapt over the wall, forgetting my rheumatic spine, that I wasn't as nimble as a mountain goat and took three strides to cross the yard. In retrospect, I wondered how I did it.

I hoped to God that the door would be unlocked. It was. I flung it open, darted through the house and pounded up the stairs, two at a time. There were three bedrooms. Which one was Nicola in? It was easily found; I followed the sound of the fearful howls.

'Shirley! Shirley! Quick! Come quick!'

Without thought for my own safety I turned the knob of the door and rushed in. It was the wrong thing to do. Terrence was standing behind a kitchen chair in which Nicola was firmly bound. Her hands were tied together behind the chair. He held her in a tight grip about her neck with his left arm, whilst in his right hand he held the point of a stiletto to the side of Nicola's face. She gurgled and grunted.

I gasped. My fear was such that my nerve was about to desert me and render me stiff with hysteria. What was I to do? Turn on my heels; leave Nicola and bring help? By then she might be dead.

Important points of my limited amount of training on how to deal with aggression flashed through my mind. In the classroom, nothing as horrible as the scene which confronted me had been described. Myself and the other carers had done role play but the flimsy scenarios were petty compared with this.

My one hope was that Betty and Ivor Green had contacted the police. If they had, the sound of their siren should be heard any minute. Surely the Greens would realise that something was wrong. If they didn't and considered the situation a hoax, I feared Terrence would kill Nicola and me.

Thoughts of not seeing Derek, our son and his family again, flashed through my mind. I had to do something to calm Terrence and do it quickly. I had to keep calm and use my powers of persuasion on him. It was our only hope. I swallowed hard, trying to appear unruffled, but whatever power of persuasion I had, if any, no longer existed.

Nicola was naked but for her panties. Her brassiere, her T-shirt which she wore under her uniform tunic, the tunic itself and her uniform slacks were scattered about the room. Her face was covered with blood where the point of Terrence's weapon had pierced her soft skin in several places on her forehead, cheeks and chin. The small nicks bled copiously as if her face had been sliced rather than nicked. The blood had dripped down the front of her and smudged her bare, young breasts. Terrence's hand was blood-stained and a few drops had stained the blue and white bedroom rug.

When I happened to look down onto the rug my heart sank. The sight of Nicola's beautiful hair scattering the floor made me gasp. Terrence had taken a weapon to her long, thick, shining plait and cut it at different lengths. He had taken more than one cut to get through the plait. Not knowing the resilience and strength of healthy hair, he must have thought he could have cut it off in one fell swoop.

When I realised what he had done, something inside me snapped.

'You evil creature,' I seethed. 'What madness made you do that?'

He appeared to squirm; he began to realise his action was beyond contempt but he tightened his grip on Nicola and kept the point of the knife near her face. She continued to gurgle and gasp.

'Well, look who's here,' he sneered. 'If it isn't the posh piss pot. Think you're going to take this home with you, do you?' He was referring to Nicola. 'Well, you're not.' He spat out a string of obscene and blasphemous swear words describing what he thought of me. Some words I hadn't heard before but I guessed they wouldn't have been flattering.

His eyes were wide with madness, his face bright pink with excitement, and the metal pieces about his gaunt features stood out. A small, glass stone in the metal ring on his eyebrow sparkled when it was touched by a slit of daylight breaking through a gap in the closed curtains.

He wore nothing above his camouflaged trousers. The tattoos I had wondered about were, as I had expected, not only covering his arms but, also, his chest and back. Coloured shapes of sheep, goats and devils.

I was terrified. The palms of my hands were wet with a cold sweat and my mouth was as dry as sand. I had difficulty in keeping my mouth moist so that my voice was steady and clear. The last thing I wanted was for Terrence to know I was afraid.

'Well, Terrence, I'm disappointed. I always thought you liked me. I always rather fancied you.'

His manner softened and he eased his grip on Nicola. 'Fancied me? What the fuck are you getting at. You fancied me?'

'Well, I'm married so I wasn't able to give you the wink or anything because I was afraid you'd think me a tart. And I know you like classy girls like Nicola. And I don't know why you think I'm posh. I have no money.'

'No, I didn't know you fancied me. Anyway, it's Nicola, this snooty bitch, I wanted. I thought she fancied me and when I asked her to marry me just now, she laughed and said I must be off my head.' As he spat out his words he shook Nicola and she winced at the wrench of her neck.

My ears were straining for the sound of a police car. In my fear I thought I heard them but it was wishful thinking. There was no sound from anywhere but in that room.

'Well, all right, Terrence, if you want Nicola to marry you and stay here why don't you be nice to her? Not hurt her.'

Nicola yelled out. 'Shirley, don't! No, no, no! I don't want to marry him!' She tried to shake her head but Terrence held her rigid with his hand gripping the hair that was left.

I went close to Nicola and looked hard into her eyes, hoping she would catch on to the ploy I was engaging. 'Well, Nicola, you've changed your mind, haven't you? You've often told me how you fancied Terrence Pritchard and how you wished he would ask you to go out with him.' She looked at Terrence. 'That's why she always asked to come here. It's you she wanted to see, not your mother: not that she didn't want to see your mother as well. She's a lovely woman and would be a nice mother-in-law. Where is your mother, anyway? Is she still in the hospital? If she is she'll be home today. We'd better clean up this room and open all the curtains. You know how she likes the curtains open.'

Terrence loosened his vice-like grip of Nicola. 'She's not coming home for a few days yet. I wanted to see Nicola so I rang up and asked that Vanessa to ask her to come. They thought my mother was home. I fooled them. I'm clever, I am.'

'Yes, you are, Terrence, but we'd better sort this room out.' He began cutting the ropes that bound Nicola.

'Why didn't you tell me you fancied me, Nicola? I wouldn't have hurt you.' He sounded pitiful. He seemed to have forgotten Nicola had laughed when he proposed marriage.

Nicola was shaking too much to respond. She looked at him with blood and tears running down her cheeks. All she could do was nod her head.

'When she's come to herself she'll tell you, Terrence,' I said. I, also, was trembling. My gut felt like jelly. I tried to control it. Any second I was going to break. The last time I'd known such fear was when I was held down by Melvyn Baker, a sex maniac, when I was working at The Nightingale Nursing Homes. I was rescued then. I hoped I would be this time. Where were the police?

I felt like screaming. Terrence was in a dangerous mood and I had run out of words to keep his mind occupied.

He went to his mother's dressing table and took paper tissues out of its top drawer. He returned to Nicola, knelt on his knees, and gently began to wipe her face. She was in a serious state of shock and stared at him, afraid to take her eyes from him in case of another tirade.

Just then, the sound of the police siren could be heard at the top of the street. It became loud as it neared 6, Duke Street.

Terrence sprang to his feet, took two large quick strides towards me and grabbed me by the front of my sweater, tightening it about my neck. The restriction caused me to gag. He threw me across the room towards Mrs Pritchard's dressing table. My body thumped against it. I winced with pain as I bounced to the floor on the impact. The dressing table wobbled and a number of trinkets and a china ornament fell to the floor. The ornament shattered into pieces. I crawled on all fours to Nicola who grabbed me vice-like against her. The rope which restricted her hands had loosened and she frantically shook it off.

We wrapped our arms about each other and became one heap on the floor, waiting for someone to save our lives.

'You rotten, fucking bitch. You called the police. They've stopped outside.'

'No, Terrence, I didn't call the police,' which was the truth. 'It must be the ambulance bringing your mother home. Quick, open the curtains while I clear the floor.' I still clung to Nicola. She was frozen to the spot.

Terrence believed me. He went to the window and pulled back the curtains, looking out at the street as he did so. He had dropped his dagger beside Nicola. I snatched it up from the floor and slid it slyly behind me. Terrence was too frightened of the police being outside to have noticed.

With no discretion the police cars entered upon the scene. One policeman banged on the door and waited. Another looked up at the bedroom windows and managed to catch Terrence looking down at them. The policeman shouted up.

'Right, then, Mr Pritchard, come down and open the door or we'll have to break in.'

The other policeman continued to bang on the door.

Terrence raged like a mad animal and was about to pound us with tight fists. I took up the knife and snarled at him.

'You touch one of us again and you'll have this right through your guts.' I lunged the knife, not aiming directly at him, but he moved towards me and it stabbed the top of his arm. Blood poured out of the wound when I withdrew the knife.

He screamed and covered the wound with his hand. Blood poured through his fingers.

'Look what you've done!' he screeched like a child as he crawled to the corner of the room where he folded himself in a ball as if he were trying to hide himself. He knew he was defeated.

'I thought you fancied me,' he wailed.

The two policemen entered the room followed by another two who had arrived in a second police car. They had entered the house by the back entrance of number five on the advice of Betty and Ivor Green.

Ivor had dutifully called them after he had jumped the back-yard wall onto the yard of number six. He had entered the house and listened at the bottom of the stairs. He knew Terrence could be dangerous; he wasn't going to risk his neck by confronting him.

To me, those policemen were as knights in shining armour. The lives of Nicola and I were saved.

With long, heavy strides, one policeman crossed the room and stood with his hands on his hips overlooking Terrence, crouched with his hands on his head as if trying to be invisible.

'What have you been up to, Terrence?' The policeman seemed to know him.

'Nothing, nothing. It was them.' He pointed to me and Nicola, who were huddled together with our arms still wrapped tightly about each other. Nicola was weeping with relief, wailing with shock. The blood from her many small cuts about her face, neck and arms was now smeared over the front of my clothes.

A second policeman knelt beside us and put his arm on my shoulder. 'It's all right, now, girls.' He turned to the policeman standing near.

'Call the emergency ambulance,' he ordered. 'And stress that this is an emergency. There've been rumours that the emergency system has failed to respond to urgent calls.'

I had taken off my blood stained jacket and covered the front of Nicola. She seemed to have forgotten her nakedness although most of her bosom was hidden between us. I was glad Terrence allowed her to keep her panties on.

'I want to dress her before she goes in any ambulance,' I told the young policeman who was on his knees beside them.

He rose from his knees and went to Mrs Pritchard's bed and took off the cover.

'Put this around her until she's dressed,' he said with sympathy in his tone. 'And you will be going to casualty, too.'

I hadn't thought of that but I was in no condition to argue.

'Come on, Love,' he said to Nicola. 'Go across the landing to the bathroom and dress.'

I looked again at the young policeman. 'Gather her clothes together, please, and bring them to the bathroom.'

There was no mistaking Nicola's clothes; they were identifiable by her beautiful hair scattered on them. Her hair had been long and thick but spread about the room as it was, in strands, it seemed to have been even thicker.

Nicola could barely stand or put one foot in front of the other to walk. The young policeman took one side of her, I the other until we reached the bathroom door.

'I'll stay here to help when you are ready,' he said.

I nodded before shutting the bathroom door and locking it.

In the bathroom Nicola spoke her first words. 'My face. Shirley, my face is scarred.'

'No, it won't be scarred. They're just tiny cuts, from the point of his dagger. They'll heal in no time.' I took a towel from the bathroom rail and gently wiped some of the blood away. I was afraid. I would have preferred not to see the depth of the wounds, but I had to clean them and stop the bleeding before she got to the casualty department. And I had nothing clean enough to put pressure on them without fear of infection.

'Honestly, Nicola, they won't leave scars.' It was a white lie. I couldn't be sure what the outcome would be. 'And your hair will grow. Now's your chance to have it bobbed to shoulder length.' I tried to comfort her. She couldn't stop shaking, even though the relief of being rescued was overwhelming.

As we came out of the bathroom, supporting each other, we saw Terrence handcuffed behind his back. He was being taken down the stairs by two of the policemen; one in front, one behind. With head bent low, he skulked as he partly turned towards us and squinted a sidelong, guilty glance. He'd put on a grey T-shirt. He reminded me of a trapped rat.

Seconds after we returned to the bedroom two female paramedics bounded up the stairs.

They were loud. 'Dear me. What do we have here then?' They went straight to Nicola, pushed back short bits of hair from her forehead and looked closely at the cuts on her face and neck.

'They seem to be mostly superficial', she said to her colleague without looking at her. 'Hand me some sterile gauze swabs.'

She opened a few small paper packets and withdrew gauze swabs and gently dabbed the wounds. There was one small cut on Nicola's forehead which, stubbornly, refused to stop bleeding.

'Put your hand on this and hold it there for a little while,' she ordered. 'Can you do that?' Nicola nodded.

The other paramedic dealt with me. 'You did a good job, Love. God knows what would have happened if you hadn't had the guts to come in and face him.'

I didn't respond. I wanted to get away from Mrs Pritchard's bedroom – a hole of Hell.

The policemen talked among themselves. I couldn't make out what they were saying and didn't wish to.

'I can go now, then?' I spoke to the young paramedic in a tone that inferred a decision rather than a request. He didn't reply.

The paramedic looked at the policeman who seemed to be in charge.

'Let's get them to casualty. Todd and Walters will stay here and go over things.'

He referred to the other two policemen who recognised me and Nicola. Excel carers were well known in the area.

I heard one policeman say to the other, 'That's Sister Phillips who used to be on 4/1 in Nevill Hall when my mother was in. She's manager for community nursing now.'

Everyone left 6, Duke Street by the front door. When I had banged on the door on arrival, not much more than an hour before, the street was like that of a ghost town; not a soul in sight. The result of the arrival of the police cars and ambulance brought most of the neighbours, who were at home at that time, to their front doorsteps. A crowd of people stood around the police car into which the handcuffed Terrence was pushed.

The onlookers bustled tightly together to get a full front view of the proceedings. One boy actually waved to Terrence and called out his name to let everyone know that he knew him. Terrence looked in the boys direction without a change of his downcast expression.

Newspaper men lurked and circulated on the edge of the crowd, like aliens from outer space, hidden behind large projecting camera lenses, loaded heavily on their shoulders. I wondered how they knew what had been going on. Someone in the street or police station must have informed them.

Their cameras clicked and the blinding light of flashes flashed intermittently. It was similar to what I had seen on television. Never did I think I would be an object of their curiosity.

Before Nicola was taken out of the room I spoke quietly to her. 'Where are your car keys? Give them to me and Derek and I will get it to your house. I'll see you in casualty; I'm going in my own car. When I see you settled I will leave. You remember our phone number, don't you?' Nicola nodded. I went on. 'Call me if you need me. I'll go and tell your mother and father what's happened before the police do. They'll be frightened if a policeman knocks your door.'

Nicola nodded vigorously. 'In my bag, in my bag!' She pointed to the floor under which Terrence had bound her.

She was carried down the stairs of the house and lifted into the ambulance in a chair. She was well wrapped up in a blanket with just her face to be seen.

Although most of the blood had been dabbed away, there was enough remaining to excite the onlookers. One woman's voice was heard above the murmurs and mutterings.

'Oh, my God,' she said, 'she's scarred for life and she's such a pretty girl.'

I, who was able to walk with the support of one of the policemen, looked daggers at the woman. I would have liked to rebuke her but I was too emotionally injured to do so.

The policeman beckoned me to the ambulance. 'I'm all right, thank you. I'll take my own car and catch up with Nicola when she's in casualty.'

'Are you sure,' he replied hesitantly. 'You should go in the ambulance.'

'No. I need to tell her parents what's happened. I don't want a policeman going there; her mother will be frightened.'

I managed to get to her parents' home and explained briefly to her mother what had happened. I didn't accept her invitation to go inside. I needed to be at the Accident and Emergency Department with Nicola.

I was with her when she was having her wounds asceptically cleaned and dressed. I stayed with her for a while when she was in a cubicle, being checked frequently.

She fell asleep which I considered a good time to leave. I let the nurse in charge know I was leaving. She and I recognised each other from when I had worked at The Nevill Hall Hospital, so I was able to leave without the rigmarole of being clerked.

Nicola, however, was detained overnight for close observations of her general condition and the wounds on her face neck and arms.

She was discharged the following day. Her parents picked her up. They had brought in clean clothes and a jacket with a hood beneath which she hid as much as possible of her injured face. She wasn't fully recovered from the horror of the previous day but with MRSA infection in the hospital it was considered wiser for her to be in her own home environment.

No-one looked at her; the hooded face didn't attract attention. Everyone was wrapped up in their own problems. It was as if yesterday hadn't happened.

Chapter 24

DILEMMAS OF THE ELDERLY

Nicola's father was a town councillor. He spoke to the police to ensure the event in Duke Street didn't get into the papers. However, the matter was out of his hands and far from closed.

Nicola and I were rigorously questioned and were warned that we would have to appear in court when charges were pressed and Terrence Pritchard put on trial.

Nicola and I dreaded the day arriving. Nicola, especially, was nervous. Her father made an attempt to avoid us appearing in court but failed.

I put on a brave face for her. 'Let's try to forget Terrence Pritchard and carry on as normal until the day we have to go to court. And the sooner the better.'

Derek was concerned. As a child and educational psychologist he had appeared in court many times as an expert witness. He knew how traumatic it could be.

'I wish you didn't have to appear in court,' he said, 'but that dangerous man has to be tried and punished. He'll be put away, of course. I'm relieved that the police turned up when they did. I dread to think of what could have happened.'

Several weeks passed before Terrence Pritchard's trial took place. Nicola and I were prosecution witnesses. We each stood in the dock and were questioned. The ordeal wasn't as awful as we expected.

Some days after the incident at 6, Duke Street, when Nicola appeared to be overcoming the dreadful event I went with her to the hairdressers. Luckily, Terrence hadn't cut Nicola's hair close to her neck but some inches below. It was of uneven lengths with some strands as long as it had been and others close to her scalp. Her thick, glossy, chestnut coloured hair was bobbed to shoulder length though there were strands which didn't reach her shoulders. The hairdresser skillfully dealt with them.

As predicted, all the small nicks of the skin of her face, neck and arms had almost disappeared except for the cut on her forehead which had been done by the force of one of Terrence's metal rings when he hit her. The ring must have been dirty and caused the cut to become infected. The cut healed long before Nicola's post-traumatic stress did. That took many months.

I went to work on the Tuesday after the Terrence Pritchard event, thinking I would be inundated with morbid questions. But I was wrong. Eileen Hunter must have instructed everyone not to do so. In a group during the mid-day break we talked about the experience of being held by Terrence Pritchard, who was deranged. It had been too dangerous an event to be discussed lightly.

It was decided that our carers should be made more aware of the dangers of working in the community and there should be some definite rules drawn up. Day seminars were to be arranged.

It was an easy guess as to whom Eileen would allocate the task of organising the seminars. Initially, she suggested that I organise and conduct them. I adamantly refused; I was not knowledgeable enough to discuss psychoses.

A closing remark was made by Eileen: 'Shirley, I wonder if your little adventure did good for our business or bad?'

'A **little** adventure did you say! A little one! I'll tell you after it happens to me again!' That remark amused everyone.

On discharge from The Nevill Hall Hospital, Mrs Pritchard was taken into a National Health Service long-stay unit. Unless Terrence was released from the institution into which he was detained – if ever he would be released, Mrs Pritchard's care had to be considered.

After the trial, Terrence was diagnosed to be of unsound mind and confined, indefinitely, to a psychiatric institution.

An assessment was made of Mrs Pritchard's home facilities and her abilities to care for herself in her own home. It was considered that she needed twenty-four hours care and was given the opportunity to choose a nursing home or to return to her own home, as was her right.

She was broken-hearted about Terrence and the stress delayed her recovery. She was convinced he would be discharged soon and life would revert to "normal".

She chose to go home, be supported by community carers and manage the best she could on her own. Twenty-four hour care was expensive and not easily provided. It was a dilemma. After a while she had to admit she couldn't manage living on her own.

As a last resort she agreed to be admitted into The Nightingale Nursing Homes until Terrence came home.

Her empty house was locked up for a long time. I was pleased to hear she had been admitted to a nursing home which I knew would meet her needs. It was at a time when there were media reports which proclaimed that many of our nursing homes were not caring for their residents as they were expected to.

During the time we waited for Terrence's trial to be heard, Derek and I found ourselves in a position of having to search for a nursing home for his ninety-two year old aunt who was totally incapacitated.

She lived in Leamington and wanted to stay there, where her few remaining friends lived.

Since Nancy's husband, Bert, died some years before, Derek had been travelling to Leamington to visit her. I knew that journey and the responsibility had become too much for him. Nancy and Bert had not been blessed with children. Derek was Nancy's nearest and dearest.

I felt that I should have given up my job and had Nancy here, living with Derek and I. That would have been difficult when Paul and the family came, though something could have been arranged to accommodate everyone.

I felt guilty and explained to Derek that we could, perhaps, manage if I had enough help from the community carers. Nancy was doubly incontinent and had little mobility. The hurtful point was that she was of sound mind. She was a delightful person; Derek loved her and she looked upon him as her god. We were careful not for her to feel she had become a burden.

'That's out of the question,' he'd said. 'Even if you had a strong back bone, Nancy would be too heavy for you. She'd be too heavy for me. I'd be happier if she decided herself to go into a nursing home. The point is – where? She wants to stay in Leamington.'

We talked to her and she agreed she was in a dilemma and had to make a choice. She couldn't be cared for in her own home and would feel safer in a nursing home.

Derek and I viewed six nursing homes in Leamington which had been recommended by a social services' officer. We telephoned each one to make an appointment to view the premises prior to visiting.

They were all below the standard we expected, even though I thought, efforts had been made to display a compassionate and caring front. The homes were shoddy, the residents sitting around the walls didn't look neatly clad and the carers looked as if no effort had been made to look professional. Some of the homes smelled unpleasant.

Nancy's residency was wanted. It meant revenue to the owners but she would have hated being in any one of those we viewed. The residents did, indeed, look uncared for and uncaring, as did the carers.

Derek despaired. I had delayed suggesting that we arrange for Nancy to come to a nursing home near us. I thought he would have been offended by my idea of moving Nancy from

Leamington. After a long, physically and emotionally draining day I put the idea to him.

'If that's possible it would solve the problem. We'll put it to her.'

Nancy agreed, so we arranged an ambulance to bring her down to a nursing home not far from where we live; where we were able to visit regularly.

She wasn't happy there. The trauma of the move affected her mind. She became confused and told me that she felt that she'd been dumped. I wondered if she misunderstood the plan for her to go into a nursing home and expected to come into our home.

She died shortly afterwards.

Chapter 25

A RELUCTANT CARER

The carers' work in the nursing homes is heavy and demanding for little remuneration. Most of the carers receive no more than the minimum wage, even though they might have been in the same position of the pecking order for a number of years.

When they remain in the job it can be said that they enjoy caring for the elderly and infirm; compassion is within them.

However, at the end of each working day, they "hand over" their residents' comfort and safety to others. They leave to enjoy their own homes and families. They are free.

Being the sole carer of a debilitated loved one in the community is emotionally and physically demanding for twenty-four hours of the day, seven days a week, twelve months of the year. There is no freedom to live an independent life and little or no remuneration. It can be too much for one person, no matter how determined he or she might be to meet the caring commitments.

Some nursing homes offer care for the needy elderly and infirm to allow a time of respite for the fatigued, worn down carer. I have seen that this arrangement is not taken advantage of when it should be.

"Please don't put me away," continues to be the cliché. The carer becomes an imprisoned slave out of love and a sense of duty. Denying that sense of duty is reinforced by the possible fear of regret when the loved one dies. This has been seen to lead to resentment.

The first time I set eyes on Victoria Heatherington was when I was on the panel for interviewing prospective nursing students into professional training at The Nevill Hall School of Nursing. She was sitting among nine other candidates in our visitor's small waiting room. A touch of nervous tension could be sensed there.

All the young ladies and one young man, were smartly groomed; all in their late teens or early twenties, except two mature entrants.

I knew how the mature entrants might have felt – old! I had entered the profession as a mature student and in all gatherings over the years in the profession I was the "geriatric", a term rarely used now.

Victoria Heatherington stood out. She wore an easy smile and a suit which didn't come from Marks and Spencer or one of the up-to-date ladies boutiques that were favoured at that time. Her thick, shining, corn-coloured hair was attractive, as well as neat. A pair of gold studs glistened on her earlobes, partly hidden by soft coils of hair. When she sat before us in the interview room I noticed she had a light-textured cream make-up on her smooth, satin-like skin and a touch of pink lipstick. She was and still is beautiful.

She interviewed well, with a cultured accent answering more or less the same questions as were posed to the other candidates.

'Your home is in, Hereford, Miss Heatherington,' Louise, our senior tutor said. 'There's a very good nurse training school there. Why have you chosen to come to us?'

'It's a good enough distance from my father as well as near enough to my mother,' she replied. 'My father wanted me to go into medicine but I'm not clever enough and my mother agrees with me. She liked the idea of me being a nurse. I hope you will consider me clever enough to be accepted here.' I thought she was being facetious.

When asked what she planned when, or if, she qualified, she said she would consider working in a developing country, possibly somewhere in Africa. I thought that would be a very long way from her parents, but I didn't comment.

Louise, senior tutor, went on, 'Then you should speak to Mrs Phillips. She did voluntary nursing there and other overseas countries.'

'But as a voluntary auxiliary nurse,' I added. 'It made me determined to become a registered nurse.'

We had four intakes of students a year. Victoria was accepted for nurse training and began with the July Group in 1986.

After the interviews the candidates gathered in one of our classrooms for tea. They chatted with excitement and exchanged names. There was much enthusiasm to begin three years of hard work. I remembered how I felt when I was accepted in 1970, over fifteen years before.

After a few months into her training Victoria and I met in the school library. It was on a Sunday and we were the only ones there, which was unusual. I was the first to speak.

'Hello, Nurse Heatherington. Researching surgical nursing, are you? I don't think you could be feeling as inadequate as I did when I was doing my surgical module, or indeed, every other module.'

She smiled. 'I couldn't imagine you feeling inadequate about anything, Mrs Phillips.'

'I'll take that as a compliment but it's true. Many a time I didn't think I'd make the course, but here I am. You're, obviously, on weekend duty or I would have expected you to go home.'

'Yes, I'm on next weekend, too. My parents have friends for the weekend so I'm glad to be here.'

I smirked, 'I know the feeling. Derek and I like the quiet life but when he was in the army, weekend entertaining was the norm.'

'Is that when you were overseas and did voluntary nursing?'

'Yes, it was. I didn't begin my training until he was on his last army posting. Anyway, I'll get on and let you get on with your research.'

Following that day we shared experiences on a number of occasions. I learned that she was of a wealthy, well-reputed family. Her father was the director of his own engineering company and Julian, her brother had followed in his footsteps in the family business. I assumed he was expected to; Mr Heathington, I discovered, was a disciplinarian.

In spite of the difference in our ages and professional status Victoria and I became close friends. I was often invited to her home, especially when the family had some special occasion to celebrate. When she was off-duty she sometimes came here, to my home.

I was pleased that she understood the need to keep our relationship discrete as other students might have considered it unprofessional. It might have been said that I would favour her written work, which had to presented after every ward experience. I ensured one of my colleagues marked Victoria's work.

When she was six months from her final examination, life changed for her. She telephoned me at home when she was on duty, which was unusual. She was crying and sounded desperately stressed.

Derek answered the phone. I heard him say, 'Victoria, what on earth has happened. Here, speak to Shirley.' I took over.

'Shirley, I'm sorry to call you at home. Something awful has happened and I have to go home. I've had permission from Sister. I'll call you when I know what's happened, if you don't mind.'

'No, of course, I don't mind. Do you have any idea what's gone wrong?'

'My parents are on a touring holiday in France and there's been a terrible road traffic accident. That's all Julian told me.'

'That's terrible. You are very emotional. Would you like me to drive you?'

'No, I'm leaving the ward now. Thank you, I'll be all right. I know the road well.'

Two days later Victoria called me at the school. 'Shirley, my mother is dead and my father is in a critical condition. His back is broken. He's being flown home today. I'll be needed here for, I don't know how long, but could you arrange a delay in my training?'

'Yes. Don't worry about your work. Concentrate on what you have to. Keep me informed, Victoria. If necessary, we'll arrange a six months break.'

I rang off, hoping the terrible circumstances wouldn't get to that.

After about three months I had another desperate-sounding phone call from Victoria. 'Shirley, can you come up. My father is insisting I terminate my training. He doesn't realise what he's expecting of me. He says I'm needed here permanently. If you can explain what has been involved in my training and explain that I must complete the course, he'll change his mind. He'll have to have the local care agencies to nurse him.'

I did as Victoria asked, thinking that I wouldn't change her father's mind and I was correct in my assumptions. He was adamant and in a roundabout way, told me it was none of my business. Victoria didn't sit her final examination after her six months referral nor did she return to Nevill Hall Nurse Training School to complete her training.

We kept in touch. I visited Victoria several times at her Hereford home. I sensed her father resented my visits. I considered it might have been that he was afraid I would entice Victoria back into nursing.

She nursed her father for over twenty unhappy years; until his death. He'd been dead some weeks before Victoria called me. 'Shirley, please come to see me. I feel dreadful. I need to talk to you.'

Before I left home I called Julian. 'I'm glad you called before seeing Victoria,' he said. 'She's confused and she's blaming herself for Father's death. On post mortem it was found that my father must have had an acute heart attack. Witnesses swear that she didn't push the handles of his wheelchair. She hadn't even reached it before it went over the cliff.'

'Thank you, Julian. I'll try to talk her round. She's, no doubt, still in shock.'

'Shirley,' Julian went on, 'will you try to convince her that it would be best if the property is now sold? She considers herself old. Daphne and I have been telling her she has plenty of time to enjoy life before she joins our father.' Daphne is Julian's wife.

I agreed with him. We chatted for a short while; he repeated the outcome of the inquest.

Before leaving I wrote a note for Derek and placed it where it would catch his eye as soon as he came home. I knew my visit to Victoria would be a long one.

When I arrived at her home I entered the house by way of the conservatory doors which were always open. I guessed there would be no-one to open the main front door. I found Victoria sitting in front of the French window in the drawing room. She was in an acute state of depression. Her appearance was unkempt and her mask-like expression aged her. She greeted me with no enthusiasm, which wasn't her way.

I put my arm about her shoulders and the response was as cold stone; as if she hadn't felt my touch. 'Why didn't you call me when your father died?' I asked. 'You should have.'

'You couldn't have done anything. It is now I need you and your advice. I don't know what to do. I killed my father.'

Although Julian had warned me, I was aghast at her determined commitment. I didn't expect her to be so forthright.

'You didn't! I will never believe that. Your mind is twisted. Tell me what happened.'

I let Victoria talk. I was saddened as well as angered by the way she had been treated. I realise there must be millions of sons and daughters, wives and husbands, who are slaves in their own homes, reluctantly sacrificing their freedom to live how they would wish. It is known there are carers who are unaware of the fact that there is financial and respite help available for them by the State. They equate to being slaves. Victoria was one of them.

She looked out onto the patio but her blank expression told me she was seeing nothing. She began, 'Well, Shirley, on my next birthday I will be forty-five. Not quite an old maid but doomed to be one. My father, Quentin Heatherington, was cremated a week ago. I sacrificed my profession, marriage and probably motherhood to care for him, which I did for over twenty years. Today, his remains were delivered to me by the undertaker. I shed no tears.

'I'm sitting in what had been one of Father's favourite chairs by the French window of the drawing room, and as you can see, I'm overlooking his patio and garden.'

I sat in a similar chair, close to her. The scene outside was beautiful even though the day was dreary and damp and a low mist lurked in the distance. I took her hand but she withdrew it. I think she wanted no intrusion into what she had to say.

'As you see, the room is tastefully arranged with fine furniture and fittings. The whole of High Trees House is fine. My mother had good taste. Father told Julian and me that, after his parents had passed away and Mother became mistress of the home, she changed an already lovely house into one of elegance and beauty. Now it is mine. I don't share it with Julian because Father paid his mortgage and stipulated that this house is to be mine.

'Father was the only child of a wealthy family. He inherited this fifteen-room Edwardian house, including servants' quarters, as well as a flourishing engineering company.

'At the bottom of what is now our rear garden, is a tall privet hedge. It can be seen if you stand up.'

I didn't stand. 'Yes, Victoria, I know. We've strolled down there together a number of times. Your mother came with us. She was beautiful and you are the living image of her.'

Victoria went on as if she hadn't heard a word I'd said:

'Well, directly beyond that, are two acres of land belonging to the house, then a green of the golf club. Father remained a member of the golf club but, of course, couldn't play as he used to. He was paraplegic since that road traffic accident, some twenty or so years ago, broke his spine and killed Mother. They were on holiday.

'Innumerable times he expressed his regret of taking that trip to France. His words grated and I often reminded him of a motto he instilled in me and my brother. *"Better to regret something you've done than something you've not done."*

'Before the accident that rendered him totally dependent on others for his existence, the gardens of High Trees House were splendid. He employed gardeners to keep them beautiful in summer and winter. Now they're just tidy, maintained that way by our part-time gardener, Bill Thomas.

'The land beyond the thick, privet hedge is divided into allotments. Father rented them to men living in the nearby village. 'Bill is one of the allotment-tenants. Looking after the gardens is part of the rental deal. He mows the lawns, back and front in the summer and clears the leaves from the surrounding trees in the autumn.

'Father once ordered me to do something about the gardens. "Victoria, you must plant flowers and keep the borders pretty and free of weeds, as Mother did. Julian should help you, as he did Mother." 'Julian, as you know, is my forty-eight year old brother.

'I reminded him, "Julian's too busy, Father. He's running the business and has a family of his own, don't forget. I'll do the gardening when I have time and that will be when I have more help here."'

'I worked a long, seven day week for my father and sometimes I couldn't hide resentment of his attitude.

"I can't afford to take on more help," he responded angrily. "I'm no longer the company's director; my income is limited. And since I paid off Julian's mortgage you'd think he'd try to do something to help here by way of a thank you."

'I inwardly fumed. Father could well have afforded more help. He expected too much of me. There were times when I wished him dead, but then afterwards I always regretted my wicked thoughts.

'Bill Thomas's wife, Ida, helps me in the house three days a week, though it needs more than the two of us to keep it as Father expected.

'He was demanding and took a lot of looking after. A nurse-carer from the local private care agency came every morning to help me with his personal care. He was always outraged by the monthly fee and expected every pound to be accounted for. He told me he didn't know why I couldn't manage on my own, but he had to be lifted out of his bed, taken to the bathroom and put into the bath and out, every morning. I couldn't manage that on my own. It was thanks to my student nurse-training that I was able to do everything else.

'Father liked sitting in this chair. When the male nurse carer came, Father was transferred manually from his wheelchair onto it.

'That was a twice-weekly morning call. On other days the carer was a female. She could transfer Father from wheelchair to chair only by using the mechanical hoist and then with my help. It's a company regulation that two experienced people use the mechanical hoist. We did do so for his morning ablutions, when she was here. Her hours of care were limited. She had other people to call on.

'Father hated the hoist and made that quite clear. He was uncooperative and grunted his disapproval. He thought it undignified being hammocked into the air. He had to accept it if he wanted to sit in this chair and enjoy the view, or to be put in and out of the bath; to be moved in and out of bed, or from any A to B.

'Between the carers' calls I had to cheat and use the hoist on my own. I ignored his complaints. I'd got used to being referred to as an uncaring weakling. If I hadn't been able to close my mind to them I'd be in a psychiatric hospital now, not sitting in his favourite chair planning my future. I would have been driven mad.

'I was his daughter but filled the role of a full-time lackey: nurse, housekeeper, cook, laundry maid, masseuse and chiropodist. He expected it; considered it my duty and thought I considered it my duty. I suppose I did, otherwise I would have left him to be looked after by various and strange carers. But I had nowhere to go and little money. I relied on my inheritance to give me a good life when Father was gone. I thought that might have been too late, though. And it is.

'Many mornings, when entering his bedroom, I hoped to find him dead. Later, I always regretted my sinful thoughts.

'The trimming and shaving of his beard he did himself. That was something he wouldn't trust me to do, but I was expected to prepare the tray with his grooming equipment, set it before him and clear up afterwards. The preparation had to be immaculate or he would cast the tray aside in anger, spilling water and items across the floor.

'How dare you treat me with slovenliness,' was an often said remark of dissatisfaction.

'He also didn't trust me to cut his white hair, still ample in spite of his age. I took him to the men's hairdresser in the village. Although a cripple, he took pride in his handsome appearance.

'I lifted Father bodily until about ten years ago when I strained my back. Our GP told him that my days of being a human hoist were over. He wasn't happy about that. He said what he often said; that he wished he had died with my mother. I didn't believe him. He took pleasure out of what was left of his meagre coping ability.

'He held a Bridge party here one evening of most weeks. During those afternoons Ida and I prepared a buffet supper for him and his friends. The silver was polished, our best china brought out and Father would inspect the spread before his guests arrived. Ida went home around six o'clock so I stood alone to be chastised for the imperfections.

'His friends constantly praised me for being a caring daughter and frustrated Father with reminders of his good luck at my having been a nurse.

'One Bridge evening, a guest called him to task over the way he took me for granted.

'She's no skivvy, you know, Quentin. Victoria's a lovely, intelligent lady. One day you'll be sorry for the way you treat her.'

'I don't treat her like a skivvy,' Father snapped. 'She's my daughter and her duty is to look after me. She knows that and has no regrets. You don't know what it's like being in this wheelchair. I've often thought of releasing its brakes at the top of the stairs and letting myself down and ending it all.'

'Don't do that, Quentin. You'll regret it if you survive and be more of a cripple than you are.' The other guests were amused by that remark.

'Father sometimes forgot to apply the brakes of his wheelchair but always remembered in time and shouted after me when he lost control.'

'Victoria! Quickly, you stupid girl. Get hold of this thing!'

'When his guests left I had the tidying up, dish-washing and clearing away to do. That was after I'd got Father upstairs in the stair-lift chair he has installed, and seen him into his soft, winceyette pyjamas, abed between freshly laundered sheets. His medication was, as always, was on the bedside table for him to take when I'd served him with a hot drink. By then I was exhausted.

'You hurry along and see to yourself now, Victoria dear, or you'll be tired in the morning.'

'Yes, Father.'

'Words spoken more than once as I glared at his container of medication and thought of overdosing him. He didn't check his pills before taking them all in one hand-scoop, including potent night sedation. He knew what medicines he took but he trusted me implicitly to set them out for him.

'It would have been easy to poison him; see him close his eyes in peaceful sleep, never to awaken again. Yet, I always regretted my sinful thought and asked forgiveness on my knees before getting into bed myself.

'Father always insisted on coming to "help" me with the shopping. It was more to ensure he had everything he needed and to stop me spending wastefully, to his way of thinking.

'He'd had the front of his Jaguar engineered with ramps so that he could wheel himself into the passenger side and strap himself in. I, of course did the driving and when he was out of the car I did the pushing, lifting, carrying, the unpacking and anything else which was needed.

'More than once I thought of pushing his wheelchair under the wheels of an oncoming heavy vehicle on the busy road we had to cross when going into the town. But would I regret it?

'If I wanted to buy anything personal I'd have to ask him for permission to add it to the cost of the shopping. He usually agreed, but with bad grace.'

'You have money of your own. Why don't you use that? When it's all gone, then ask me for money. You'll have my house and half of all I've got left when I join Mother. Can't you wait?'

'No, Father, I wouldn't ask unless it was necessary. And please stop reminding me of what I'll get from you when you're dead. Have you ever thought that I might die before you? I know exactly how you've arranged your estate.'

'He sulked for days after that but accepted my caring ministrations. The atmosphere depressed me. I wished myself a thousand miles away.

'What a grand, brave old man. He keeps going in spite of it all,' was often said, or words similar in meaning, by people we came into contact with.

'Yes, he is, isn't he,' I always replied, inwardly seething. Father was crippled not senile. He sensed my frustration.

'I'm sorry I'm such a burden to you, Victoria. It's a good thing you were a nurse when I became this useless bit of a man. You gave up your career to look after me. I'm sorry about that but what else could I do?'

'He lied, but he's not sorry now. He's dead. Patricide is a dreadful sin and the gates of Hell will be open to me. I can't clear my mind of the evil deed. I killed him and I regret my action, though according to his philosophy, he would have believed I should feel better having done it. I think he would have changed that way of thinking had he the foresight to know his fate.

"Better to regret something you've done than something you've not done."

'I can hear him saying it as clearly as if he were sitting beside me and I shudder. I regret what I've done and will never find peace. Father has been dead for more than three months, yet it feels as if he's still here. Perhaps he is.

'After the drudgery of being his dutiful daughter, at his beck and call for over twenty years, I find it hard to adjust to the fact that at any minute he won't call me to do or get something for him.

'I'm not pretty to look at any more. I'm slim but rather on the skinny side. My hair is still thick and curly but now dulled with streaks of grey; the onset of ageing. I've been told that I have an appealing smile, though not recently. When I was nurse-training I was told I'd inherited Mother's lovely features. My first aim now is to recover them, as far as is possible.

'I was devastated, six months before my final professional nurse examinations, when Julian and our father insisted upon me resigning and returning home.

'At that time I was in love with Alistair Granger, a third year medical student, and he with me. We kept in touch by telephone and letters but it was inevitable that I would lose him, and I did.

'He came twice to High Trees House to see me. Each time Father was rude and over-demanding, making it clear to Alistair that he wasn't welcome. The second time Alistair came he asked Father for permission to marry me. Father told him I was needed here, to forget he ever met me and not to come back.

'My conscience was torn between caring for my father and my desire to marry Alistair. Out of loyalty to Father I said and did nothing to strengthen Alistair's advances. He never came again and I was heart-broken. Father didn't notice my misery, or if he did, he ignored it.

'I had done what Father and Julian said was my duty. I resigned from nurse-training and returned home to nurse Father after the fatal road traffic accident which killed my dear mother and rendered him paralysed.

'I think I gave up easily because of the sadness of losing Mother. She hadn't wanted to travel by road through France;

she wasn't a good traveller, but Father wanted to show off his new Jaguar. He insisted they go by road and ferry-crossing but he always regretted it. His regrets are over now.

'Father's funeral was delayed because of the routine post-mortem and an inquest into the cause of the "accident" which ended his life.

'The outcome was cut and dried. "Death by misadventure". There were plenty of witnesses.

'The "accident" occurred when Father and I were spending two weeks' annual holiday at the grand Sea View Hotel in Cornwall.

'The hotel is situated not far from the cliff-edge and has a prominent view of the bay directly below and the nearby picturesque fishing village. The hotel building is designed to accommodate the disabled. It is staffed by skilled nurses and an in-house doctor, but there is a stipulation that every disabled guest be accompanied by his or her own carer.

'The packing for the holiday was no mean task. All Father's aid equipment had to be taken and he insisted on his toiletries and clothes being immaculate.

'I suggested that we hire a taxi to take us to the hotel. It was a long drive to Cornwall and the taxi-man would help with the heavy luggage. Father seemed to have forgotten that our GP told him I had a back injury and should avoid lifting and carrying.

'Pay for a taxi, Victoria!' He was appalled and shouted at me. 'The holiday is already costly but it's the only hotel I can cope with. The Sea View is a pleasant place because there'll be people we know there; people like myself. I can't afford a taxi and I see no reason why you can't drive there. After all, it's just once a year and I **do** need a holiday.'

'So, as usual, I drove. It took over four hours, but as it happened I enjoyed the holiday once I'd recovered from the journey and got Father settled.

'I enjoyed socialising with the other carers; most of them younger than I. The difference between myself and them was that they were there out of choice; not enslaved, as I was.

'One morning, as I pushed Father along the cliff-top path, he instructed me to stop his wheelchair beside a bench where a couple of other Sea View guests were dozing in the warm sunshine. Father enjoyed discussing the problems of their various ailments and they seemed to like his company. However, that day he seemed particularly sleepy so they chatted to him only for a short while before moving on. They both had electric mobility-scooters so were independent of their carers at that time.

'Father fell into a deep sleep, as I'd expected, having given him a high dose of sedative instead of his usual analgesic. I knew the couple he chatted to thought it kind to let him dose; they knew I was nearby. I had left him to join a group of carers sitting on the grass some yards away.

'The sound of our laughter stirred him. He awoke disorientated, in a confused daze and inadvertently released the brakes of his wheelchair.

'I deliberately ignored the wheelchair as it began to free-wheel down the steep approach to the edge of the cliff. No-one else noticed because they had their backs towards it. Father was too sedated to call out for me as he usually did. He wasn't aware of what was happening.

'The runaway wheelchair gained impetus as it sped downwards. On catching sight of it, people saw me react with panic. I screamed and ran towards it as fast as I could.

'Too late. I managed to grab the tip of one of the handles of the wheelchair and everyone watching in horror, saw me try to pull it back. It had gained too much momentum to be controlled. I fell heavily and managed to stop myself rolling dangerously near the edge of the cliff. People ran towards me and pulled me back to safety.

'I hadn't tried to pull Father's wheelchair back; I had pushed it forward. The wheelchair tipped over the edge and smashed to pieces on the rocks below, where the inflowing tide began to wash over them. Father's battered body was found later that day. I'm sure he felt no pain and was too sedated to feel fear.

'It was just as I'd planned, but immediately I regretted what I had done. I trembled with fear but my reaction was considered to be shock of what had happened to Father, not to what I had done to him. Everyone considers patricide one of the most heinous of crimes. Did anyone see me push Father? Apparently not. People were solicitous and I had all the help necessary to deal with the tragic "accident".

'Father is gone now but I don't feel free. I sense his presence in every room. In my sleep I hear him calling me.

'V i c t o r i a! Where are you?' I awake shaking with fear.

'Sometimes I hear the creak of his wheelchair trundling through the corridors of the house, but I know it's not real; it is guilt playing tricks with my disturbed mind. Father is dead. His ashes are in a silver urn on the mantle-shelf in his study. I've checked, several times.

'As long as I live in this house, Father's spirit will, too. He will never allow me to live a life of my own. I feel his haunting presence.

'I sometimes ask his forgiveness; he might hear me. "*I'm sorry, Father. Please forgive me. I regret what I did.*" As I sit here in his favourite chair I am planning a future without him. Perhaps I'll miss him when the realisation that he is gone forever accommodates in my dulled brain – if it ever will.

'Ida Thomas is still working in this beautiful house; my house. She fusses over me, feeling sorry for me. She wonders what I will do as a free woman; past my prime but with a handsome financial inheritance to enhance my existence. Ida knew the sort of exciting life I had forsaken to care for Father. She knows my regrets of having to care for him. She frequently praised me for my dedication to his well-being. Over twenty years of my life I gave to him. I did it because I knew Mother would have wanted it that way. I hope she wasn't watching over me when I gave Father's wheelchair that last push. I wouldn't want her to know what I did, but I don't mind my brother, Julian, knowing. He hated our father. For many years he, too, wished him dead.

'"You must never blame yourself, Victoria," Julian told me. "Father was always meddling with the brakes of his wheelchair. You simply turned your back for a few minutes to enjoy the company of others and he released them. You're a saint to have put up with him for so long. You have nothing to reproach yourself for."

'"But I do, Julian. Do you remember the principle Father lived by and what he instilled in us when we had a decision to make?"

'"You mean, *Better to regret something you've done than something you've not done?"*

'"Yes, that's what I mean." He was wrong. I did something which I will always regret and it will torture me until the day I die.'

Victoria's account of what happened ended with a sigh and a long pause. My eyes held tears that hadn't yet fallen. I embraced her.

'Julian is right, Victoria. You didn't push your father nor did you over-sedate him. You've explained how you gave his medication – in a small pot and he put them in his mouth all at once.'

'Yes,' that's right,' she said. 'You remember that?'

'I do and I don't think for one second that your father didn't know what was in that pot. You think you killed him because you've thought of doing it sometimes.'

For the first time, Victoria turned her head towards me and looked directly into my eyes. She noticed that I was tearful.

'Now I've upset you. You are crying; something that I haven't done after Father.'

I sniffed and put a paper tissue to my eyes. 'Perhaps you will when the reality of what happened gets through to you. Julian is right. "You have nothing to reproach yourself for."'

Victoria looked at me and the hint of a smile crossed her lovely face. 'Let's go into the kitchen and have some tea and cake. Mrs Thomas has baked me a fruit loaf. I've talked so much, I'm quite hoarse. You can suggest how I should plan my future. Daphne wants me to stay with them for a while; perhaps I will.'

'That's more like my Victoria,' I replied. 'And you can come down to see Derek and me, now you don't have your father to care for. He's with your mother now and I'm sure he is happy.'

Victoria actually laughed. 'Yes, he's most probably scolding her or giving her orders.'

Victoria lived happily ever after. She had done her duty and did it well, though reluctantly

Chapter 26

THE INCREDIBLE VIOLET

On 22nd April, 2014 I had the honour and pleasure to be a guest at the birthday celebration of Mrs Violet Lewis. She was aged one hundred and five that day.

It was held at The Penpergwm Nursing Home, situated on the outskirt of the pretty village of Penpergwm , where she has resided since shortly after her hundredth birthday.

Mrs Lewis has been my friend for thirty years or more. I met her through Derek's business partner, Ruth.

On her birthday Violet appeared as she had all the years I'd known her. She wore a dress which she had tailored herself when she was able to use her sewing machine, her hair was immaculate, (she'd had it styled and set the day before) she sat upright in her chair with a table in front of her, awaiting a special birthday cake.

'Hello, Shirley,' she said. 'Thank you for coming.' At the age of one hundred and five I am surprised that she always recognises me, in spite of her failing eye-sight, as she did all her friends and members of her close-knit, devoted family. I've lost count of her many offspring.

The birthday entertainment included a "sing-a-long" of old-time music hall songs. Songs which she and I are familiar with. She remembered the words of the songs; I didn't and I am more than twenty years younger than she.

The party was held in a large, bright room overlooking well-kept lawns surrounded with splendid trees in full bloom.

Her residential companions sat around her and when all her guests had arrived the room was almost elbow-to-elbow. The local press, with their flashy cameras had to wriggle in and about to get good pictures of her. The pictures appeared in the local newspaper the following week.

We were served with tea and fancy pastries before the grand entrance of the birthday cake, which had to be seen to be believed. It wasn't round, square or tiered, but in three parts; 1 * 0 * 5, iced with pink and blue designs on a large, rectangle silver base.

There were many woos! and ooohs!.

The digital cakes didn't have a hundred and five candles decorating their tops but there were many. Violet made a wish before dousing them all with the help of Ruth. Violet was handed a cake-cutter and she, at a hundred and five, cut neat slices until her hand weakened.

Her mobility is poor but not worn out and she is able to stand and walk short distances with a Zimmer frame. Without prompting she stood up that day and with a smile, thanked everyone for coming.

'Thank you, thank you. You are so kind. Thank you,' was the limit of her ability to give a speech. There were tears in many eyes.

It was an unforgettable afternoon.

At her age, it is not surprising that her mobility is limited but she is a determined lady and often tries to be independent. Inevitably, she falls and has done several times in the past year. She had overcome the gentle falls until approximately six months before her birthday, when one morning she got out of bed without assistance, became dizzy and fell. This time more heavily than previously, when she had held on to the nearest piece of furniture and eased herself to the floor.

A fractured hip was suspected. She was admitted to the casualty department of the nearby Nevill Hall Hospital where she was X-rayed and no fracture was obvious. However, in view of the bruising sustained, pain and her advanced age she was admitted to an infamous assessment ward and was cared for there until a bed became available on a medical eight-bedded unit. She was retained there for observation and possible delayed shock.

The following day, in keeping with her spirit, she had improved and requested "to go home". It was considered detrimental at that stage so she agreed to do as was advised. She settled into the ward and enjoyed the company of the other patients. Violet enjoyed conversation and being among people. Ruth told me something I hadn't known about Violet – that she was afraid of being alone.

Two days after admission to that ward Violet developed a temperature and complained of feeling unwell. On investigation it was found she had contracted an infection ((MRSA) and had to be isolated. Ruth and I were furious but the staff didn't seem to care. Such an incident couldn't have been new.

Ruth asked the nurse in charge if the source of Violet's infection was known. She shrugged her shoulders. 'These things happen. She might have had it before she came in.'

Ruth was even angrier and reminded her, the ward sister, that Violet was a resident of a nursing home and there was no-one there with an infection. The nurse shrugged her shoulders. She was a young foreign lady; from the Philippines, I guessed.

Ruth came to the conclusion that in the Philippines shrugging of the shoulders must be a gesture of politeness. I knew it to be a gesture of a lack of interest which I had become familiar with; an example of the bad attitudes of nurses I'd had to deal with when I relied on hospital care for Derek.

Violet was moved from the eight-bedded unit into a single ward near the nurses' station. The single ward reminded me of a prison cell. It had no clock, though there was a patch on the wall where one had been. There was no radio or television, the large windows were without curtains and the room's drab cream-coloured walls added to the bleakness. There was, of course, a bed, a bedside locker, a bedside table and a hard upright chair beside the bed.

Ruth was there when her mother was transported, on her bed, up to the single ward. She was held up outside for a while, until the bed already in the ward was taken out and down to the eight-bedded ward which Violet had agreed to tolerate until she was discharged. She couldn't understand why she couldn't go home and disliked, intensely, being on her own.

'Ruth, why am I being moved?'

Ruth explained to her mother that she had an infection and had to remain until the infection had cleared.

'I don't have an infection. Why am I being moved?' she looked pleadingly at the nurse who was helping to manoeuvre the bed. 'Please take me back.'

'You be a'right, Violet. We jus' outside door.'

Ruth left the ward in tears and called in to tell me on her way home.

'My mother will hate it in that single ward. She'll be afraid. She needs to be among people. I dread to think how she'll feel tonight.'

That night Violet became frightened as Ruth predicted. She became confused, disoriented and demanding. She persistently pressed the nurse-call button and her behaviour became aggressive.

One of the nurses had chastised Violet in broken English, which she couldn't understand, before closing the door of her room. Violet has a quiet voice, as would be expected of a person of her age, but she shouted as loudly as she could.

'I want to go home! Take me home!'

She was eventually, sedated, and slept so soundly, that when Ruth went in the following morning, around eleven o'clock, her mother was still under the effect of the sedation and had wet her bed. She complained about her treatment of the night before and cried when she said she couldn't understand what the nurse was saying.

Her breakfast was untouched on the bedside table, out of her reach and it looked as if she hadn't had a drink for some time. The glass of water was, also, out of her reach. Her lips were cracked and her mouth was parched.

Ruth asked the nearest nurse to tell the ward sister she wanted to speak to her.

'Sister busy now. I go find her soon. Violet OK?'

'No, she is not OK! And I would be grateful if you tell the sister I would like to speak to her, now.' Ruth tried to keep calm.

Tight-lipped, the nurse obeyed. In minutes the ward sister entered the drab ward to find Ruth with a glass of water to her mother's lips and trying to rouse her to drink.

'How did my mother become so drowsy. She's an early riser and has never needed sedation, because that's how she appears to me; as if she's been drugged.'

The sister's hackles rose. Her attitude indicated annoyance.

'The night-staff had trouble settling your mother and they had other patients to deal with. She was trying to get out of bed. They were afraid she'd get injured.'

'She has become injured,' Ruth replied. 'She's had no breakfast or anything to drink for hours. My mother has her dentures taken out every night and soaked in Steradent. Just look at the state of her mouth.'

The sister took a closer look at Violet's face. 'All right, Mrs Eastman. I'll get her nurses in. Would you mind waiting outside while they care for her?'

'Not at all,' Ruth agreed. 'And then I'll pack her things and take her back to Penpergwm m House.'

'You can't do that, Mrs Eastman. Your mother is infected and until we are sure she is clear she cannot be discharged. She wouldn't be allowed into the nursing home with an infection.'

Ruth was defeated. 'With MRSA, which she caught in this hospital: I'm appalled. Please find out if she is clear today. I'll ring later.'

She told me she left the ward feeling like a dog with its tail between its legs.

After three days, when Ruth had been given no information of the infection being cleared, I asked if I could visit Violet. I wanted to see my dear friend but I was fearful of how I would find her. I went during an afternoon visiting time.

Before I entered Violet's side-ward I approach the duty desk which was situated close to it. Two nurses were sitting with their elbows on the desk. One was a male nurse. They were both, I thought, Philippinos. They looked bored.

'Good afternoon, Nurses,' I said in a high, hard tone. Each stood up with a jerk.

'I've come to see Mrs Violet Lewis. Where is she?' I knew where she was.

They both pointed to the open door of her ward.

'Good,' I kept up the tone. 'At least her door is open. She likes to see people about her, doesn't she?'

With quizzical expressions they slowly nodded and I felt their eyes following me as I walked towards the entrance. I stood on its threshold and turned my head towards them. 'How is she?' I asked abruptly. 'I hope she's well enough to be discharged tomorrow because she not doing well here.' Derek would have said I must have sounded like a sergeant major on parade.

'No tomorrow,' the female nurse replied. 'She got infection.'

I stalked into Violet's room before I spoke again in my authoritative tone.

'Well, she has an infection but she hasn't had her tea, has she?'

'She got tea,' the young man said as he looked onto Violet's bed-table. A cup of tea and a plate with a piece of cake stood untouched, out of her reach.

'Oh', he said, 'carer not put it close. I give Violet her tea, now.' He proceeded to push the bed-table nearer.

'It's all right. I'll help her now I'm here,' I snapped.

Violet was sitting with her eyes closed in a hard, upright chair. She opened them at the sound of movements about her.

'Hello, Mrs Lewis,' I reverted to my normal tone.

'Ruth,' she murmured, 'Take me home. It's awful here.'

'It's me; Shirley, Violet. How are you?' She didn't recognise me.

One of the nurses brought me a chair and I sat close to her and began encouraging her to sip the cold tea. She pushed my hand away.

'Where am I?' she asked. My heart sank. Sitting for most of the day alone for hour upon hour had had an adverse effect on her mind.

I chatted for a while until Glyn, her son came in.

He smiled and greeted me before addressing his mother.

'Hello, Mother. Are you better today?'

'Yes, and I want to go home.' I recognised Glyn's disappointment. 'No, you're worse. The sooner that infection is clear, the better.'

I noticed Violet began wriggling on her chair. 'Is your backside hurting you, Violet?'

'No,' she replied, 'please take me home.'

I was reminded of Emily Burgess, an elderly resident of The Nightingale Nursing Homes, where I had worked some years before. She repeatedly and constantly said she wanted to go home. One freezing, cold night, unknown to any of the staff, she escaped and wandered into the town. Fortunately, she was found before anything bad happened to her.

Seeing Glyn was upset brought tears to my eyes. I had to leave. I didn't want Glyn to recognise my hurt and resentment of his mother's treatment.

On my way out I stopped at the duty desk where the two nurses were now writing in the nursing documents.

'Is Mrs Lewis's skin broken? I asked harshly. They looked questioningly at each other and slowly shook their heads. 'Does she have a pressure sore?' I know I sounded irascible. One of them began flicking through the documents, I guessed, looking for Violet's nursing report. The nurse quickly read the information before looking at me.

'No, no pressure sore; skin intact.'

'Well it won't be for long if she remains on that hard chair with no cushion on its seat.'

She began to look ruffled. 'OK. I put cushion. I make her comfortable.'

I think she wanted to tell me to be she would act when I was out of her sight.

Before I left I pointed out something that would mean nothing to those two nurses, but I said it anyway. 'That lady, Mrs Violet Lewis, is one hundred and four years old. You should be proud of the privilege to nurse her. You won't come across anyone like her again.'

I felt sad and useless as I left that terrible ward.

I called Ruth and told her of my visit to Violet and admitted that I was unhappy about her condition and care. I tried to comfort her by mentioning the fact that it wouldn't be too long before Violet ended the course of antibiotics she'd been prescribed and she will surely be discharged the following day. But she wasn't.

That afternoon when Ruth visited, she overstayed the visiting time, being loath to leave her mother alone. She was given no definite date for her mother's discharge.

She heard the ring of the bell which heralded the end of visiting time, but she ignored it. After a while a nurse appeared at the open door of Violet's ward and rang the bell loudly, saying nothing before stalking away. Five minutes later the nurse repeated the ringing of the bell and later still a third, loud ring. Ruth was at the end of her tether. She walked close to the bell-ringer, a nursing-aide, and loudly threatened her.

'If you come near here again and ring that bell I will wrap it about your bloody neck!' The nurse looked shocked for a few moments, said nothing, but cocked a snoot as she walked off. Ruth left her mother when she decided to.

I laughed when Ruth told me. She said it felt good to let off steam. Violet was discharged the following day.

She had been in the hospital for ten days and when she arrived back at The Penpergwm Nursing Home she was a changed woman. She was confused, aggressive, incontinent, didn't recognise any of the staff and she couldn't stand. The inactivity had rendered the muscles of her legs too weak.

Fortunately, an excellent physiotherapist worked at The Penpergwm Home. She was skillful and compassionate and after daily movements and encouragement, Violet was able to stand independently again and walk a few steps with a Zimmer frame. Her total continence didn't return but for a lady of her age she did well. She was no longer totally confused and slowly began to recognise people again.

Some weeks ago, since being discharged from the hospital, she had an illness and we were worried. However, she overcame it and we hope to see her on her one hundred and sixth birthday. On her hundred and fifth birthday, she was astounding.

Chapter 27

ON THE OTHER SIDE

I retired at the end of 2002, just before my sixty-ninth birthday. My aim was to practice for another year; until I made the round seventy. However, I wasn't reluctant to let go of the strong ties to my profession; my priority was Derek. I wanted to be at home with him permanently. His health was deteriorating and I wanted to care for him. I regret not having taken the step earlier.

Three years at Excel Community Care was my last place of nursing and nurse training. During the last six months there, my circumstances were such that I had to make several visits with Derek to the hospital. I was not, generally, impressed by the practice of our nurses. Some had been trained under the auspices of the academic, bureaucratic system of nurse training which had begun some twenty years before. It has been recognised that Project 2000 hasn't turned out to be a change for the better. From what I have seen, heard and read it has been a disastrous failure.

I regret having to express my anguish and disapproval of what has happened because the majority of ward sisters, ward managers, carers, nursing-aides, or whatever they may be called, are loyal, hard-working nurses and have that essential and important key – compassion. However, I have heard many of them expressing their adverse opinion of the current nurse training.

The media continues to wallow in broadcasting the failing of the caring profession and it seems that we are losing the confidence and prestige we once had.

"*Don't believe in all you read in the newspapers*", is the well-used cliché and I did not believe all I read. I assumed the horror stores to be exaggerated. Not only must I admit to being wrong but have witnessed more horrible incidents than those I have read about.

In spite of the powers that be, eventually, admitting to the failure, the syllabus of current nurse training has been changed at least twice. Yet the cruelty and unexplained, inexcusable neglect of hospital patients and nursing home residents continues.

At my breakfast table on Thursday 27th August, 2009, the headlines of *The Daily Telegraph* spoiled my appetite. Not only did they turn my gut but alarmed me.

I knew Derek would be needing constant hospital treatment. Anger overtook my disgust and I decided I would defy that rule of strict visiting times if, or when, his care would not be as it should. His care was faultless during only two urgent admissions and one of them started badly.

Derek had an advanced degree of renal failure and needed intravenous therapy to correct an acute episode. A bed wasn't available on a medical ward so he was, initially, admitted to the hospital's assessment ward, prior to being allocated a bed on a medical unit.

I had heard how bad that assessment ward was from a number of people who had had the misfortune of being patients there. I've heard it being called "a torture chamber" and worse.

We were kept there for hours after being clerked (examined) by a young doctor. Derek's condition had deteriorated before an obese consultant flew with the flaps of the front of her ubiquitous white coat fluttering into the confines of Derek's screened bed. She reminded me of Dawn French as The Vicar of Dibley. The young doctor must have contacted the consultant for advice about Derek's treatment;

hence the long delay. It would have reduced our concern had we been warned.

'Right,' she said. 'Your kidneys need flushing out. The treatment is aggressive and dangerous. If you arrest, do you wish to be resuscitated?'

We both understood his poor condition but being told he could die that night made us both stiff with fear. He answered affirmatively.

The Vicar of Dibley went on. 'For twenty-four hours all your medication will be withheld. You will have an intravenous infusion, a urinary catheter … '

At that point I held up my hand and switched her off. She looked surprise.

'What?' she asked, tartly.

I waved the flat of my hand close to her face. 'No urinary catheter,' I said with determination.

'What?' she said again, 'Why not?'

'There is no need for a urinary catheter. My husband does not have urinary retention, he is not unconscious, he has no difficulty urinating. No catheter.'

'Then how do you suggest the output is monitored?' she asked, looking none too pleased. She referred to the amount of fluid that would leave his body by urinating.

'Measuring output is a nursing procedure and I am a nurse. I will monitor the output because I fear there will not be a nurse available to do it.'

'Very well,' she said, 'as you wish.' She flew away leaving her minion (the young doctor who had examined Derek) to write up the suggested treatment. He looked tired; I guessed he'd most probably been on duty for too many hours. But his compassion was obvious. He recognised our distress.

Derek was, eventually, allocated a bed on Medical Ward 4/1, where many years before I was the ward sister. I and a porter took Derek on his bed up from "the torture chamber" to Ward 4/1. I remained at his bedside as he was taken into a four bedded ward near the duty room.

I stalked into the duty room, out of bounds to visitor unless invited, to reinforce my instructions about there to be no catheterisation. Derek was too ill to have argued and I expected to be rebuffed.

The ward sister was sitting at the desk. I was pleasantly surprised, as was she.

'Shirley!' she said in a high tone of surprise. 'I won't say how nice to see you because you are here with Derek.'

Julie had been a second level nurse (SEN) when I was her ward sister. She had studied her way up the career ladder and I knew her to be a first class nurse.

Just then, the night staff arrived on duty. Three of them remembered me and seemed surprised to see me "on the other side". I was relieved and explained the situation.

Sister Julie Harris insisted. 'I know maintaining a fluid balance chart is our responsibility and it will be done by us. You go home and rest. You will be called if or when necessary.'

They appeared a large group as they all stood together; day and night staff. They formed a semi-circle around me outside the duty room; all looking neat and smart and professional in their appearance and attitude. Some of them addressed me as Mrs Phillips, remembering me as being part of the staff of the School of Nursing.

'Please, Nurses,' I said before leaving, 'care for him well and measure and test every drop of urine that leaves his body and every drop that goes in.'

'We will, we will,' was chorused.

When I visited Derek the following morning he looked and felt much better. The treatment had resulted in no complications.

'You know, Shirley, the nurses even measured the milk in my cornflakes and the juice in a small dish of peaches,' Derek said. I was grateful.

The thought of that one incident of hospital care restored my confidence in the current nursing. I recognised that most of the staff were not of a young group but of an age who worked by the standards of pre-Project 2000 training.

That favourable admission was the best. It was followed by too many bad experiences and at the time I write I cannot see an end to the present desperate situation in the world of nursing. The media continues to confirm my opinion.

"Cruelty, squalor on NHS", headlines of *The Daily Telegraph,* Thursday, August, 27th, 2009. That was five years ago and I haven't read or heard evidence of improvement. The damning report suggested to me that nursing will never redeem the respect and confidence of which we were once proud, unless the present system of training is scrapped.

Rebecca Smith, a medical editor of *The Daily Telegraph* states that, "While the criticisms cover all aspects of hospital care, the treatment and attitude of nurses stands out as a repeated theme."

It would seem that she agrees with my suggestion for the current form of nurse training to be scrapped and to start again. When it was suggested by Andrea Spyropoulos, the President of the Royal College of Nursing, that new recruited nurses spend a year carrying out basic physical care, she considered it would take back nursing a hundred years.

From my experience of thirty years in the profession, witnessing its decline, I am almost of the opinion that a year of ward-based nurse training would not be a retrograde step.

Such a measure could cause a recruiting problem unless the applicants are offered attractive terms. That might incur more cost and our Chancellor wouldn't like that.

Headlines of *The Daily Telegraph, August 2009.*
* *Million patients suffer appalling care.*
*
* *Catalogue of rude nurses, dirty wards, cancelled*
* *operations.*

Rebecca Smith states in the article that The Patients Association claims that millions of people across Britain have been the victims of appalling care.

A horrifying catalogue of elderly people having been "*left in pain, in soiled bedclothes, denied adequate food and drink and suffering from repeated cancelled operations, missed diagnoses and dismissive staff", is now not hard to believe.*

Most of that statement appears to be the fault of uncaring, badly trained nurses. But to whom should the finger be pointed in the case of patients suffering from repeated cancelled operations? It seems possible that there is a deficiency of surgeons or they are not available because they are busy feathering their nests in the private sector.

The late Claire Rayner, OBE, was president of the Care Quality Commission when this dreadful indictment hit the headlines of *The Daily Telegraph.* She declared that "she was trained as a nurse with one of the patients who had suffered. She was horrified by the appalling care she had before she died".

Claire Raynor came from a generation of nurses who were trained at the bedside and in whom, she said, "the core values of nursing were deeply inculcated".

Over the past decade I am persistently hearing and reading complaints from patients and relatives of the appalling, disgusting treatment in our hospitals and nursing homes.

From the point in my life of leaving formal nurse-training, I became the nurse of a most important patient: Derek, my husband. There were times of despair, relief, discourtesy and appalling disgust.

It began in 2002. Between then and 2013 Derek's hospital admissions were many. Each admission was followed by numerous out-patient appointments and being supported by our local National Health Service general practitioners and primary health care teams. When in their care, Derek was treated with skill and compassion for which I will always be grateful.

As I have already stated, there were several emergency admissions and, I can affirm that we can be proud of our excellent paramedical teams. In spite of the error in nurse training, I think we must continue to support our National Health Service.

Being Derek's nurse and carer for over ten years, I found the nursing care in the general hospital on most wards not as it should have been.

There were bad times when he had to be admitted to receive essential treatment, which I was unable to provide at home.

I would have liked to remain with Derek beside his hospital bed until I needed sleep, but I would have been in the way of the staff having to carry out the caring tasks. This, of course, I have understood and have not, at any time, been given a choice, anyway. When asked to leave, I left.

Ann Clwyd, the Member for Parliament for Cynon Valley, told the Cardiff and Vale University Health Board that her husband was treated no better than "a battery hen". An apt description, I thought.

Following the reports of her claims of her husband's treatment I am reminded of the cruel way my husband was treated.

On one of my evening relatives' visiting times, he said, 'Shirley, I have dislocated my hip and no-one will believe me. I think I should escape and come home with you. There is one nurse on this ward who is evil and I don't feel safe.' Derek would never have described anyone as "evil" unless he strongly felt it.

'Who is she? What is her name?' I intended to seek her out but she had gone off duty as had the ward sister – not that complaining would have made a difference. The NHS is inundated with thousands throughout the nation.

One afternoon I visited him to find him sitting in a chair beside his bed. In spite of being in unrelieved pain he smirked at an incident which had happened that morning: an elderly gentleman in the bed next to him appeared to be dangerously ill. Yet, at around ten o'clock a nurse approached him and proceeded to prepare a chair beside his bed whilst shouting at him to wake up and that he must "sit out".

Derek was disgusted. He felt sorry for the gentleman. 'He is so ill he can barely hold his head up,' he told me. 'I thought it wrong to get him out of bed, but of course, I am in no position to criticise. I daren't.'

'Come along,' said the nurse loudly. 'Sister said I must help you out of bed.'

The poor elderly gentleman was too ill to object. He sat in his chair, no-one seemed to know or care that he was suffering and too ill to press the buzzer, which would have called his nurse.

Just before the lunch trolley arrived, the ward sister entered our four bedded-ward. The nurse "caring" for us, "our nurse", was with her.

'Mr James!' shouted Sister. 'Why are you out of bed. You are on total bed rest.' She looked, threateningly, at the carer and angrily at Mr James, as if he had been a naughty boy.

'Why is Mr James out of bed, Sally?'

'Sister, you told me to get "the hip" out of bed.'

Derek solved the confusion in as loud a voice as he could muster. 'I'm "the hip" he's the "gut"!'

The nurses looked at each other accusingly and stalked out of the ward. Derek said he heard them chuckling as they strolled down the corridor.

The lunches were given out, dining time was over and the meals' trolley taken away before two nurses entered with a trolley to wash Mr James and help him back into bed.

One of the first professional principles I learned as a pupil nurse, nearly forty years ago, was not to forget that "the patient is a person". No longer, "the heart" in the middle four-bedder, "the diabetic" in top ward, "the leukaemia" in first side ward, "the stroke" in bottom ward … etcetera.

The patient is to be addressed by his or her title, Mr or Mrs, unless invited to be informally addressed by another name.

That is one of the many characteristics of courtesy and professionalism which is not practised enough these days. Judging from the attitudes of some nurses, I doubt that their lecturers at the universities have an understanding of the importance of communicating with ill people in an appropriate manner.

When I visited Derek the day following the dreadful error of Mr James's care, a different patient was in his bed. As well as being in pain, Derek was emotionally upset. Mr James had died during the night.

Derek had dislocated his hip. It was diagnosed after four days.

After leaving Excel Community Care I kept in touch with the staff. I was invited to their celebrations, whatever and whenever they were, and Erika, my NVQ assessment partner often called on her way home. It was she who told me when and where Mr Drake, my last patient, had died.

'He died at home,' Erika told me, 'as he chose to, but it would have been better if he had agreed to go into a nursing home. He was afraid. He'd been brain-washed by what he'd heard and read about of the cruel treatment of residents in the nursing homes. He was of the understanding that his house would have to be sold to finance his residential care in a nursing home.

'He needed twenty-four hour care and didn't get it. He died in that dirty house, cold, hungry and lonely.'

I agreed with Erika. 'He would have been no less lonely in a nice nursing home, even surrounded with others but, at least, he would have been warm and given regular meals.'

Mr Drake's existence until he died is not an isolated one. The scaremongering of the media is ongoing and it is apparent that it wallows in the sordidness of the shameful events of bad nursing. It is being seen as having created a new problem which has arisen in caring for the elderly and infirm. It is, that on hearing the horror stories of the neglect and cruelty meted out to residents, some of them and their relatives have become afraid of going into nursing homes. They, unnecessarily, perish to death, often alone, as did Mr Drake and as do thousands of others.

The revealing of the current nurse-training being a mistake and the suffering of patients from poor nursing, often with neglectful, demeaning, painful and cruel treatment by *The Daily Telegraph* in 2009 has done nothing to improve matters.

The serious complaints made by Labour MP Ann Clwyd over the disgraceful and cruel treatment of her husband when on a hospital ward was in 2013; four years after the indictment of *The Daily Telegraph.*

The reason, especially, for one of her allegations being unacceptable escapes me: "I saw a nurse in the corridor and asked her why my husband wasn't in intensive care. She just said, 'There are lots worse than him'".

I wonder how bad the nurse expected Mr Owen Robert's condition to be before he received special care. He was dying. What is worse than that? "There was an, almost, callous lack of care".

First Minister Carwyn Jones considered some of Ms Clwyd's allegations to be "unattributable" and couldn't be investigated when he must have, or should have, known that a special investigation confirmed that her husband died of "hospital-induced pneumonia".

I cannot but comment: *"There is none so blind as he who does not wish to see."*

My sight is not perfect but keen enough to have seen bad nursing practice in this year of 2014. I don't know what has been done or suggested by the powers that be to correct or even improve the situation, but it hasn't been enough.

God willing, the future will see a miraculous turn for the better and we will not have to concern ourselves about the care of our children and those that will come after them.

SUMMARY

The completion of this book is July 2014. It is the end of my writing of life as a nurse teacher, an assessor of future nurses and promoting the quality of life of the elderly and elderly mentally infirm citizens in the community and nursing homes. Also, I have written of myself as a carer on the "other side". I cared for a dear husband for over ten years.

I relate again to the unfair treatment of Ann Clwyd, Member of Parliament for Cynon Valley for "stirring a hornets' nest" when she spoke out about the bad care her husband received and died as a result of. Indeed, his was not an isolated case. My husband's death in 2013 could have been avoided. My knowledge, (though now limited in the light of progress) of thirty years in Nursing, allowed me to recognise the mistakes that were made. The traumatic ending of his life on a badly run ward is making my grief harder to bare.

The future of the nursing profession is in jeopardy. In my opinion it has deteriorated in the past year, unless a change for the better has occurred of which I am not aware.

Christine Patterson, writer, medical consultant of *The Independent* (July 1914) looked at what has happened to Nursing. She asks, how did we come to this? The reforms which began in the 1990's were supposed to make nursing care better. Instead, there is a widely shared sense that this was how today's compassion deficit began. She has experienced bad nursing care herself.

When Project 2000 was introduced, the system of State Enrolled Nurses (SEN) was replaced by health care assistants, who were not registered, or formally trained.

Now, in many areas, the nursing diplomas are being phased out and it is planned that all qualified nurses will have a degree. I fear, then, that our profession may be further denigrated.

I am reminded of the words of my first nursing tutor in 1970. "First class nurses we need, not third class doctors". Her words didn't fall on deaf ears.

I have experienced the bad effects of the bureaucratic and academic error of taking training away from the bedside.

The national news on 2nd July, 2014, announced concern about the increase in complaints of National Health Service care and treatments throughout the nation.

Too many nurses lack the necessary knowledge, professionalism and compassion, irrespective of the type of training they were given, pre or post Project 2000. I have spent enough time in the caring world to have recognised this

I am gratified to admit that I found most of the nurses throughout the hospitals displayed the qualities expected of them. It is a pity that it takes one rotten apple to spoil the lot. Unfortunately, there are too many rotten apples and bad habits have rubbed off. "If you can't beat them, join them.'

This was said to me by an ex-nurse student who is now a ward sister. Should she read this, she will recognise herself.

The nursing homes throughout the country vary in quality. The residents are, predominantly, cared for by untrained nurses of various titles: carers, nursing-aides, nursing assistants. They are expected to learn from experienced nursing colleagues, also untrained. A redeeming factor of this is that they are learning in the right place, where patient contact is at its best.

The Daily Telegraph , *2010* reported, 'Nursing homes for elderly residents were among the worst for quality of care, with nearly one in five rated "adequate" or "poor". It has been said that significant investment will be needed for nursing homes – even if the goal is to maintain the status quo.

My suggestion is that the status quo be improved:

* More trained nurses to care for the elderly and mentally infirm (Currently, the law,... accepts that one registered nurse is adequate to be in charge of a nursing home during day and night duties).

* More stringent selection of applicants into Nursing. This, not necessarily considered by the number of GCSEs or A levels on the curriculum vitae of the applicant.

* Enhance the financial terms and conditions of training. (This might increase the number of applicants to the profession).

* Nurse training must be predominantly, ward-based.

* The discontinuation of the writing of long assignments based on research during training. Let the researchers do the researching and allow the students to concentrate on practical nursing management but benefit from the nursing research that has already been accomplished and has been proven to be effective. This does not infer that nursing should not be research-based after qualifying.

* Clinical teachers should be permanently attached to the wards and departments.

* Return to two levels of nursing; State Enrolment, State Registration.

* Annex schools of nursing to the hospitals.

The above suggestions are my personal views and opinions, formed from what I have witnessed, read and heard. I would gladly stand corrected when, or if, necessary.

A continuation of the current training will not correct the problems we see in hospitals and nursing homes today. But, I hope I am wrong.

END